hoices & hances

The Western History Series

SERIES EDITORS

Carol L. Higham
University of North Carolina at Charlotte

William H. Katerberg
Calvin College

D1602310

Choices and Chances

A History of Women in the U.S. West

Sheila McManus

University of Lethbridge

A CO-PUBLICATION OF

HARLAN DAVIDSON, INC.
773 Glenn Avenue
Wheeling, Illinois 60090
www.harlandavidson.com

THE BUFFALO BILL HISTORICAL CENTER
720 Sheridan Avenue
Cody, Wyoming 82414
www.bbhc.org

Except as permitted under United States copyright law, no part of this publication may
be reproduced or distributed in any form or by any means, or stored in a database or any
retrieval system, without prior written permission of the publisher. Address inquiries to
Harlan Davidson, Inc., 773 Glenn Avenue, Wheeling, Illinois 60090-6000.

Visit us on the World Wide Web at www.harlandavidson.com

Library of Congress Cataloging-in-Publication Data

McManus, Sheila.
  Choices and chances : a history of women in the U.S. West / Sheila McManus.
      p. cm. — (The western history series)
  Includes index.
  ISBN 978-0-88295-277-2 (alk. paper)
  1. Women--West (U.S.)—History. I. Title.
HQ1438.W45M37 2010
305.40978—dc22
                                                                        2010038884

Front cover art: "*New Gold.*" Gold Leaf and Acrylic on Canvas, 2008 by Marla Alli-
son. Four women admiring adornment inspired by Laguna Pueblo pottery art.
The artist is from Laguna Pueblo, NM, and conveys the history of her home via con-
temporary art. More information available at www.marlaallison.com
Back Cover, bottom photo: Susie Shot in the Eye, Sioux, in elk tooth dress, ca. 1890s.
Buffalo Bill Historical Center, Cody, Wyoming; Gift of George D. Kolbe, P.35.142
Cover Design: Linda Gaio, Harlan Davidson, Inc.

Manufactured in the United States of America
12 11 10   1 2 3 MG

In memory of two engineers,
both of whom believed that a woman
could do anything she put her mind to

My dad
Kevin F. McManus, 1940–2005

My partner
Jennifer A. Hanes, 1973–2006

Contents

Acknowledgments

Without a doubt, the first person I have to thank is Carol Higham for talking me into this in the first place. Her faith in me was astounding. She and Will Katerberg were patient and persistent editors (even when I did not make their job easy!), and the book is better for it. I am deeply indebted to the historians whose work informs every page of this book. Although I could not thank you individually in footnotes, I included as many of you as I could in the "Suggested Readings" sections at the end of the chapters. The good stuff here comes from you and your decades of bold, feminist historical scholarship; any errors are wholly mine. My good friend Leslie Hall was the first person who really understood what I was trying to do in this book, and her understanding gave me a huge boost when I needed it most. I have been enormously lucky to have Dr. Patricia Chuchryk, award-winning sociology professor and dog guru extraordinaire, in my life the past few years as a mentor and a friend. She has shaped my approach to teaching more than I can even put into words, and helped give me the confidence to trust my instincts in the classroom and with this book. Shaunere Lane, her family, and the absolutely magical guest cottage at the Brown Creek Ranch west of Claresholm, Alberta, gave me and this book three days of peace and quiet in the summer of 2009. The book turned a big corner that weekend, and

I am heading back next time I am having a bad writing slump! This book, and the series to which it belongs, would not have happened without the support and assistance of the Buffalo Bill Historical Center (BBHC) in Cody, Wyoming, and Andrew J. Davidson of Harlan Davidson, Inc. The BBHC staff made my all-too-short research trip both efficient and enjoyable, and many of the images in this book are from the center's extensive collection. Linda Gaio at Harlan Davidson helped me fill in the gaps in the list of images, and generously included me in the design process for the book's cover. Catherine Cocks gave the book the best copy edit I could have asked for. I am also very grateful to artist Marla Allison, who graciously allowed me to use her beautiful painting *New Gold* on the cover.

And finally, I want to thank my partner, Gene Thibault. You propped me up when it was hard to stand and you make me keep a foot in this world. Muchas gracias, mi amor.

—Sheila McManus
University of Lethbridge

Preface

In 2007 I taught a class on the history of the United States West to a great bunch of students. To get the conversation started one day, I asked them a simple question: what would the history of the West look like with women at the center? I covered three blackboards with notes as they talked for the next two hours, and after the class was finished, I sat in the classroom and wrote down everything on those boards. By the time I got home that day, I knew I had to throw out everything I had already written for this book and start over, because the students were really on to something.

My students talked about themes more than chronology and stressed agency (that is, a woman's ability to make choices and take action even in difficult circumstances) and opportunities more than victimization or marginalization. They argued that the traditional political narrative should move into the background and be seen in relation to the women who made it possible. For example, my students insisted that if women were at the center of the narrative, then we would see sex trade workers as more than just "prostitutes"; we would also see them as workers, mothers, wives, sisters, daughters, friends, and community members. My students challenged me to write a book that put women at the center of the story and looked at the familiar political narrative from women's points of view.

This book takes up their challenge. It insists that women were active participants in every facet of the history of the West and that their actions and choices helped shape the way that history was made. Until the 1970s historians knew very little about women's active participation because for a long time historians of the West focused mainly on what men did, and mostly white men at that. Historians knew a lot about only one half of the history of the West but could not see the whole picture. They just did not see the full range of women's roles and contributions until the first generation of women's historians started pointing them out.

Beginning in the 1970s, historians of western women began to expand our view of the history of the region dramatically. At first much of their work concentrated on women in various supporting roles: Native American women who helped white men find their way across the continent or white women who followed their husbands westward and tolerated the poor conditions in stoic silence. The historians also wrote about white women who founded institutions and fought for the right to vote. It was easier for the first women's historians to write about these women because they were performing respectable and appropriate roles: they were helping men, helping their communities, or asking for a political right that men already had. This approach was a way to squeeze a few "good," respectable women into the history books, and it did not require thinking about that history in a different way or changing the central narrative at all. A few more women could be squeezed in by focusing on the "bad" ones: the women who worked as prostitutes in mining towns, for example.

Either way, men and their activities remained at the center of the story. The "good" women helped white men achieve their personal or national destinies and the "bad" women did jobs that had to be done when there were not enough of the "good" ones around. Our knowledge of the West included a lot more about women, but they were still usually white women who remained peripheral to the real action: the things that men did.

What started off as a trickle of work on western women in the 1970s is now a flood of dynamic, insightful, and multicultural scholarship. We can now see a much fuller and balanced picture of the history of the U.S. West, and by placing women at the center of the story this book highlights the fact that women were active participants in and creators of that history. Women of all races, ethnicities, classes, and religions were workers and explorers, mothers and adventurers, miners and ranchers, activists and environmentalists, community leaders and housewives. They made the best choices they could, often with few options, and they took chances to make better lives for themselves, their families, and their communities. Women's experiences paralleled and overlapped with the experiences of men of their races, classes, and religions but were also very different from men's because gender mattered enormously. By including the experiences of many different women, we can now see and appreciate a richer, more complex, and more realistic story than the older histories. The West simply would not have developed the way it did without women.

This book emphasizes three themes. My students inspired the first, agency and opportunities, when they objected to women always being portrayed as passive victims. What struck me as I was writing this book was how often women created their own opportunities despite bad situations and seized the smallest chances for a better life even when their circumstances looked pretty bleak. A key feature of the mythology of the West is that it is the land of opportunity, where success is just handed to individuals. Women discovered that this certainly was not true for them, but many refused to accept the constraints they faced and challenged such limits. They felt that their lives were supposed to be better in the West, and they were determined to make them better.

This emphasis on agency is not meant in any way to downplay the fact that many western women suffered horribly throughout the region's history and there was often little they could do to stop the rapes, murders, starvation, disease, or internment they faced.

This truth brings us to the second theme of this book, choices and constraints. Although women made conscious, deliberate decisions about their lives and resisted the brutality whenever and wherever they could, there is no doubt that women made those choices within historical circumstances that placed greater limits on them than they did on men. They were paid less money than men even when they did the same job; they were the targets of sexual violence; and they lived in a world in which gender and racial norms usually gave them a very short list of acceptable behaviors and options.

The third theme in this book is continuity and change, because for all the dramatic changes over the centuries, striking similarities shape most women's experiences, even across the divides of race, class, and religion. For example, most women in most cultures do most of the childcare, just as most women in most cultures are not supposed to be public political leaders. However, child rearing responsibilities today are not the same as they were even one hundred years ago, and they mean different things and take different forms for women who live in different places or who come from different racial or class backgrounds.

These three themes and the remarkable diversity of women who helped shape the history of the U.S. West are central to the following chapters. Chapter one focuses on Native American women for whom "the West" had always been home. They enjoyed a high level of agency and opportunities in their communities, as well as respect for their skills and knowledge. Those skills helped keep the earliest white male arrivals alive, and chapter two discusses the period of early contact between Native American women and white men across the West. For some women this was a time of rapid change and significant new constraints on their status and activities, while others had more time to incorporate the changes into traditional patterns of life and culture. Chapter three looks at the experiences of Native American, Spanish, Mexican, African American and Anglo-American women across the Southwest and California from the eighteenth to the nineteenth century, as they lived through and had to adapt to successive political regimes. For all of these women, these were centuries of dramatic changes and ever-increasing constraints, yet they continued to find ways to resist, to shape the changes as much as possible, and to carve out new opportunities, however small. The nineteenth century was particularly cruel for Native American women across the West, as their options, population, and land base continued to shrink; chapter four examines their experiences and survival strategies. The dispossession of Native Americans helped clear the way for the huge influx of white Americans that started with the overland trails discussed in chapter five. The trails have long occupied an important place in the history of the West because they marked the start of rapid and widespread white settlement, and the emphasis in this book is on the mix of choices and constraints that shaped women's westward journeys.

Women often only appear in the history of mining as sex trade workers, but chapter six shows that their choices and contributions went far beyond prostitution. In the harsh, boom-and-bust atmosphere of mining towns across the West, women created a wide range of unique economic opportunities for themselves. Similarly, women homesteaders and ranchers took advantage of land laws in the late nineteenth century and made western land a new part of their individual, family, and community strategies. Chapter seven examines those opportunities and their effects.

The fact that most women in the West got the vote before most women in the East has often been one of the few reasons why western women got any attention at all in the older histories, but chapter eight traces the many different ways that western women were politically active. Women were determined to make their communities better, and no issue was too big or too small for them to tackle. Women carried that activism and determination into the towns and cities of the West. They had more economic opportunities in the cities than men did, as well as a new and different set of constraints, and chapter nine discusses women's urban experiences and responses.

Chapter ten looks at the profound effect the Great Depression of the 1930s had on women of all racial and ethnic groups and the ways they survived and resisted the economic and environmental catastrophes that had a permanent effect on the West. World War II provides some of the most striking examples in this book of women's determination to seize whatever opportunities they could find and create new ones when they had few options. The war was a turning point for women across the West, and chapter eleven examines the changes and continuities that women experienced as a result.

Does the history of the U.S. West look different with women at the center? As a matter of fact, it does.

A Word about Terminology

There is a big gap between the words used in the past to describe people and the words that are used today. The words used in the past are generally wildly inaccurate historically and often were used pejoratively. Therefore, they are not particularly appropriate in a modern history textbook. There is as yet no unanimous agreement among historians about the contemporary usage and meanings of many of the words used to describe the racial and ethnic background of peoples in the past, so this book will err on the side of simplicity. It uses "Native American" to refer to all peoples of aboriginal descent, except when "Indian" is part of a title or is used to refer to pre-twentieth century perceptions of Native Americans. "Euro-American" is used in the earlier chapters as a collective term for white people of European descent; "Anglo" and "Anglo-American" are used later in the book to describe whites of non-Spanish, Euro-American descent. "African American" and "black" are used interchangeably. The book uses "Spanish-Mexican" to refer to non-aboriginal women from the region known as New Spain (the northern reaches of Spain's North American empire, now the southwestern United States, California, and northern Mexico) before Mexican independence. It uses "Mexican" and "Mexican American" to refer to Mexican-born and

American-born women, and it uses the more modern "Hispanic" to refer to Spanish-speaking communities as a whole. "Asian" and "Asian American" are used to refer collectively to people of Chinese and Japanese descent, and the specific national term is used where accurate and appropriate. And finally, women's own words are used as often as possible and with as little editing as possible; I have not added "[sic]" (a term that signals an error in an original document) because I do not want to interrupt the flow or affect the original character of a woman's voice.

Suggested Readings

Albers, Patricia, and Beatrice Medicine, eds. *The Hidden Half: Studies of Plains Indian Women.* Washington, D.C.: University Press of America, 1983.

Armitage, Susan, and Elizabeth Jameson, eds. *The Women's West.* Norman: University of Oklahoma Press, 1987.

Irwin, Mary Ann, and James F. Brooks, eds. *Women and Gender in the American West.* Albuquerque: University of New Mexico Press, 2004.

Jameson, Elizabeth, and Susan Armitage, eds. *Writing the Range: Race, Class, and Culture in the Women's West.* Norman: University of Oklahoma Press, 1997.

Jeffrey, Julie Roy. *Frontier Women: The Trans-Mississippi West: 1840–1880.* New York: Hill and Wang, 1979.

Jensen, Joan M., and Darlis A. Miller. "The Gentle Tamers Revisited: New Approaches to the History of Women in the American West." *Pacific Historical Review* 49 (1980): 173–213.

Klein, Laura F., and Lillian A. Ackerman, eds. *Women and Power in Native North America.* Norman: University of Oklahoma Press, 1995.

Myres, Sandra L. *Westering Women and the Frontier Experience 1800–1915.* Albuquerque: University of New Mexico Press, 1982.

Riley, Glenda. *The Female Frontier: A Comparative View of Women on the Prairie and the Plains.* Lawrence: University Press of Kansas, 1988.

Schlissel, Lillian, Vicki L. Ruiz, and Janice Monk, eds. *Western Women: Their Land, Their Lives.* Albuquerque: University of New Mexico Press, 1988.

Taylor, Quintard, and Shirley Ann Wilson Moore, eds. *African American Women Confront the West, 1600–2000.* Norman and London: University of Oklahoma Press, 2003.

CHAPTER ONE

The Women's West before Contact

In the centuries before European contact, Native American women enjoyed a level of equality, opportunity, and respect in their communities that newcomer women would not achieve for centuries. Native American cultures had clear gender norms for women and men just as European cultures did, the key difference being that Native Americans regarded women's roles as equally important as men's and allowed women far more individual agency within those norms. The enormous geographic diversity of the West was matched by a diversity of Native American cultures, yet one thing those cultures all had in common was a belief that women's and men's contributions and relationships should be balanced and reciprocal. Women controlled their own economic activities and personal relationships, and they played many important social, ceremonial, and political roles in their communities.

Equal from the Very Beginning

This egalitarianism and respect is reflected in Native Americans' earliest stories, most of which describe a balanced world in which both men and women are necessary to achieve a harmonious community. Some groups go further and give women a primary role in human creation. The Pawnee of the central Great Plains, for example, believe that the first thing in the world was the Power. The Power was everywhere and nowhere, thought and planning, man and woman. The Power created the female Morning Star with the help of the Sun and then created the male Evening Star with the help of the Moon. The Power then created the South Star and the North Star, with other smaller stars to help them. The Power went on to make the rest of the natural world, but it did not make any people. Morning Star called all the star gods and the Sun and the Moon to a council to make a plan to create people. The council decided that Morning Star and Evening Star should mate, and Morning Star gave birth to a daughter. She was the first human being, as her mother had been the first star. Next Moon and Sun mated, and they had a son. According to the Pawnee, this is how the first two people were made, a story that gives equal importance to the female and male roles in creation.

In another example, one that puts more emphasis on women's roles, the Pueblos of the Southwest believe that in the beginning two females were born underneath the earth. Their father Uchtsiti had made the world from a clot of his own blood, and he planted the two girls in the earth. While they grew in the darkness Tsichtinako (Thought Woman) taught them and cared for them, and she gave them each a basket from their father. The baskets held seeds and symbols of all the plants and animals that were to exist in the world. Their father had given them the baskets so that they would bring life to everything in the baskets and rule over the world. Thought Woman told the sisters to plant the four pine tree seeds they had in their baskets. One tree grew so tall that it pushed a hole through the earth. Before the sisters climbed up, Thought Woman taught them how to praise the Sun with prayers and songs. After the girls made it to the surface and prayed to the Sun, Thought Woman named one sister Iatiku and made her Mother of the Corn clan. She named the other sister Nautsiti and made her Mother of the Sun clan.

In a third example, the Arikara of the upper Missouri River believe that Mother Corn led people up out of the earth, where humans and animals all lived together as a big band of wanderers.

The six Native American culture areas of the American West.

Mother Corn took charge and sent birds and animals out to find a better world to live in, and the skunk and badger dug upward until they found the sun and skies. Mother Corn then led the people on a long march westward, parting an ocean for them so that they could walk through on dry land, until they came to a wide open prairie. The fish, birds, and animals agreed to give as much of their power as they could to Mother Corn before they left the humans to live apart. Mother Corn was grateful because this gift meant that the humans would be able to get food and clothing from any animal and continue to look to animals for sustenance as well as spiritual strength.

Most Native American tribes have similar stories stressing that women and men have balanced and complementary roles. There were hundreds of different tribes and dozens of different languages spoken in the area that would become the American West. Each tribe had an economic and social structure suited to its geographic region and available resources, and its spiritual worldviews recognized and valued women's roles.

Ethnohistorians divide the North American continent into twelve broad culture areas, six of which fall into the region that would become the U.S. West. The local environment determined the available resources, so even though tribes in the same region might have spoken many different languages, they usually shared many significant cultural traits. The Southwest culture area extends from the southern edges of present-day Utah and Colorado southward through Arizona and New Mexico, includes parts of Texas, California, and Oklahoma, and continues into Mexico. This area was home to groups like the Pueblos, Navajos, and Apaches. The California culture area corresponds roughly to the present-day state of California and the Baja California Peninsula in Mexico, and it was home to tribes like the Pomo and Miwok in central California. The Northwest Coast culture area is more than 2,000 miles long, running along the Pacific coast from the Alaskan panhandle to the northern limits of California, and is only about 150 miles across at its widest point. It had a very dense population, including the Coast Salish and Chinook tribes near its southern end. The Columbia Plateau and its two great river systems, the Columbia and the Fraser, define the Plateau culture area of present-day eastern Washington, northeastern and central Oregon, southeastern British Columbia, northern Idaho, western Montana, and a small portion of northern California. This region was home to such groups as the Columbia, Nez Perce, Cayuse, and Flathead. The Great Basin culture area consists of the huge natural desert basin covering most of present-day Utah and Nevada, parts of Colorado, Wyoming, Idaho, Oregon, California, and small parts of Arizona, New Mexico, and Montana. The Paiute, Ute, and Shoshone were three of the tribes who lived in the Great Basin. The Great Plains culture area is the biggest of the six, stretching from the Mississippi River valley in the east to the Rocky Mountains in the west, and from the northern edge of the Great Plains in Canada to southern Texas. It was home to groups like the Kiowa and Comanche in the south, the Omaha, Cheyenne, and Sioux in the middle, and the Mandan, Hidatsa, and Blackfeet at the northern edge.

In spite of the remarkable environmental and cultural diversity found in these different areas, the Native American women living in them had many roles, experiences, and opportunities in common. Most Native American cultures' gender norms tended to be egalitarian: women did different things than men, but their societies generally valued and appreciated their contributions and roles just as much as men's. Women were both the mothers of the people and the ones who fed the people, and in most Native American cultures these roles afforded them a high level of respect. Their choices and the level of respect they enjoyed are evident in four areas: economic contributions, family relationships, ceremonial and political power, and the availability of alternative gender roles.

Economic Contributions

As the creation stories suggest, one of the main reasons why Native American cultures valued women so highly was because of their roles in creating and sustaining their communities. Across the continent Native American women were responsible for gathering plants for food and processing the animals and fish that the men hunted and caught. In these *hunter-gatherer* cultures, as they are called, women often directly contributed half of the food their people ate and made the other half edible. This broad generalization obscures a lot of regional differences, however. The exact roles women played in collecting, processing, storing, trading, and distributing food varied considerably according to their specific local economy. For example, tribes that were purely hunter-gatherers tended to be nomadic, in that they followed seasonal patterns of migration to maximize their food sources. By contrast, groups such as the Mandan and Hidatsa of the Upper Missouri and the Pueblos of the Southwest were agriculturalists who relied primarily on plant foods grown and harvested by women, supplementing the plant foods with whatever meat men might provide from hunting. Agriculturalists were not nomadic because they did not need to travel far for food; at most they would move between summer and winter villages.

The local environment and its resources shaped women's economic activities in other ways. In the Columbia Plateau region, for example, fish was a staple food for the aboriginal people because the rivers provided the most abundant salmon runs on the continent south of Alaska. Men fished and hunted during the appropriate seasons, while women gathered plants from spring until fall and prepared all the food for storage and winter use. The diet in most of the area consisted roughly of half plant and half animal foods, which meant that women and men contributed equally to their communities' food supply.

Native Americans on the Plateau followed an annual pattern of migration to fish and dig roots. Roots had to be dried or baked in the spring and summer camp areas, then stored and later transported to the winter camps. Each woman carried a load of four or five hemp baskets weighing about 30 pounds each (for a total of 120–150 pounds), which she tied in clusters on her back. When the women had collected enough roots, they dug a round pit two and a half feet deep, into which they put four or five flat stones, followed by a large amount of dry wood and then a layer of small stones. When the wood burned down to the embers, the small stones dropped to the bottom of the pit, indicating that the pit had reached the right temperature. The women then layered in earth and branches until the hole was almost full. They put the roots on top and covered them with more branches and dry pine needles, piled the whole pit with earth, and built a large fire on top. The roots remained in this earth oven for twelve to twenty-four hours. Communities had a lot of respect for the women who became experts at this complicated process and for the food it produced. In the early spring villages held a First Roots ceremony, one of several sacred First Foods ceremonies. The chief or an elderly man would appoint four or five women to collect and cook the first ripening roots. After the women prepared the food, the community gathered to pray to the Creator and then ate the cooked roots.

On the Plateau men were not involved in women's gathering activities, but women always helped with certain aspects of the men's fishing and hunting. Women provided the necessary building materials for the men's salmon weirs (a dam or trap set into a river to catch the fish) and processed what the men caught. Women accompanied the fall hunting expeditions to set up camp, cook the food, help drive prey animals toward the hunters when needed, and pack the carcasses back to camp, where they butchered and dried the meat. After each hunt the community gave a share of the dried meat to a member of each family, usually a woman, who had exclusive decision-making authority over its use, trade, or storage.

Among the Southern Paiute in the Great Basin, the division of labor between men and women was far less rigid than in most other Native American cultures, because the scarcity of food meant that women and men often had to work together to get enough food for the tribe's survival. Rabbits were the most common animal portion of the diet, with the occasional addition of mountain sheep, deer, antelope, tortoise, quail, or other game. Men hunted the larger animals both individually and in groups, while women trapped the smaller animals. Men helped to gather pine nuts and harvest legumes from the mesquite tree. Women processed and stored all the food and were responsible for distributing it to their families and neighbors. Women also tanned hides and made rabbit-skin robes for winter clothing and trade; wove a range of household items, including baskets, mats, and cradles from vegetable fibers; and made their own tools and additional items for interband and intertribal trade.

On the northern Great Plains, nomadic hunter-gatherer tribes such as the Lakota and Blackfeet usually accorded a higher status to men's activities, but they still valued women's economic contributions and the women owned and distributed the things they produced. The Lakota considered men's work (warfare and hunting) to be more glorious and important than women's work (processing the buffalo meat and hides, managing the household, and raising the children), but men respected women for doing their work well. Blackfeet women made, and therefore owned, the tipis in which each family lived. Women who specialized in certain skills, such as bead work, exchanged or sold their products to other women. Some women grew wealthy by acquiring objects of fine craftsmanship, surplus clothing, and so on, and that wealth helped distinguish their family from others.

Unlike the nomadic tribes of the northern plains, the Mandan, Hidatsa, and Arikara tribes settled in fairly permanent villages along the upper Missouri River valley. They grew corn and vegetables instead of following the buffalo herds as the Lakota and Blackfeet did. A woman who lived in a village on the upper Missouri River followed a seasonal cycle, as did women in hunter-gatherer societies, but she was not nomadic like them. In the spring adult women, along with their daughters, prepared their garden plots and planted the crops. Once the seeds had been planted, women began preparing for the summer hunt. The hunt was a sort of working holiday, because it gave women a chance to travel, see new things, and meet new people. To ensure her husband's success in the hunt, a wife prepared the goods for him to use in the pre-hunt ceremony to ensure a successful venture. The women also helped the men butcher the meat and prepared the hides after the hunt. The work was balanced with festivity, however, because a good hunt meant there would be plenty of meat until the gardens began to produce corn and vegetables.

For women, the rest of the summer involved tending to the fields and gardens. At harvest time, the women and girls gathered the corn and other vegetables and prepared them for storage. Harvesting usually began in August with the squash and ended in October with the ripe corn. When the crops had been gathered, the women closed their big summer lodges and moved their families to smaller winter quarters in the river bottoms, where wood was more plentiful and the winter winds less severe. Women either built a new winter lodge or repaired an old one. In the early spring before the ice broke up, families moved back to the big summer lodges. Women owned the fields, the agricultural tools, and the lodges.

Women from the Mandan, Hidatsa, and Arikara tribes not only produced enough corn and other vegetables for their own families, but they also generated a substantial surplus that the tribe traded for buffalo hides, horn spoons, and other goods produced by the neighboring nomadic, buffalo-hunting tribes. Enjoying a reliable food source and located at the center of a huge trade network that stretched from Mexico to Canada and from the Pacific Ocean to the Great Lakes, the three tribes were well placed to carry on a profitable trade. The men did most of the ceremonial trading, by which they established and maintained good diplomatic relations with other tribes, while the women did most of the individual, practical trading.

In all Native American tribes, women's main economic contributions involved processing and gathering food and producing household goods for their families, but many women also produced a surplus to trade with other families and tribes. Women could become wealthy, just as men could, by being energetic and ambitious enough to gather or produce additional food or goods for trade. Like men, women were actively involved in trading, typically exchanging food items, baskets, dressed animal pelts, and clothing. Through trade a woman could acquire horses and household goods, markers of wealth and status for her family. Some of the food items women produced were particularly valuable commodities. On the Plateau, for example, women pounded dried salmon into a powder, which took a long time but created a very valuable food product that kept indefinitely. During some trade negotiations in the eighteenth century, well after Europeans had arrived and Plateau tribes had adopted horses, one salmon skin filled with pounded salmon powder was equal in value to a good horse.

Even children could trade their own products if they wanted to. According to one account, a little girl from the Plateau traveled east across the mountains to the Great Plains with her parents on a trading expedition. She brought some dried salmon eggs she had prepared to trade for a doll from a Blackfeet girl. Unfortunately, fighting broke out between the Plateau and Blackfeet adults before the girls could complete their trade, much to their disappointment.

In all Upper Missouri cultures, men and women both had defined roles to play in their village societies and economies, but each had to rely on the other. Men hunted, and women turned the buffalo carcasses into food, hides, and tools. Women farmed, and men used the surplus agricultural goods to establish good relations with other tribes. Men fought off enemies, but women built and maintained the village palisades. As these examples suggest, although women and men had very different economic roles and responsibilities, all the cultures acknowledged and respected women's work and women had a high degree of agency when it came to their work.

Family Relationships

Women's roles in food production and trade meant that their labor was critical to the survival of their people. This same recognition of and level of respect for Native American women's economic activities was mirrored in many cultures by women's central roles in kin networks and residency patterns. Many groups traced their family descent through their female relatives and ancestors and lived closer to them than to their male relatives. Groups who traced their lineage through their mother's side are called *matrilineal*; for example, among the Mandan and Hidatsa, kinship and residency were determined through the mother and matrilineal clans controlled any property not claimed by a specific family. Groups who traced their lineage through the father's side are called *patrilineal*, and those that trace it through both sides are called *bilateral*.

The same system is used to describe residency patterns. If a newly married couple lived with the bride's family, the group was *matrilo-*

cal; if the pair lived with the groom's family, it was *patrilocal*; and if it alternated, the couple was called *bilocal*. In some instances the newlyweds lived on their own or with family members who were not their parents. Perhaps one-quarter of the aboriginal groups in what is now the U.S. West were matrilineal, including the Arikara, Navajo, Cherokee, Crow, Hidatsa, Hopi, Mandan, Pawnee, Wichita, and Zuni. Tribes were more likely to be both matrilineal and matrilocal if they were agricultural because, as described above, women in farming villages were in charge of producing and distributing most of the food on which the community depended.

Most Pueblo households in the Southwest were matrilineal, usually consisting of a grandmother and her husband, her sisters and their husbands, her daughters and their husbands, and various young children. Pueblo women worked together to build their own and each other's houses, and they added additional rooms when daughters married. Women stayed in their birth home their whole lives, but men moved from house to house according to their stage in life: they lived in their mother's house until they got married; then they went to live in the house belonging to their wife's mother. Pueblo girls married when they were about seventeen and boys when they were about nineteen. Young adults were free to meet and court each other, but the man had to take the first step toward getting married. He would tell his parents whom he wanted to marry, and if his parents and kin agreed with his choice, the senior members of his household would gather and deliver the necessary marriage-validating gifts to the girl's household. If the girl's kin agreed to the marriage and accepted the gifts, each person who accepted a gift had to give one in return. In this way the two households exchanged equal amounts of wealth. After the gift giving, the families would conduct a marriage ritual. Marriage was not a monogamous, lifelong commitment for the Pueblo people, however, and either party was free to leave the relationship if she or he was unhappy in it.

The Pomo of California were bilocal, and newly married couples alternated between their parents' villages for the first few years after marriage, usually settling permanently in the bride's mother's village. This pattern gave the couple the chance to develop a wider kin network and maximize their access to any specialized skills that either side of the family might possess. Within each village extended families lived together in one large house. Pomo families measured their wealth in baskets, beads, and blankets woven of tree squirrel or rabbit skins, and these items were kept in the house and distributed by the oldest female, who often owned the house.

On the Plateau, marriage worked a little differently. Although such tribes as the Columbia, Nez Perce and Cayuse often had a bilocal residence pattern similar to that of the Pomo, married couples generally lived with the groom's family. Parents usually arranged their children's first marriages, but individuals chose subsequent marriage partners on their own. A marriage began when a couple started living together, and it ended when one of the individuals took his or her personal items and left the home. Both men and women had an equal right to divorce, and many individuals had several spouses in one lifetime. Divorce did not lead to economic hardship for either partner, because he or she could move in with kin or live independently. Women had the means to support themselves, if they wished to, through their own gathering and trading. Some Plateau men were wealthy enough to have more than one wife, which is technically called polygyny but is more commonly referred to as polygamy. Polygyny was an important social and economic institution in many Native American groups because in some situations it could help provide some stability for a community. For example, if a group had fewer men after a long period of warfare, polygyny guaranteed that women could still marry if they wanted. Plural wives were often sisters or cousins who were friends and allies, a pattern that could enhance a community's stability and cohesion. Wives who were not related to each other might become unhappy rivals, but an unhappy wife could divorce her husband easily.

First marriages for Plateau peoples were, as mentioned, arranged by their parents, but if a young woman or man was unhappy with the prospective spouse, he or she could choose to elope with a preferred lover and thwart parental authority. To arrange a marriage, a young man's mother would make the proposal to the young woman's mother. If the mothers agreed, the two fathers would make their arrangements. After a few days the girl would move in with her new husband and his parents, or he might move in with her and her parents. A few days after the couple began to live together, the families would exchange gifts. The groom's family gave food and other goods traditionally provided by a male for his family to the girl's relatives, and the bride's family gave to the groom's relatives the foods and other goods that a woman traditionally provided for her family. This marriage trade marked the beginning of a relationship between the two families.

Power was shared relatively equally in Plateau marriages, with neither partner having an automatic or institutionalized advantage over the other. And although European observers assumed that women were subordinate to their husbands in polygynous marriages, this was not the case among Plateau peoples. Men would sometimes seek plural wives as a sign of prestige or vanity, while a woman might enter a polygynous marriage with the intent of driving off the other woman. Polygynous marriages were often unstable, except for those involving sisters or cousins. In rare cases, a wife or co-wives would choose an additional wife for their husband because the woman had a particular skill that the family needed.

In Plateau societies a child born to a young, unmarried woman was accepted by the mother's kin without condemnation. The new mother could keep the child or choose to have a married couple adopt it. Grandparents exerted great influence on children, whether raised within their households or not, and they often gave the child its first name. Children lived with their grandparents while their parents were busy with their annual round of economic tasks, and grandparents provided stability for children whose parents went through a series of marriages and divorces, a common phenomenon. Grandmothers wielded the most power because they were the managers of the household and everyone consulted them about the goings-on in the extended family. Childlessness did not lower a woman's status, because she was still considered a mother and grandmother to her siblings' children.

South of the Plateau in the Great Basin, the Paiutes determined their ancestry bilaterally. Newly married couples usually lived with the bride's family, but later moves typically were bilocal. Parents arranged the first marriages for their sons and daughters at or before puberty. Individuals arranged their own subsequent marriages. Premarital sexual experiences were common and acceptable. Polygyny was rare among the Paiutes, usually consisting of sisters marrying the same man, and divorce was frequent and could be initiated by either partner.

Further north and east, the Lakota of the northern Great Plains had three kinds of marriage and residence patterns. First, a woman and a man might elope before their families exchanged any gifts to sanction the relationship. These couples usually lived first with the husband's family. Second, a couple could marry by mutual agreement, which entailed an exchange of presents between the two families. These couples usually began their married life with the wife's family. Third, a husband could earn his wife by giving a large quantity of valuable goods to her family. Lakotas considered this method the most honorable because it showed how much a man valued the woman he wanted to marry and the aspiring husband would have to work hard for a long time to acquire the wealth required. In theory a girl's male relatives, especially her brothers, had the power to choose her marriage partners, but in practice girls chose their own husbands. Husbands and wives owned their personal goods individually, while the wife owned the home and domestic goods. As in all other Native American cultures, divorce was simple and either party could initiate the separation. The Lakota believed that women were more sexually demanding than men but, unlike the many other Native American groups that permitted or encouraged sexual activity before marriage, the Lakota expected women to be virgins when they married for the first time, and they held women responsible in all cases of premarital pregnancy or adultery.

Upper Missouri women were usually matrilocal, and their society was organized into matrilineal clans. Although village chiefs were all men, their positions depended on the support of their matrilineal clan, and villagers made important decisions by consensus. Women usually outnumbered men by about three to one because so many men were killed during hunting or warfare. For this reason a man often married his wife's younger sisters when they were old enough. The women would share the work and care for each other's children if one of the mothers died. Women usually gave birth in their mother's homes, and the child's naming ceremony took place either in the child's mother's lodge or in a public ceremony conducted by the sister of the child's father. Because women of childbearing age had a great deal of work to do, maternal grandmothers cared for the young children. When a girl was about seven or eight, she started to follow her mother into the woods to gather wood and the fields to tend to the crops.

If a woman did not want to marry her older sister's husband, she could seek a relationship with another man. If he reciprocated her feelings, he would offer her two or three horses and she would leave her mother's lodge to live with her husband. If she had female relatives in a lodge with no men, she might bring her husband to live there, and she would later inherit the lodge and fields. If her husband had no sisters, she could choose to work in his mother's lodge and eventually inherit it. A woman living in her husband's lodge was in a much less secure position than one in her mother's lodge, however. If she disagreed with other family members or her husband died, she had to leave the lodge, often taking only her clothes and children with her. Her deceased husband's brother might agree to marry her and protect her children, but she always had the option of returning to her mother's lodge. No woman had to support and raise her children on her own, because she could always count on the support of her matrilineal clan. If a married woman got sick and was not able to maintain her lodge and gardens or care for her children, others in her household or clan would take over those responsibilities until she recovered. If she died, her sisters, mother, and grandmothers would take care of her children, and her property would revert to the clan if no one claimed it.

Similarly, in the Southwest Navajo, Hopi, and western Pueblo women controlled their own property and bequeathed it to their children. The women who headed the clans made the final decisions in all economic and domestic matters. Communities respected grandmothers for their wisdom and mothering skills and viewed them as the most important informal influence on younger family members. Plateau mothers had an equal say with fathers in raising their children and arranging children's first marriages. The men and women of both families also had important roles in celebrating a couple's marriage. For example, in the centuries after Europeans arrived, the fathers of the newlyweds exchanged horses to finalize a marriage agreement, and the women gave more gifts several months later to confirm the relationship.

Further evidence of women's high status in Native American communities was the fact that domestic violence was rare and, when it did happen, women had a range of acceptable ways to respond. For example, Plateau communities thought it was shameful for a man to beat his wife. The extended family would tell the man either to change his behavior or divorce his wife if he could not get along with her. Rape was also rare, and the community would usually hand a rapist over to the women of the village to be tormented and humiliated before banishing him. In the case of adultery a Plateau man could kill his wife's lover with no fear of reprisal, but usually people would tell him either to ignore the affair or divorce his wife without resorting to violence. A wife could not kill her husband's lover, but she and her female friends were entitled to attack a rival and drive her away.

Another example of Native American women's agency was their ability to define and control their own sexuality, instead of having it defined for them in relationship to their husbands. Most cultures equated sexuality with fertility and regeneration, and they also saw it as a way to connect to the spiritual world. For instance, the Pueblos believed that women's sexuality empowered them, and it was theirs to share or withhold. Sex helped incorporate a woman's husband into his wife's matrilineal community, and it produced the children who would care for women when they were older.

Native American communities across the continent organized their families and marriages in different ways, but none of them forced women into an inferior or dependent position or imposed significant constraints on them. Most Native American women could marry whomever they chose, leave the marriage when it no longer suited them, had the economic skills to support themselves and their children, and could rely on the help of their kin when they needed it, without any disgrace or disrespect.

Ceremonial and Political Power

The high degree of agency and respect Native American women enjoyed in their economic and family lives extended into the ceremonial and political realms. Native American women and men usually had distinct ceremonial and political roles, just as they had different economic roles. However, communities did not exclude women from their ceremonies and political decisions because they were women, and women's contributions were necessary for much of the community's ceremonial and political life. For example, Paiute women could be shamans with the same prestige and status as male shamans, although there were usually more male shamans than female. Plateau boys and girls acquired guardian spirits in equal numbers and were both sent out on spirit quests, suggesting equal access to the spiritual world. Pomo men and women also had equal access to spiritual power.

Even in the patrilineal groups on the plains, women played critical ceremonial roles. Among the Lakota, for instance, women gained status by participating in the Buffalo Ceremony and Virgin Fire rituals. Only a holy woman could sponsor a Blackfeet Sun Dance, and Blackfeet believed that women were intermediaries through whom sacred power was granted to humans. This crucial role was evident in medicine bundle openings: only a woman could unwrap and rewrap a holy bundle, and she handed the powerful objects inside to the male celebrant. Plains women also made elaborate ceremonial objects, including the tipis and robes used for sacred ceremonies, the containers that held items needed for rituals, and gifts such as quilts that were given at honoring ceremonies. Women of the Blackfeet, Dakota, Lakota, Arapaho, and Cheyenne had different spiritual and ceremonial roles from men, but their roles were no less important than those of men.

In the three Upper Missouri tribes, men performed most of the rituals and ceremonies, but women made most of the preparations. By growing the corn that fed the tribes and fueled their trade network, the women ensured that their people had the leisure to perform their rituals and the wealth to gather impressive amounts of goods and food for the events. The practice of the tribal religion, which recognized the earth and all its bounty as female, depended on women and their work. Men had more leisure to give to ceremonial activities between their hunting or war expeditions, and so their rituals were more numerous and more elaborate than the women's, but these events were not more important than those of women.

Native American women's political power can be hard to recognize now, because we assume that political involvement involves formal processes like elections and office holding. In most Native American tribes before contact, women exercised informal and indirect power. For example, on the Plateau women and men earned informal political power by demonstrating superior skills. Good providers, whether male or female, had more influence in the community than those who were less successful economically. Direct authority, however, was not equally available to men and women. Chiefs were almost always male, but they were chosen by an assembly of all the male and female adults in the community. During these assemblies people asked the most respected community members for their opinions of the candidates, and they listened to women's opinions as seriously as those of men. An assembly discussing whether to go to war might exclude women because the men would be doing the fighting, but women often participated in those discussions because they would have to provide the necessary food supplies.

Plateau chiefs usually had multiple wives who produced a surplus of food and goods that the chiefs redistributed to tribal members and guests during meetings, funerals, and other formal occasions. Male leaders therefore depended on their wives' economic contributions to maintain their status. When a community considered a candidate for the chieftainship, it took into account the character of his wife or wives. A chief's wife advised him on important decisions and served as chief when he was away. When he died, she nominated his successor, usually their son, and in some groups she acted as chief for a year during the mourning period.

Paiute women also participated in the process of choosing headmen. The job often passed through female kin ties, meaning that a man was more likely to be chosen if he was related to the previous chief through his mother or aunt. Community members debated each man's character before they made a final decision. Pomo women also participated in choosing their village's headmen, although Pomo chieftainship was likely to pass from father to son. Even hereditary chiefs needed the support of everyone in the village. A female relative, but not the headman's wife, acted as an official hostess and organized women's activities.

By contrast, women who lived among northern Great Plains groups like the Lakota and Blackfeet had less formal and informal power than women who lived along the upper Missouri River and on the Columbia Plateau. For example, in Lakota communities gender—whether a person was male or female—was the most important attribute defining an individual, and the Lakota thought that women were less important than men. Women controlled domestic matters, whereas men dealt with the dangers of life outside camp. Only men could lead the community, and all-male councils made the decisions. These Plains groups were exceptions to the common pattern across the continent, in which most Native American women enjoyed ceremonial and political power equal or nearly equal to that of men.

Alternative Gender Roles

Some Native American women also exercised a surprising amount of agency in defining their own gender. Women in some tribes could adopt alternative gender roles without being scorned by their communities. These alternative gender roles included the uncommon "manly hearted woman" role in the northern Great Plains and warrior women in some other groups. Because many aboriginal cultures allowed a wide latitude in the definition of self, they often recognized the existence of more than two genders. A person's gender and sexual role was not necessarily fixed over the course of her lifetime. It was more common for someone with a male body to assume a female role (generally referred to as a *berdache*), but in a few cultures some people with female bodies took on male roles.

For example, if a woman showed a particular aptitude for hunting or other men's work, many tribes supported her. Among the Blackfeet, although women usually had less status than men, an older, elite, wealthy woman who was or had been married could become a "manly hearted woman." Such women had distinguished themselves in property ownership, participation in ceremonies, and domestic affairs. They had often been favored children who dominated games and played boys' sports, and they became independent, outspoken, assertive adults. Having acquired wealth through a combination of inheritance and hard work, they had the means and status to sponsor important celebrations and dances. They ran their own households and, if they were still married, dominated their husbands. If their husbands abused them in any way, manly hearted women would fight back, shame their husbands in public, or leave the marriage. Younger men were eager to court a manly hearted widow because of her wealth, status, and reputation for sexual prowess. Blackfeet people simultaneously admired, criticized, and feared manly hearted women.

Some Native American groups permitted women to become warriors if they showed enough bravery and skill. Most of these warrior women helped the wounded and rescued male relatives during battle if needed, but they did not miss a chance to kill an opposing warrior. Some women chose to participate as full warriors. Their communities usually did not see such women as having ceased to be female, nor did women warriors have an unusual or lower social status. Women participating in warfare were not unheard of among the northern Great Plains tribes because of the great individual prestige that could be gained in the masculine arenas of warfare and raiding. For example, when Woman Chief of the Crow and Running Eagle of the Piegan (one of the three Blackfeet tribes) displayed in childhood their preference for masculine activities, their families respected their choice.

Woman Chief was born about 1814 into the Gros Ventre tribe in what is now southeastern Montana. The Crow captured and then adopted her when she was a young child. Around the age of ten, she began to express an interest in men's activities, and her Crow stepfather encouraged her by teaching her to hunt and ride. Woman Chief's career as a warrior appears to have begun in her teens. During a Blackfeet attack on the Crow, her people took refuge in a nearby trading post. When the Blackfeet expressed an interest in negotiating, Woman Chief was the only one who would leave the post. Instead of talking, the Blackfeet shot at her. She escaped unharmed and managed to shoot at least three of the attackers in the process. A year later she led her first raid against the Blackfeet, during which she and her party stole some seventy horses. In the ensuing battle, she managed to kill and scalp one Blackfeet and "count coup" (hit but not kill an enemy, a show of superior skill) on a second man, whose gun she seized. As her daring accomplishments mounted, her people sang songs about her bravery and the tribe's elders came to believe she had a charmed life. She took the name Woman Chief, and men invited her into their councils.

Woman Chief only wore men's clothing when she was at war, but she claimed many masculine privileges in addition to fighting. She became wealthy by stealing horses and married four wives to process the numerous hides she obtained through hunting. Her wealth in horses and wives reinforced her status as chief. When she took over her family's lodge after her stepfather's death, she ranked third among 160 heads of families. The Gros Ventres killed her in the summer of 1854 when she was approximately forty years old.

Although several of the northern Great Plains tribes had a tradition of accepting alternative gender roles for women, it was less common for such behavior to lead to a wholesale change in gender role such as Running Eagle's. She was born into the Piegan tribe of what is now northern Montana sometime during the early 1800s, and became the most famous warrior woman among the Blackfeet. As a little girl, she was called Brown Weasel Woman. Her career as a warrior began when she was in her teens, when the Assiniboine (a neighboring enemy tribe) attacked a small hunting party and she saved her father's life. Later on a raiding party against the Crow, she stole eleven horses and killed a Crow warrior. After this victory, her people allowed her to sing the Victory Song and held a Scalp Dance in her honor. She became so successful as a warrior that she won the right to tell her own war stories around the fire. Following a major battle with the Pend d'Oreille (another enemy tribe), she became the only woman in the tribe's history to receive a male name, Running Eagle, and the tribe invited her to join the Brave Society of male warriors. Because of her skills and good fortune, she soon began leading raiding parties, and many Piegan warriors happily followed her.

Her ability to become a warrior had a spiritual element as well as a martial one. As a young woman Running Eagle had had a vision in which the Sun gave her supernatural powers in exchange for her promise never to marry a man. This vision both legitimated her gender role change and made her a holy person. She invited a young widow into her household to care for her siblings and take care of the domestic labor.

One account of Running Eagle's death around 1850 says that Flathead Indians, a common target of Piegan horse raids, killed her during a raid on one of their camps west of the Rockies. The Flatheads had heard that a woman planned to lead the raid against them, so when a Flathead warrior spotted Running Eagle, he shot and killed her. Another account of her death says that the Pend d'Oreilles killed her when she led a large war party against them in retaliation for their earlier attack on a group of Piegan warriors. Both stories emphasize that she died a warrior's death.

One unusual Kutenai woman whose people did not accept her gender role change at first was Qanqon-kamek-klaula. According to Kutenai oral tradition and the accounts of European fur traders, she was born sometime around 1790 in what are now the borderlands between British Columbia and Idaho. Her childhood name was Ququnok-patke or "One Standing Lodge Pole Woman," because she was taller and stronger than the other girls. When she was in her teens, the white fur traders of the North West Company first entered the region and she married a French-Canadian fur trader named Boisverd around 1808. The marriage lasted only a year, after which she returned to her people. When she got home, she stated that her husband had turned her into a man. She claimed a new name, Ko-come-ne-pe-ca or "Gone to the Spirits," to stress the spiritual nature of her transformation and the new spiritual powers she possessed. She began to wear men's clothes, carried a gun as well as a bow, and pursued intimate relationships with widows and older divorced women. She was very possessive of her wives and would beat them if she suspected them of being unfaithful.

During an unsuccessful horse raid shortly after her change, an incident led to Ko-come-ne-pe-ca to adopt the name Qanqon-kamek-klaula or "Sitting in the Water Grizzly." When her group of warriors crossed a creek, she hung back so that she could cross alone and unobserved. Her brother spied on her because he did not believe that her sex had really changed. She saw him watching her and sat down in the water to hide her body, at which point he left to rejoin the group. When she caught up, she announced that she had chosen the new name, but her brother replied that he would only call her Qanqon, making fun of both the name and her claim to have been changed into a man. Her brother was not the only person who did not accept her new appearance or names. Gender role change for women was not common among the Kutenais, and they were initially suspicious of her behavior and claims. She was not accepted by her people until after she had spent several years living and acting as a man.

Between the time of her gender change (about 1809) and her death in 1837, Qanqon-kamek-klaula pursued a variety of masculine activities, including participating in horse raids and trading expeditions, acting as a guide for white travelers, and working as a prophet, healer, interpreter, and mediator. She generally passed as male among whites, and they often perceived her and her current wife as a married couple. When she prophesied epidemic disease in the 1810s, she became unpopular among many Plateau tribes. She never returned to a feminine appearance or way of life, and by the end of her life she had garnered some respect from her own people. Blackfeet raiders, traditional enemies of the Kutenai, killed her in 1837 during an ambush.

Cross-gender behavior and warrior women were the exceptions and not the rule in Native American societies. Nevertheless, these three women are striking examples of the fluid gender roles of Native American societies, even among those that esteemed masculine warrior identities, and the ways those gender roles sometimes allowed women to make unusual choices.

For thousands of years women were valued members of most Native American cultures across the West. Women's economic, social, and spiritual roles gave them choices and status that were different from but usually equal to those of men. Native women's equality and independence were two of the hardest things for European newcomers to understand when they began to explore the region. Nothing highlighted the differences between Native and European ways of life as much as their views of women, and Native American women would not be able to retain their high status and egalitarian communities under the impact of the newcomers' arrival.

Suggested Readings

Ackerman, Lillian A. *A Necessary Balance: Gender and Power Among Indians of the Columbia Plateau.* Norman: University of Oklahoma Press, 2003.

Albers, Patricia, and Beatrice Medicine. "The Role of Sioux Women in the Production of Ceremonial Objects: The Case of the Star Quilt." In *The Hidden Half: Studies of Plains Indian Women,* edited by Patricia Albers and Beatrice Medicine, pp. 123–140. Washington, D.C.: University Press of America, 1983.

Deloria, Ella Cara. *Waterlily.* Lincoln: University of Nebraska Press, 1988.

DeMallie, Raymond. "Male and Female in Traditional Lakota Culture." In *The Hidden Half: Studies of Plains Indian Women,* edited by Patricia Albers and Beatrice Medicine, pp. 237–266. Washington, D.C.: University Press of America, 1983.

Ford, Ramona. "Native American Women: Changing Statuses, Changing Interpretations." In *Writing the Range: Race, Class, and Culture in the Women's West,* edited by Elizabeth Jameson and Susan Armitage, pp. 42–68. Norman: University of Oklahoma Press, 1997.

Gutiérrez, Ramón A. *When Jesus Came, the Corn Mothers Went Away: Marriage, Sexuality, and Power in New Mexico, 1500–1846.* Stanford, CA: Stanford University Press, 1991.

Hungry Wolf, Beverly. *The Ways of My Grandmothers.* New York: Quill, 1982.

Klein, Laura F., and Lillian Ackerman, eds. *Women and Power in Native North America.* Norman: University of Oklahoma, 1995.

Medicine, Beatrice. "'Warrior Women'—Sex Role Alternatives for Plains Indian Women." In *The Hidden Half: Studies of Plains Indian Women,* edited by Patricia Albers and Beatrice Medicine, pp. 237–266. Washington, D.C.: University Press of America, 1983.

Peters, Virginia Bergman. *Women of the Earth Lodges: Tribal Life on the Plains.* North Haven, CT: Archon Books, 1995.

CHAPTER TWO

Contact between Natives and Newcomers

Contact with Europeans affected all Native Americans profoundly, but it affected women and men differently. European products, diseases, and their fundamentally different social and spiritual norms changed Native American women's lives dramatically. The number of choices and opportunities that Native American women retained and the new constraints on their lives varied according to when and how the contact occurred, which European power was involved, gender norms in the women's home communities, and the ways in which their economies intersected with those of the newcomers. There were, however, some powerful similarities across the continent in terms of the changes and constraints that Europeans introduced. In some cases women carved out new opportunities for themselves or maintained a high degree of continuity with their traditions by incorporating change on their own terms, but overall the number of women and their status declined drastically as a result of European colonization. As they changed their trading practices to accommodate the newcomers, Native American communities began to devalue women's economic contributions and put more emphasis on male traders and their goods. Most of Native America's egalitarian and matrilineal cultures were forced to adopt European patriarchal norms, some quickly by violence and some slowly through gradual colonization. Europeans often saw any alternative roles, such as the warrior or manly hearted woman, as aberrations, and women's social, political and ceremonial contributions declined in both frequency and importance. Sexual violence, which was rare among precontact Native American cultures, became a fact of life for Native American women across the West. And yet, even as European and American expansion and conquest marginalized Native American women, the newcomers also depended on women's productive and reproductive labor.

The Spanish

Native American women in what is now northern Mexico and the U.S. Southwest first encountered European men in the early 1500s, when Spanish conquerors and slave traders entered the region looking for gold, silver, and slaves. Contact with the Europeans was sporadic throughout the sixteenth century but became more frequent and violent in the seventeenth century. The Spanish often stole the food and supplies they needed, by force if necessary, and assaulted Native American women while they were at it. As a result, women and their communities lost the products of their labor and got little or nothing in return.

If a community fought back against the assaults and thefts, the Spanish retaliated by attacking it and burning it down. In 1598, for instance, the Pueblos of Acoma, the "Sky City" in what is now New Mexico, stood up to the Spanish and were punished harshly for it. When the Spaniards were not satisfied with the supplies the people had given them voluntarily, they entered the city to take what they wanted and assaulted a young woman in the process. Acoma's warriors retaliated, killing most of the soldiers before the survivors jumped off the edge of the mesa. The Spanish sent more soldiers in January 1599 to punish the residents of Acoma. The soldiers killed about eight hundred men, women, and children, and took another eighty men and five hundred women and children prisoner. The Spanish cut one foot off each adult man, sentenced all prisoners over the age of twelve to become Spanish slaves, and took the younger children as servants. There would be no more rebellions against Spanish demands until the massive Pueblo Revolt of 1680, during which the Pueblos drove the Spanish out of the province. Spain did not try to reconquer the region for more than a decade.

In the 1690s, the Spanish began to build a series of *presidios* (military forts) along the northern edges of their claims to establish a defensive ring against the encroaching English, French, and Russians, as well as what they called the *indios bárbaros* (barbarian Indians) such as the Comanches, Navajos, and Apaches. But the presidios were more than just military outposts; the Spanish hoped they would speed the colonization process by providing a safe place for Spanish women to settle. Spanish officials believed that Spanish women would play important roles as models of appropriate feminine behavior and as mothers of a new population that would help the government hold on to what it had claimed.

In 1769 the Spanish moved to take control of California. One year earlier the Spanish authorities had learned that Russia was establishing colonies along the Pacific Coast in California. In response, a small force of Spanish soldiers and Franciscan friars established the first presidio and Catholic mission in California in present-day San Diego. Between 1769 and 1784, the Spanish established presidios and missions at Monterey, San Francisco, Santa Bárbara, San Gabriel, San Antonio de Padua, San Luis Obispo, and San José. Historians disagree about the amount of force that the Spanish used to get the Native Americans to live at the missions, where they were to be converted to both Catholicism and European social norms, but once they were there the Spanish used whatever force was necessary to make them stay. The colonizers whipped any Native American who refused to work or was caught after running away.

The main reasons why so many Native American women were sexually assaulted during Spanish colonization were that most of the male newcomers were soldiers who were accustomed to using to violence to get their way and authorities took few concrete steps to stop the systemic rapes. In colonial settings around the world, rape was the ultimate act in the subjugation of indigenous peoples; armies and conquerors used it to subordinate women and make indigenous men look weak and helpless. In Spanish California Friar Junípero Serra warned the authorities that if they did not do more to stop the attacks, the peaceful Native Californians were going to unite in an attempt to drive out the settlers. The authorities repeatedly told the soldiers not to harass and rape Native women, but the men did not stop. Sometimes the Spanish soldiers killed Native American men to get at the women. Secular and spiritual officials claimed that they could not control the soldiers' behavior, but they also recognized that terror and violence were useful ways to subdue a population. Most of them placed little value on Native American women anyway, but some of the missionaries felt differently. The frequent attacks not only hindered their work and caused many Native Californians to flee into the mountains, but they also demoralized the priests, stalled the establishment of additional missions, and had a negative effect on the Native Californians' health. Women and girls were the first to get deadly sexually transmitted diseases like syphilis, which could cause infertility, be passed on to children, or kill the women outright; the combination led to massive population losses.

The friars pleaded with the Crown to punish the offenders and send marriageable Spanish women from Mexico. The church also asked the government to encourage marriage between the soldiers and newly converted Native American women, the *neofítas* or neophytes, but there were few of these relationships. In 1772, three years after the first Spanish incursions into California, two neophyte couples settled in San Gabriel. Spanish civil and religious leaders hoped the couples would be role models for the newly converted Native Californians. The Native Californians often were happy to see the couples simply because they had yet to see any women or families among the conquerors. One of the women was María Dolores, who came to San Gabriel with her husband Sebastián. She did not stay long, however. Perhaps in response to the harsh living and working conditions, she, Sebastián, and another man ran away from the mission and later perished in the desert.

California's Native American women responded in a variety of ways to the violence. Some sought protection by marrying a Spaniard or entering the missions voluntarily. Others engaged in prostitution, which had been unheard of before European contact, to try to get some compensation from the men who assaulted them. In the early years of colonization, Native American women outnumbered men in the missions, suggesting that the women chose the institutions to try to avoid the sexual assaults or having to marry a Spaniard. Tribal customs obligated women who were raped to undergo a long purification, such as sweating and drinking specific teas. A woman who became pregnant as a result of rape might try to induce an abortion or commit infanticide. In 1772 a partially blind woman who had been raped and impregnated by Spanish soldiers at San Diego tried but failed to abort the child. She resolved to kill it at birth, and nothing the priests said or did could stop her. The priests vigorously condemned these practices, but they admitted that it was impossible to stop them so long as the soldiers continued to rape the women.

Many Native Americans also complained directly to the Spanish authorities about their mistreatment. In 1773 a Native woman and an eleven-year-old girl from La Soledad, a *ranchería* (Indian settlement), went to see the priests at nearby San Diego Mission. Through an interpreter, they stated that three Spanish soldiers had raped the girl and her ten-year-old companion, who had died of her injuries. The priests reported the attack to the military authorities, who promptly had the three perpetrators arrested. Under questioning by the authorities, the girl said that she and her friend had been out digging roots when the men attacked them. After assaulting them, the soldiers gave the two girls some beads and left. The ten-year-old died two days later. Military authorities jailed the three men, although one later escaped. Nearly five years later, after the case had wound its way through every level of the Spanish government in Mexico, officials decided that since the only evidence for the assault was the child's testimony, the two men still in prison should be freed. In spite of the girl's courageous decision to complain to Spanish authorities about the attack, the courts legitimated the soldiers' actions by dismissing the case.

Native American communities responded to incidents of vicious rape just as Friar Junípero Serra feared: they attacked the missions repeatedly from the 1770s to the 1820s. In 1775, about eight hundred Kumeyaays, tired of the frequent sexual assaults and missionary supervision, attacked the San Diego Mission. They burned it down and killed three Spaniards, including Friar Luís Jayme, who had tried to stop soldiers from raping Native American women. The Kumeyaays' actions demonstrated that they recognized all of the Spaniards, even those who opposed the rapes, as part of the problem.

In October 1785 a group of neophytes and other local Native Americans attacked the San Gabriel Mission near present-day Los Angeles. A woman named Toypurina, a Gabrieleña medicine woman who claimed to have special magical powers, was one of the two key leaders of the rebellion, along with a neophyte named Nicolas José. Toypurina and José convinced Christian converts at the mission and Native Americans from six nearby villages to participate in the fight by telling them that Toypurina could kill the Spanish with her magic. A soldier overheard them discussing their plans on the night before their planned attack. The Spanish arrested the two leaders, along with several of their coconspirators. During questioning, she stated, "I hate the padres and all of you for living here on my native soil…[and] for trespassing upon the land of my forefathers and despoiling our tribal domains." After she spent two years in prison at San Gabriel, Spanish authorities sent her into exile at the mission at San Carlos de Borromeo. Her male coconspirators were flogged as a warning to other would-be rebels.

In addition to the violence and sexual assaults that characterized the Spanish conquest throughout the Southwest and California, the colonizers also seized Native American women and children in slave raids across the Southwest. Native American groups had captured women and children in raids for centuries before contact, but the numbers rose considerably after the Spanish arrived. Between 1700 and 1850 Spanish raiders captured thousands of Native American women and girls and took them to their settlements in New Mexico. In 1800 these women and girls represented about one-third of the total "Spanish" population. In retaliation, the Comanches and Navajos attacked the colonizers' settlements and seized Spanish women and children. Spanish authorities estimated that the Comanches might have had five hundred Spanish captives by 1830, and the Navajos had more than three hundred a half-century later. Prepubescent girls made up two-thirds of all captives on both sides. In addition, into the mid-nineteenth century, Native American groups continued to take slaves from each other and sell them to the Spanish and later the Mexicans. New Mexico's settlers valued female slaves more highly than males and would pay twice as much for them. The Spanish settlers perceived male slaves as dangerous troublemakers, and, given the scarcity of Spanish women, they needed female slaves to bear children, perform household labor, and produce surplus domestic goods for sale.

Whether the raiders were Native Americans or Spanish, the captives usually spent the rest of their lives in their captors' communities, and their status could range from slave to family member and anything in between. Spanish women and children usually became full members of a Comanche or Navajo kin group. Spanish captors expected Native American women and children to convert to Christianity and assimilate into the Spanish community, but they never accepted Native women as equals. The captured women in both cases eventually had children whose fathers were members of the host society, and those biracial children, called *mestizos,* often grew up as full members of the society. If captured women were lucky, they could use their own skills and their biracial children to improve their status. Sometimes they even became important negotiators between the two cultures.

Women of the Southwest and California bore the brunt of Spanish colonization because the raiding peoples of the southern and central Great Plains, groups like the Comanches and Navajos, blocked Spanish attempts to move northward in the seventeenth and early eighteenth century. Plains women instead had intermittent contact with French and British explorers and fur traders in the eighteenth century and with Americans in the early nineteenth century after the 1803 Louisiana Purchase.

Native American Women and the Fur Trade

The fur trade on the Great Plains and in the Pacific Northwest in the eighteenth and nineteenth centuries brought male Euro-American traders and Native American women into contact with each other because the men and their trade could not have survived without women's labor. Unlike the Spanish colonizers, these Euro-American men entered the West without priests or soldiers to back them up and had to rely solely on Native Americans' goodwill and trade. Unlike women in the Southwest and California, Native American women who encountered French and British fur traders retained a high degree of agency for a long time. At first they made the fur trade adapt to them instead of the other way around, and they incorporated new opportunities into their existing cultural patterns. Most of the guides, translators, and diplomats of the fur trade were Native American women, and many married fur traders. They also produced the finished, tradable skins. There was far less violence against women in the northern fur trade because it could not have succeeded without Native American women's skills and labor and the goodwill of their tribes.

Women's roles in the fur trade were a logical extension of their precontact trading practices, which were described in chapter one. However, the fur trade also began to alter women's role in trade. Even the earliest and indirect contact with whites began to do so in two ways: first, all of the European groups preferred to trade with men because they were male-dominated societies, and second, in the sixteenth century the Spanish introduced a valuable new trade item: horses. As horses became a central element in Great Plains cultures during the 1700s, the animals replaced food and clothing as the main trading items, and they were usually controlled by men. Women continued to trade food and other goods, but this trade became less important. In response, women expanded another important means of exercising power: they used marriage and kin relationships to facilitate and strengthen trading connections.

European fur traders deliberately sought out Native American women for short- or long-term relationships because they were invaluable as guides, interpreters, diplomats, producers, and sexual partners. The best-known Native American guide in the nineteenth century was the Shoshone woman Sacajawea ("Bird Woman"). She was born in what is now western Montana and was the daughter of a Shoshone chief. A Hidatsa band captured her sometime around 1801, when she was approximately twelve years old. In the fall of 1804 she was about fifteen and married to a French trader named Toussaint Charbonneau. She was pregnant with her first child when the Americans Meriwether Lewis, William Clark, and their "Corps of Discovery" arrived at the Mandan and Hidatsa villages on the upper Missouri River, near present-day Bismarck, North Dakota.

These horticultural villages were trading hubs for the entire region, and French fur traders had already established themselves as the most frequent Euro-American visitors. French traders across the northern Great Plains already knew the personal, political, and economic benefits of having a Native American wife. Some accounts say that Charbonneau won the teenaged Sacajawea in a gambling game, while others say he bought her at a local slave market. Either way, he was certainly counting on her labor and knowledge to help him succeed as a trader. Lewis and Clark hired Charbonneau to join their expedition as their interpreter, with the understanding that she would come, too. She gave birth to her son Jean-Baptiste in February 1805, and two months later the family headed west with the Corps.

Sacajawea proved to be much more useful than her husband. She was the expedition's guide and survival expert, as well as its interpreter and diplomat in dealing with the many Native American tribes it encountered. When the expedition arrived in her home territory, she learned that her brother was now one of the Shoshone chiefs, and she convinced him to give them horses to help their journey to the coast. The corps made it to the shores of the Pacific in the fall of 1805 and began the return journey the following spring. There are several different versions of her life after the expedition returned to the Mandan villages in the summer of 1806. One story is that she and Charbonneau went all the way back to St. Louis and William Clark officially adopted her son before she returned to the Upper Missouri and died in 1812 at the age of twenty-three. Another version is that the family stayed in the Mandan villages, never going to St. Louis. A third story says that she went to live with the Comanches, then went back to her own Shoshone people, and eventually died on a reservation in Wyoming in 1884 around the age of one hundred.

Far less is known about the Ioway woman Marie Aioe Dorion. She guided an expedition funded by businessman John Jacob Astor from St. Louis to the mouth of the Columbia River in 1811–12. The German-born Astor founded the American Fur Company in 1808 and was determined to have the first American fur trading post on the west coast to compete with the existing Russian and British coastal trade. Around 1806, Marie Aioe met and married the *métis* (half-French, half-Native) fur trapper and trader Pierre Dorion, Jr., in the Red River region of what is now southwest Arkansas. While in St. Louis in the winter of 1810–11, he signed up for Astor's expedition. Dorion insisted that his wife and their two small children come along. They left St. Louis in March 1811 and, as Sacajawea had been for Lewis and Clark, Marie became a critical asset to the expedition. She helped guide the Astorians, as this group of American fur traders were called, to the coast while she was pregnant with her third child. The baby was born in December 1811 but only lived a few days. The group arrived at the Pacific in the spring of 1812 and founded Fort Astoria. Marie and her family stayed until the fall of 1813, when Astor sold the outpost to the British. She and her family then headed east with a large group, intending to meet with another group of Astorians in western Idaho before returning to St. Louis. Along the way Native Americans attacked them repeatedly, until she and her two children were the only survivors. She kept them alive through the winter while traveling more than 250 miles to what is now southeastern Washington. Although she eventually met the other Astorians who were heading to St. Louis, she decided to stay in the West. She settled at Fort Okanagan near the present-day Washington–British Columbia border and married another trapper. When that marriage ended, she headed south to Fort Walla Walla, where she married the fort's interpreter, Jean-Baptiste Toupin. In the early 1840s the family moved southwest to the Willamette Valley, near present-day Salem, Oregon, where she died.

One of the few non-Native women who played an important role in the fur trade was Marie-Thérèse Choteau. As the head of one of the leading trading families in St. Louis in 1803, when the United States purchased the Louisiana territory from France, Choteau was an influential woman who created unusual opportunities for herself in a male-dominated industry. Her family had already made a lot of money trading in the Missouri Valley while it was under Spanish and then French sway, and the Chouteaus quickly developed new connections with the Americans. In 1808, she and Manuel Lisa founded the Missouri Fur Company to exploit the rich resources of the Upper Missouri region. This merger made Choteau one of the most important early investors in the American fur trade.

Native American women again played critical roles when William Ashley, a St. Louis businessman and the first lieutenant governor of Missouri, developed the "mountain man" system in the 1820s. This system involved men living, trading, and trapping on their own instead of as employees of a fur company. Although the stereotype of mountain men and fur traders portrays them as rugged individualists surviving alone through harsh mountain winters, they would not have survived at all, let alone prospered, without their relationships with Native American women. Those relationships gave the fur traders social and sexual companions, as well as trade advantages. Nearly 40 percent of American, French-Canadian, and Anglo-Canadian mountain men in the northern Rocky Mountains married Native American women, and another 20 percent who traded further south married Mexican or Mexican-American women. Some 80 percent of these marriages lasted on average fifteen years and produced three living children. Trappers who married a second time were even more likely to take a Native American wife.

Native American women often chose to pursue the Euro-American traders as sexual partners because of the men's technological and material wealth. These women had traditionally acted as traders and cultural mediators for their families and their tribes, so their decision to marry Euro-American traders represented continuity in a time when the fur trade brought changes and new opportunities. Native American women could increase their own material wealth and that of their families by marrying Euro-American traders. Great Plains families expected their new relatives to participate in traditional resource-sharing and gift-giving practices, and Euro-American traders quickly learned that they had responsibilities to their new kin as well as to their new wives. Many Native American women also used cross-cultural marriage to try to understand the outsiders and the changes they brought.

Class and status also shaped these relationships, in that Native American women from lower-status families tended to marry lower-class employees of the fur companies, whereas higher-status women married upper-class European men. Class overlapped with race, as the lower racial status of black, Spanish-Mexican and métis men in the fur trade made it harder for them to get and keep Native wives. This racism went both ways, however; by the late nineteenth century, Native women were less popular as marriage partners for white traders than their biracial daughters. Euro-American men believed that the métis daughters of Native American women and white men were better cultural brokers than their mothers had been earlier, and they were more desirable as marriage partners because of their higher racial status.

The length and quality of fur trade relationships varied widely. Some relationships were short-term, ended by either partner after a season or two. Sometimes wives went east with their husbands when the latter left the trade, and some husbands stayed in the West with their wives. Many marriages lasted until one partner died. The Assiniboine woman Hai-kees-kak-wee-yah was the second wife of trader Edwin Denig, and they stayed together until his death. In his will he left everything he owned to her and their children. The Blackfeet woman Natawista married Alexander Culbertson in 1840, after he sent nine horses to her family as proof of his respect for her. They stayed married for nearly thirty years. At their home in Illinois in the 1850s, she erected a tipi and dressed in Blackfeet clothing during the summer. In 1853, Natawista insisted on accompanying her husband when he was invited to join Isaac Stevens, the new territorial governor of Washington, who was charting a railroad route from St. Paul to Puget Sound and needed help negotiating with the many Native American groups along the route. As Sacajawea and Marie Dorion did only a few decades earlier, she was a key intermediary between her people and Euro-Americans. Her efforts helped convince the Blackfeet to allow the railroad to go through their lands.

Another Native American woman whose experiences as a fur trader wife made her into a cultural and political broker was a Lakota named Wambdi Autepewin. She married Honoré Picotte, the general agent for the American Fur Company's Upper Missouri Outfit, in 1838 when she was eighteen. In 1850 she left Picotte and married Charles Galpin, another trader. When he was promoted later that year, she suddenly found herself in the upper levels of fur trade society. In September 1866, U.S. Army General Alfred H. Terry asked her and her husband to visit Yanktonai and Oglala camps along the Little Missouri River to open treaty negotiations. She helped defuse the tensions between the Army and these Sioux tribes, at least temporarily. She gained a reputation as a skillful cultural and political intermediary and was again invited to participate in peace talks between the United States and the Lakota, another Siouan people, in 1868 at Fort Laramie. She was able to convince most, although not all, of the Lakota bands to sign the treaty that established the Great Sioux Reservation.

Although the fur trading companies encouraged relationships between their employees and Native women to promote trade, Great Plains women retained control over their sexual agency to a much greater degree than women in the Southwest and California. Native American men and white men had little power over women's economic and sexual activities as long as women occupied the culturally acceptable role of wife as trader and political intermediary. Through their roles as mediators, economic informants, cultural transmitters, companions, producers, and consumers, Great Plains women could gain status and become agents of change in their home communities. But the fur trade also eventually weakened Native American societies. Natawista helped clear the way through Blackfeet territory for the railroad, and Autepewin helped confine the Lakota to reservations. Few Native American women in the mid-nineteenth century had as much influence as these exceptional women, but every Native American woman in the Upper Missouri was affected by the fur trade.

The Great Basin

Native American women living in the Great Basin were one of the last groups to have sustained contact with whites. When white men arrived in the region in the mid-nineteenth century, however, Paiute women suffered a similar level of sexual violence in their encounters with the newcomers as the women in the Southwest and California had a century earlier. The Northern Paiutes had little direct contact with whites until the 1840s, when overland migrants to the west coast suddenly cut trails through their territory. The number of white men rose even faster after the migrants discovered silver in Paiute territory in 1859. As white miners, ranchers, and settlers poured into the Basin, they destroyed the Paiutes' traditional resource base and Paiute women's safety. The women's custom of working alone or in groups while they gathered food now made them vulnerable to attacks, particularly when they were close to mines. The Paiutes modified their economic activities to avoid whites, but they could not get far enough away from the mines and still find enough to eat. The nineteenth-century Paiute writer, activist, and interpreter Sarah Winnemucca, who devoted much of her life to publicizing Euro-American violence against the Paiutes, wrote that women and men had to work together in larger groups to protect the women and girls from rape.

As it had been in the Southwest, rape was central to the white colonization of the Great Basin and its peoples, and it led to violent reprisals by Native communities. The Paiute War of 1860 started after four white men raped two young women who had been gathering roots. The tribe responded by killing the four men, and local whites then demanded that the Paiutes be confined to the Pyramid Lake Reservation. Similarly, the Bannock War of 1878 began after several white men gang-raped a young Paiute woman. The Paiute men shot the suspected rapists. As punishment, American authorities forced the Paiutes to leave their Nevada homeland and move to the Yakima reservation in eastern Washington state.

The historical and economic contexts of Euro-American colonization determined Native American women's experiences with the white male newcomers. For example, in the sixteenth and seventeenth centuries, the Spanish wanted to conquer the Southwest in the hopes of finding the same kind of mineral wealth they had found in Mexico. They expanded into California to try to prevent other imperial powers from controlling the area. The Spanish authorities rarely worried about fostering good relations with Native Americans because they believed they had enough military strength to simply conquer anyone who got in their way. As a result, sexual violence was a central feature of the Spanish conquest. By contrast, fur traders to the north depended so heavily on the labor and goodwill of Native American women and their families that they treated indigenous peoples in a much less violent manner.

These differences aside, the colonial encounters in the West were similar in many ways. These similarities included the introduction of new goods for trade and consumption, the birth of biracial (métis or mestizo) communities, and the introduction of European patriarchal ideologies about the appropriate behavior of men and women. Each of these dramatically transformed Native American women's lives and those of their descendents.

Transformations

Although there is no doubt that the newcomers introduced a range of new constraints and difficulties into Native American women's lives in the centuries after contact, women also found new possibilities in the trade goods and economic opportunities that the newcomers brought. In the Southwest, many women embraced spinning wheels and looms because these tools made producing blankets easier and faster. The Spanish introduced new crops, including wheat, oats, and peaches, that Native people soon integrated into their diets. Women also quickly adopted the Spanish method of raising domesticated animals like sheep and goats. Not only did the animals provide a steady food source, but they also provided raw material for blankets and rugs that could be traded for the European-made tools, cloth, beads, and other items that the women preferred to the ones they could make themselves. Domestic production of some items dropped as a result of the new availability of European goods, while other locally made products became more valuable because of Euro-American demand. Women started producing larger quantities of the products they could trade with Europeans, such as food, regional specialties like rain hats in the Northwest, Paiute baskets, Pueblo pottery, Navajo rugs and blankets, and dressed hides and warm winter clothing on the Great Plains. Contact with Europeans also introduced waged work for women, who often cleaned houses and gardened at fur trade posts or worked in the fish canneries along the coast.

One trade item that had a huge impact on the lives of many Native American women, especially on the Great Plains, was the horse. After the Spanish introduced them to the Southwest in the sixteenth century, horses spread northwards rapidly. Native peoples across the continent began incorporating the animals into their cultures and economies well before they met any Europeans. Native American men benefited more economically and socially than women did from the introduction of the horse, because horeses became a masculine way of accumulating and demonstrating wealth. Horses made it easier for a hunter to kill more buffalo on a single expedition, for instance. Although horses enabled women to move camp more easily, the animals also added a host of new tasks. In particular, women usually had to feed the horses during the fall and winter. Women also had to work harder and longer to process the increased amounts of meat and hides that resulted from the larger number of buffalo that men on horseback were able to kill. Polygyny became more common because if a man was wealthy enough to own many horses and a good enough hunter to kill many buffalo, he needed more than one wife to care for his horses and process buffalo meat and hides.

Other things the Europeans brought, such as their diseases and gender norms, proved extremely destructive in the long run. The Americas had no epidemic diseases before contact, so Native Americans had no resistance to diseases like smallpox and measles to which most European, Asian, and African peoples had some immunity. These diseases killed somewhere between 60 and 90 percent of the Native American population of the Americas. Indigenous peoples who lived in sedentary agricultural communities, as in the Southwest, suffered more than the ones who lived on the Great Plains in smaller and mobile communities. The Pueblo population dropped from 60,000 in the early seventeenth century to just over 9,000 in by the end of the eighteenth. About 20,000 of them died in a 1636 smallpox epidemic. In 1640 another wave of disease killed another 3,000 people. By that decade, only forty-three of the one hundred fifty towns that existed in the region in 1598 still existed. During California's mission period, the Native American population between San Diego and San Francisco declined from 72,000 to 18,000. The first big smallpox epidemic to hit the Upper Missouri country in the early 1830s killed one-third of the Blackfeet and nearly decimated the Assiniboine. Frequent rapes meant that Native American women were the first to be infected and killed by sexually transmitted diseases, such as a virulent form of syphilis, that the European men brought with them.

Whereas diseases killed Native American women and men quickly, the Europeans' destructive new gender norms worked more slowly to undermine Native cultures and the status of women. Converting to Christianity entailed the imposition of European ideals. To begin with, women were supposed to be dependent on and submissive to their husbands, and property belonged to men, not women or communities. Women were expected to conform to a much stricter set of rules about sexuality than men, such as being chaste before marriage and celibate after they were widowed. Compounding the limits on their economic and personal lives, women now found themselves excluded from the most important political and spiritual roles. Finally, as this chapter has shown, violence against women became commonplace. Thus the imposition of European gender norms lessened the esteem in which Native peoples regarded women and their social contributions. It severely eroded the direct and indirect influence that women had exercised over their communities' economies, politics, social organizations, and spirituality, and it curtailed their sexual and reproductive choices.

For example, being conquered by the patriarchal Spanish meant that many Pueblo women lost their rights to land, seeds, the labor of their children, and even the children themselves. Household ownership and land rights that women had held passed to men. The

Spanish forced a fundamental change on the Pueblos' division of labor: traditionally, Pueblo men did the spinning and weaving and women built the houses. However, the Spanish insisted on turning men into builders and women into weavers because that was the European norm. Before contact, most Pueblos were matrilineal, but the ones who had the most contact with the Spanish became patrilineal or bilateral. Only the Pueblos who resisted Christianization the most, like the Hopi and Zuni, remained matrilineal.

Women living in Great Plains tribes that were already patrilineal and male-dominated, such as the Blackfeet and Lakota, became more dependent on men. The fur trade displaced older, more egalitarian means of obtaining food and other goods, and women had to work harder to process goods (like buffalo hides) that they did not get to trade. Among bilateral Great Plains groups like the Arapaho, Cheyenne, Comanche, and Shoshone, women's status seems to have declined much less.

Without a doubt, the biggest changes that white colonization imposed on Native American women in the West were those involving sex, marriage, and children. A key goal for Christian missionaries was to force Native American women to adopt European notions of heterosexuality, chastity, monogamy, modesty, and shame. Europeans and Euro-Americans frequently used rape as a weapon of colonization, as discussed above. But even when the sex was consensual, misunderstandings still arose because Native Americans and Europeans had very different ideas about sexuality. As discussed in chapter one, most tribes accepted and even encouraged premarital sex and a variety of sexual preferences and behaviors, and had a single standard for sexual behavior for men and women. In sharp contrast, European cultures regulated and punished women's sexuality to a much greater extent than men's and placed strict limits on what constituted acceptable sexual behavior for women. Same-sex sexual relations took place in many Native American tribes, and the persons involved were not condemned the way they were in European cultures. It was extremely difficult to get a divorce in Europe but it was easy to end a Native American marriage.

California provides some excellent examples of continuity and change in traditional sexual and marriage practices. Native Californians had a very different understanding of appropriate sexual practices than Spanish Catholics. For example, Native Americans accepted polygyny, which appalled the Catholic priests. Generally, only wealthy high status men could support multiple wives or needed the additional labor that extra wives provided. In tribes in which the multiple wives were sisters, the missionaries considered the marriages incestuous. When a polygynous man entered a mission, the missionaries forced him to choose one wife to marry in a Catholic ceremony. The priests wanted the men to marry their first wife, but the men usually chose one of their younger wives, believing that they were more attractive or could bear more children or do a better job of caring for their husbands in their old age. Records from seven missions in northern California show that between 1769 and 1834, the Spanish priests remarried more than two thousand Native American couples. But a Catholic ceremony did not mean that the participants replaced their traditional values with Catholic ones. Many women who entered the missions never remarried, suggesting that they might still have considered themselves married polygynously. Traditional practices persisted a long time, even among people who did not resist missionization.

Moreover, the imposition of Spanish Catholic ideals made marriage both more important for women and more difficult to achieve. Many women in the missions regarded marriage as a way to improve their living conditions. Unmarried women had to live in supervised dormitories, but married couples lived in private, single-family homes. However, the missionaries insisted that mission residents could only marry other Catholics, which radically restricted women's choices of marriage partners. Earlier generations had used marriage to extend kinship ties, but younger Native Californians who lived in the missions had limited options compared to those their parents had enjoyed.

Divorce was easy for men and women in Central California, as it was in Native American tribes across the continent, and divorced people were free to marry again. The Catholic missionaries did not approve of either practice. They considered divorce unacceptable and considered subsequent relationships to be illegitimate. Believing that the low Californian birth rate resulted from a high rate of abortions, the priests severely punished any woman who had a stillborn child, including flogging the woman. Sadly, the actual cause of the low number of children being born was that the soldiers were infecting many Native women with syphilis. The priests were also horrified by the prevalence and acceptance of same-sex acts and relationships.

In all contact zones across the West, voluntary and involuntary sexual encounters often resulted in biracial children. In the Southwest, the Spanish colonists devised an elaborate racial hierarchy based on each individual's proportion of Native American, Spanish, or African blood. Biracial and multiracial children usually occupied the same rung of society that their mother did, although some people retroactively redefined themselves as more "Spanish" and worked their way up the hierarchy by erasing their Native American mothers and grandmothers from the family history. In northern Great Plains fur trading communities, the children of Native American mothers and white fathers were generally considered Native Americans, but their fathers often insisted that they receive a Euro-American education. Over the years, this familiarity with European culture enabled many mixed-race individuals to redefine themselves as white.

Native American women's experiences during contact were not monolithic. Encountering a Spanish soldier in the seventeenth-century Southwest differed greatly from encountering a French trader or Anglo-American "mountain man" in the nineteenth century on the Great Plains. Women controlled the encounters and seized new opportunities when they could, and they resisted and adapted to the new constraints when they couldn't. By doing so, they helped their cultures and traditions survive.

Suggested Readings

Brooks, James F. "'This Evil Extends Especially to the Feminine Sex': Captivity and Identity in New Mexico, 1700–1846." In *Writing the Range: Race, Class, and Culture in the Women's West,* edited by Elizabeth Jameson and Susan Armitage, pp. 97–121. Norman: University of Oklahoma Press, 1997.

———. *Captives and Cousins: Slavery, Kinship, and Community in the Southwest Borderlands.* Chapel Hill: University of North Carolina Press, 2002.

Gutiérrez, Ramón A. *When Jesus Came, the Corn Mothers Went Away: Marriage, Sexuality, and Power in New Mexico, 1500–1846.* Stanford, CA: Stanford University Press, 1991.

Hurtado, Albert L. *Intimate Frontiers: Sex, Gender, and Culture in Old California.* Albuquerque: University of New Mexico Press, 1999.

Lansing, Michael. "Plains Indian Women and Interracial Marriage in the Upper Missouri Trade, 1804–1868." *Western Historical Quarterly* 31 (Winter 2000): 413–433.

Newell, Quincy D. "'The Indians Generally Love their Wives and Children': Native American Marriage and Sexual Practices in Missions San Francisco, Santa Clara, and San José." *Catholic Historical Review* 91, no. 1 (2005): 60–82.

Peters, Virginia Bergman. *Women of the Earth Lodges: Tribal Life on the Plains.* North Haven, CT: Archon Books, 1995.

Stremlau, Rosemarie. "Rape Narratives on the Northern Paiute Frontier: Sarah Winnemucca, Sexual Sovereignty, and Economic Autonomy, 1844–1891." In *Portraits of Women in the American West,* edited by Dee Garceau-Hagen, pp. 37–62. New York: Routledge, 2005.

CHAPTER THREE

Women in the Spanish-Mexican Era

For Native American, Spanish, Mexican, African American, and Anglo-American women, each of the three governments—the Spanish, the Mexican, and the American—that ruled the Southwest and California from the eighteenth to the mid-nineteenth century brought a different set of changes, constraints, and opportunities. Native American women in California experienced dramatic upheavals as the mission era came to an end in the decade after Mexico won its independence from Spain in 1821. They found themselves at the bottom of an increasingly complex racial hierarchy, especially after the United States seized California from Mexico in 1846. As new residents of the United States by conquest, Spanish and Mexican women found themselves in the position that Native American women had occupied during the initial phases of European colonization: the Spanish and Mexican women were able to seize some new opportunities even as their status declined overall, and they became valuable as cultural mediators and wives for the conquerors. For African American women the change in governments brought a rapid decline in their rights and opportunities and a rapid increase in constraints. Anglo-American women sat at the top of the racial hierarchy, playing new roles while simultaneously replicating old ones. Within a short span of time, these groups of women began to interact with each other more often and in more intense ways.

Native and Hispanic Women in California in the Eighteenth and Nineteenth Centuries

Colonizing California marked a critical turning point within Spain's policies: for the first time the Spanish government systematically included non-Native women in its plans and considered them necessary for their success. The Spanish government privileged Spanish-Mexican women over Native American women from the beginning. Although most of the Spanish-Mexican women settling in California in the eighteenth century came from the lowest rungs of society at home, in this new region their lighter skin color and availability for marriage in a predominantly male society gave them a much higher status. In 1774 eight Spanish-speaking women came to California from Mexico, all either already married or of marriageable age and expected to marry a soldier. The Spanish authorities expected them to teach the *neofitas* or neophytes (Native American women who had converted to Catholicism) about Spanish Catholic family life and gender norms: cooking, cleaning and sewing; being subservient to men; respecting the sanctity and permanence of marriage; monogamy; and virginity before marriage and chastity in widowhood. The settlers were supposed to help suppress polygyny, alternative gender roles, abortion, and infanticide. Initially, these efforts had only limited success, because only one of these eight women stayed in California. The rest went back to Mexico with their families as soon as their husbands' six-year contracts ended.

The Spanish government even began encouraging civilian communities that were not under the direct control of the priests, which did not please the missionaries. Only six years after opening its first mission in California, Spain paid the first group of *pobladores* (town settlers) to settle in California in 1775. The group of 240 people included thirty-four women, twenty-nine of whom were married to soldiers on the expedition and another three were married to other settlers. Only two single adult women accompanied the expedition, a widow and the teenaged sister of one of the male settlers. The average

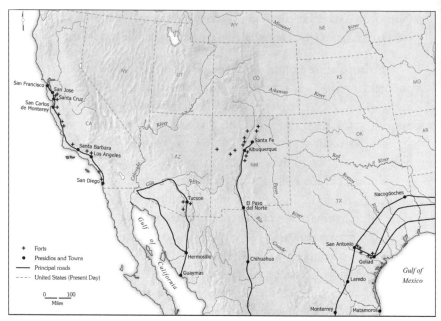

New Spain

age of the married women was twenty-eight, and they had an average of four children each. This expedition effectively doubled the Spanish-Mexican population in California. Two years later, in 1777, Spanish authorities founded San José de Guadalupe with fourteen families, and in 1781 they established La Reina de los Angeles with eleven families. Many of these new settlers had racially mixed backgrounds and came from the lower levels of Mexican society, but they still considered themselves superior to and fundamentally different from the local indigenous population. They called themselves *gente de razón* (people of reason)—meaning civilized, Christian, and from a European background—in contrast to Native Americans. More expeditions followed in the early 1780s, each with its own small contingent of women.

The Spanish-speaking women who settled in the pueblos (towns), presidios (forts), and missions in the late 1700s were essential to the social, cultural, and biological reproduction of Spanish society at its northern edge, whether they were *mestiza* (women with European and Native American parents, whose mothers were usually Native American), *mulata* (a woman with African and Native American parents, and again it was usually the mother who was Native American), or *casta* (a broad mixed-race category). Their role as mothers was particularly important because the last sizeable colonization party arrived in the 1790s, and for the next forty years the number of inhabitants rose mainly through natural increase. In 1800 the government shipped a few more families and twenty orphans (ten male and ten female) to California, intending the female orphans to marry soldiers. All the girls eventually married and stayed, but few other settlers came. The Spanish-Mexican women performed their role as mothers admirably; from 1790 to 1821 the number of Spanish-Mexican people in California grew from 990 to approximately 3,200.

Spanish-Mexican fathers arranged almost everything when it came to their daughters' betrothals and marriages, usually when the girls were between thirteen and fifteen. The Catholic Church preached that women were inherently lustful, sinful creatures, and men believed that women would not try too hard to resist being seduced. Men had to protect the purity of daughters and wives to maintain their honor as fathers and husbands, and therefore girls had to be married off at a very young age to contain their innate sexuality within the respectable institutions of marriage and motherhood. In 1776, for example, Sergeant Ygnacio Vicente Ferrer Vallejo got engaged to his future wife, María Antonia Isabela Lugo, shortly after she was born. He married her when she was fourteen and he was forty. Spanish law required males to be at least thirteen and females at least eleven before they could legally marry, although rare exceptions did occur for girls. Across New Spain from 1694 to 1846, 25 percent of women married before they were fifteen and 80 percent by twenty. Fewer than 10 percent of men married before age fifteen, and only 25 percent married by twenty.

If a woman's husband gave his permission, she could make legal transactions and act with complete freedom in her legal dealings. More importantly, a married woman retained control of any property that she had acquired before marriage, and her husband could not legally force or threaten her into any legal transaction. Spanish-Mexican women had more legal rights than Anglo-American women in the United States, but those rights gradually disappeared after the American takeover in 1846.

Some women managed to create lives for themselves outside of the roles that their patriarchal society dictated, and some found ways to take advantage of the favorable Spanish property laws to maintain or increase their own landholdings and economic activities. A small number of women worked outside the home for pay, and others rejected marriage completely. Somewhat paradoxically perhaps, the mission system (which wanted to turn Native American women into submissive dependents) helped create these opportunities for Spanish-Mexican women, because the missions had to hire women to teach and care for the Native women and girls living there. For example, like most Spanish-Mexican women, Eulalia Pérez had married in her late teens and was a mother by the time she and her husband settled in San Diego in 1802. In 1818 as a widow with six children, she started working as the principal cook at the San Gabriel Mission to support herself and her family. She eventually became the midwife, head cook, keeper of the keys, and general supervisor of food and clothing production at the mission. These roles gave Pérez a degree of authority over the men at the mission that was very unusual in Spanish-Mexican culture.

Another woman, Apolinaria Lorenzana, carved out even greater opportunities for herself by working at the missions. She was four years old in 1800 when the authorities sent her and her young widowed mother along with a group of families from Mexico to California. Her mother married a soldier there and moved back to Mexico with him when his service in California ended. Lorenzana spent the rest of her childhood moving between foster families and taught herself to write around the age of fifteen. Determined to pass her knowledge along to other children, she never married and created an independent life for herself as a nurse and teacher in the missions. When a man proposed marriage to her, she wrote that she "did not feel inclined toward matrimony (knowing full well the requirements of that holy institution) and so I refused his offer." Instead, she cared for and taught multiple generations of women and was highly respected by the Californio community for her work with children. Lorenzana's position as godmother to dozens of girls both reflected and helped her to maintain a high status in her community. Over the course of her life, she also acquired three ranches. The first two she received from the government, which only very rarely gave land to women. Lorenzana bought the third one herself, but she lost all three to a swindling American after the takeover of California.

For Native American women in California, the transition from Spanish to Mexican rule in 1821, after Mexico's decade-long struggle for independence, meant the end of the mission era. Spain had closed most of the missions before 1821, and Mexico closed the rest of them over the next fifteen years. Few Native Americans remained devout Catholics once the missions' coercive power disappeared. However, the Mission Indians also lost what had become their homes. Spain had given the missions significant landholdings, but the new Mexican governor of California gave most of that land to a few hundred leading Hispanic landowners, not to the Native Americans who already lived there. In 1821, the Native American population in California was somewhere between 100,000 and 150,000, with about 21,000 living in and around the missions.

Not only did California's Mission Indian women lose their homes in the early- to mid-nineteenth century, but they also lost their status as valued partners for immigrant men. In the first few decades after European contact, Native women often had been the only available marriage partners, and they had skills and knowledge that men needed to survive and prosper. Non-Native men generally chose white or bi-racial women as soon as they could. Between 1770 and 1854, only forty marriages between Native American women and newcomer men were recorded at three northern California missions. These marriages represented fewer than five percent of all marriages recorded in that period. Native American women retained their value as marriage partners a little longer in the interior, where fur traders, entrepreneurs, soldiers, and ranchers had little white female companionship and needed Native American women's economic and cultural knowledge. For example, John Sutter, who owned the land in the Sacramento Valley where gold was found in 1849, left his wife and children behind in Switzerland and had several Native American lovers in California. These relationships were common before the 1850s, but white Californians later erased them from the region's history because they did not want to acknowledge the role that Native women had played in the state's history.

One Native American woman's choices and chances in California depended entirely on her race and class, demonstrating some of the dramatic changes Native American women experienced even in the space of one woman's lifetime. Victoria Bartolomea Comicrabit was born into an elite family on a *ranchería* (Native American settlement) near the San Gabriel Mission around 1808. The priests permitted Victoria to live with her parents until the age of six or seven, when the priests moved her to the mission's nunnery. There, she learned Christianity, reading and writing, and basic Spanish household skills. She got extra attention from Eulalia Pérez, the mission's key keeper (discussed above), who chose Victoria as one of her assistants. When Victoria was fifteen, mission staff encouraged her to marry another neophyte, Pablo María, of a neighboring ranchería. Victoria kept working at the mission after she married and soon gave birth to her first child. The couple had three more children and received the plots of land from the mission to which they were entitled as neophytes.

Victoria remarried a year after Pablo died in 1835. As a widow and a landowner, she had more control over her life and her decision to remarry was her own. Her second husband was Scottish-born trader Hugo Reid. He adopted all of her children, and she took his last name, marking her integration into the local elite. Marriage to a

European man also increased the distance between Victoria and her children and their Native American background. Although Victoria often managed the couple's property, Reid's poor business decisions undermined their wealth, eventually forcing them to sell much of their land. Their marriage was also increasingly strained, as Hugo began to regret having married a Native wife. Victoria died in poverty in 1868. As her life illustrates, even Native American women who were highly assimilated could not escape the effects of the racial hierarchies that developed in California in the nineteenth century.

African American Women

Those hierarchies also had a dramatic and negative effect on African American women. At least 18,500 Africans and their descendants lived in New Spain (Spain's northern territories in North America, now Mexico, California, and the U.S. Southwest) by 1550, and a substantial mulatto and black population, both enslaved and free, lived in region. Black Mexicans were aware that moving further north could have a detrimental effect on their rights and often took steps to prevent it. In 1600, for example, Isabel de Olvera, a free mulatta, joined an expedition heading north as a servant to a Spanish woman. To protect her status as a free woman of color, she filed a deposition before she left that stated:

> I am going on the expedition to New Mexico and have some reason to fear that I may be annoyed by some individuals since I am a mulatta, and it is proper to protect my rights in such an eventuality by an affidavit showing that I am a free woman, unmarried and the legitimate daughter of Hernando, a negro, and an Indian named Magdalena....I therefore request your grace to accept this affidavit, which shows that I am free and not bound by marriage or slavery. I request that a properly certified and signed copy be given to me in order to protect my rights, and that it carry full legal authority. I demand justice.

The document was a clever pre-emptive strike against whatever racism she might encounter in the north. She also needed to record her racial heritage because as the child of a Native American mother, Olvera could not be enslaved under Spanish colonial law.

Perhaps because of the legal problems people of African descent could face in Mexico's northern colonies, their numbers there remained small. In 1750 the approximately two hundred families who lived in Albuquerque, New Mexico, included fifty-seven in which one of the spouses was mulatta or mulatto. Some households included mulatta servants, although most of the servants were Indian women. For example, fifty-year-old mulatta Juana Carrillo and her husband, sixty-year-old mulatto Bartholomé Lobata, had two daughters and were raising two mulatta orphans. Other mulattas appear in the Albuquerque census as widows or single heads of households. For instance, thirty-five-year-old Juliana García headed a household that included five children ranging in age from two to fifteen, one Indian servant, and an orphan. The 1790 census of Los Angeles revealed that of a total population of 141 people, twenty-two were listed as mulattos. That number included Anna María Carasca, her mestizo husband José Ontiveros, and their seven-year-old daughter. In 1792 fewer than two hundred free women of African descent lived in northern Mexico: 167 mixed-race women and nineteen black women, out of a total Hispanic population of 2,500.

Some enslaved women achieved freedom in the northern colonies. In 1783, Doña Manuela García de Noriega dictated a will providing for the emancipation of her slaves after her death. She instructed that her mulatta slave María Antonia should be freed when Manuela died and that María's daughter Juana should be freed after she had served Manuela's niece until the latter's death. Manuela wanted the rest of the slaves to remain with her husband until his death, at which time they were to be freed.

Women of African and mixed descent formed tight and supportive social and kin relationships with others of similar heritage, and they used the Spanish legal system to protect themselves or gain their freedom when they could. For example, a free mulatta named Antonia Lusgardia Hernández, a resident of Spanish colonial Texas, filed a petition with the governor explaining that she and her daughter had lived in Don Miguel Nuñez's household. While living there she had another child, a son, and Nuñez was the father. Fleeing mistreatment, she took her children and went to live in Alberto Lopez's household. Nuñez took her son from her, claiming that Hernández had given the boy to his wife. Hernández pleaded with the governor to make Nuñez give her son back. In her petition she wrote that she was "a poor, helpless woman whose only protection is a good administration and a good judicial system" and that she wanted "to make use of all the laws in my favor" to get her son back. Her petition worked. The governor ordered Nuñez to return her son, on the condition that she provided a good home for the child. For Antonia, the legal system worked to protect her rights as a mother.

The transition from Spanish to Mexican rule briefly raised the status of black women in the Southwest before American rule brought dramatic losses in rights and status. Small numbers of free blacks continued to migrate to the Southwest, particularly Texas, in the early 1800s. They were soon outnumbered by the tens of thousands of black slaves that white Americans in Texas (called "Texians" at the time) brought with them starting in the 1820s. In 1824 the newly independent Mexico adopted a constitution that explicitly banned slavery, but the influx of white Americans and their slaves quickly made a fiction of that legal protection. Between 1830 and 1835 the Texian population rose from 7,000 to nearly 30,000, including 3,000 African American slaves. This increase swamped the approximately 4,000 Mexican-born, Spanish-speaking Tejanos in the area. While welcoming Americans to settle in the region, the Mexican government insisted that they accept the constitutional ban on slavery. Texas was prime cotton-growing land, however, and white slave owners were not going to let Mexican law deprive them of the labor they needed to make money on cotton, especially when Mexico itself did little to enforce the law. When the Republic of Texas won its independence from Mexico in 1837, it enshrined the institution of slavery in its new constitution.

Slave women in the nineteenth century thought that being taken to Texas was worse than remaining in the upper South, because slaves were usually treated more harshly in the former. Former Texas slave Mary Gaffney recalled that "slavery time was hell!" Adeline Marshall remembered that in Texas "you went out to the field almost as soon as you could walk." In spite of the harsher conditions for African American women in Texas, however, they resisted racial oppression when and where they could. In 1838, a woman named Sally Vince took her new owner, Allen Vince, to court for keeping her enslaved after her previous master's will had freed her. A county judge confirmed her freedom and ordered Allen to pay the court costs. In 1847, a woman named Emeline and her two children also went to court to gain their freedom, and again the court granted it, plus one dollar in damages. Some enslaved women escaped southward to Mexico, because that nation would not allow escaped slaves to be recaptured. Other important forms of resistance and community-building included the 1846 founding of Galveston's First Colored Baptist Church by nineteen slave and free men and women. For black women, whether free or enslaved, the transition from the Spanish empire to Mexican and then American rule brought a sharp decline in their status and freedoms.

Changing Legal Systems

As Native American and black women across the Southwest in the first half of the nineteenth century struggled with this rapid decline in their status and faced a tightening web of social constraints, Spanish and Mexican women experienced a more uneven set of changes when the West became American territory in 1846. Some fought to keep older legal systems working in their favor, while others made the most of new economic and social opportunities.

The Anglo-American legal system sharply reduced the rights that women had enjoyed under Spanish and Mexican rule. Spanish law protected certain property rights for women as long as they respected prevailing gender norms, but the American system had few legal protections for women and their property because of a British common law concept known as *coverture*. This term meant that when a woman married she disappeared as a legal entity; she did not have a separate legal or economic existence apart from her husband. Coverture drastically limited her property and child custody rights, her right to separate from or divorce her husband, and so on. By contrast, Spanish and Mexican law allowed women to retain a separate legal identity when they married. As legally recognized persons, Mexican wives could buy, inherit, and maintain property on their own, and they could enter into contracts and sue in court, none of which they could do under the American legal system. Women's legal rights had limits, however, even under the Spanish and Mexican systems. For example, husbands still had greater property rights and, as the heads of households, controlled the children, made decisions regarding the couple's communal property, and could control but not alienate certain segments of a wife's own property. A Spanish-Mexican wife generally but not always needed her husband's consent to sign or enter into a contract.

Only after their husbands' death did women escape these limits on their rights. Spanish-Mexican widows got half the wealth accumulated by the couple during the marriage, as well as any remaining dowry (the property a woman brought to her marriage). They could buy and sell land and inherit their husbands' military benefits. They often gained the right to administer the inheritance of any minor children until they became adults. The law also granted widows additional protection for their property rights because they were now single mothers who were more vulnerable without a husband to protect them. However, widows' small window of legal opportunity could close quickly if relatives or other community members believed that they behaved inappropriately. They could exercise a small, specific set of rights, but they were certainly not equal to men in terms of property rights and protection.

Land was a critical asset for widows because they could sell, exchange, farm, or ranch their land. Most widows had small landholdings, but a handful had larger properties. For example, widow

Juana Lujan was one of the largest landowners in the jurisdiction of
Santa Cruz de la Cañada, New Spain, in the early eighteenth century. She accumulated her wealth using the same strategies that men
did: she had acquired some of her land legally by buying it and some
of it illegally by encroaching on neighboring Pueblo land.

The legal system could either help or hurt widows, depending
on the local officials involved, and women tried to use it to their
advantage by changing how they represented themselves. In 1696,
a young widow named Isabel Jorge described herself in court as a
"poor widow" with children who needed to gain control of land
that she believed was hers. After winning that case, she petitioned
the court again three years later to revalidate the grant, on the same
grounds that she was a "poor widow burdened with children." She
represented herself quite differently in 1733, when she and two male
neighbors complained about another neighbor who wanted to build
an irrigation canal through their land. When the defendant accused
her of being manipulated by her two neighbors, she portrayed herself
as a strong, mature woman who was more than capable of managing her land. The same legal system that had protected her interests
when she was younger now allowed her to exercise a degree of independence in protecting her own interests.

Widows used their unique legal position to take care of themselves and also to provide for their daughters and granddaughters.
For instance, when Santa Fe widow María Martin died in 1769, her
will transferred her "house and the adjacent piece of land" to her
daughter, "because she is a woman and because she is poor and for
accompanying me during my life, never having left me helpless."
Widows often bequeathed land to their daughters and granddaughters, giving the younger women an asset to help overcome their legal,
economic and social disadvantages. The younger women typically
had to earn that asset in a gender-specific way, however, by caring for
the older women.

As Americans took control of California in 1848 after the Mexican-American War, women's legal status changed, even though the

United States promised to uphold existing property rights in the Treaty of Guadalupe Hidalgo that ended the war. Under the new American legal system, *Californianas* (the female members of Californio society) still had the right to hold separate and community property, but a woman's individual class, racial status, and economic resources shaped her ability to defend herself in court. As in Texas and Louisiana, where the Spanish had also once ruled, in California in the 1840s authorities began to splice the existing Spanish-Mexican legal system with American common law, which curtailed women's property rights. In the end, only sixty-six women managed to keep their land after the Americans took over, and most of them were the widows or wives of foreigners. Women continued to try to make the legal system work to their advantage, though, including transferring property to sisters and daughters. Will-making became the primary means of preserving inheritances and keeping property out of the hands of the Anglo-Americans.

The Conquest of California

Spanish-Mexican women's struggle to maintain some control over their property included direct efforts to recoup their losses after the American conquest of California. For example, women as well as men filed claims to be compensated for property that U.S. soldiers destroyed during the invasion. In the pueblo of Los Angeles alone, forty-three individuals, including fourteen women, claimed property damage estimated at 5,580 pesos. The women reported damages averaging 121 pesos, whereas the men's claims averaged 134 pesos. Native Americans, whether Christian converts or not, did not bother to report any damages, no doubt because the American authorities did not think that they deserved compensation. Only non-Indians were entitled to reparations, and non-Native women used this fact as best they could. The widow Juana Rendon, for example, not only cited the loss of kitchen and bedroom furnishings, but also one cart of firewood and another of corn, several bushels of beans, fifty pounds of potatoes, onions, and chili peppers, as well as a copper pot and cooking utensils. She stated bluntly that she deserved compensation because she was "a widowed woman who has a young, strong child whom I have to support until she reaches of age." Josefa Cota, another widow, informed the local authorities that she was "helpless" and lacked "the means to replace what I have lost." Cota had recently sold her rancho and invested the proceeds in her home in the pueblo, but now some of her property had been lost. She complained that despite the determined efforts of her servants to stop the American troops from damaging her house, the soldiers broke two windows and the shutters and took food and other household items.

María de las Angustias de la Guerra was a member of one of the leading Californio families who lived in Santa Barbara before the American takeover. She was very critical of the Mexican officials who, she believed, had mishandled the American threat. In her view, the women of California had known that the Americans were up to no good, but the men chastised them for voicing their concerns. She was equally critical of the Mexican military response once the fighting started, saying that Mexico's soldiers "performed no more service than the figurehead of a ship." In 1846 she protected a man, José Antonio Chavez, who was fleeing from the American troops. The Americans burst into her home while her husband was away and pointed a gun at her during their hunt for Chavez, who was hiding under a pile of blankets on which her newborn daughter was sleeping. De la Guerra calmly denied knowing his whereabouts. Not even her elite social status protected her from the invading Americans, but she thwarted them in her own way.

Like de la Guerra, María Paula Rosalía Vallejo de Leese had been born into California's elite Spanish-Mexican social and economic class, and she never forgave the Americans for the takeover. She was from the prominent Vallejo family, whose ancestors had helped to found the first Mexican settlements in California. Decades after the U.S. conquest, she was still bitter: "Those hated men [the Americans] inspired me with such a large dose of hate against their race that though twenty-eight years have elapsed since that time, I have not forgotten the insults heaped upon me and not being desirous of coming in contact with them I have abstained from learning their language." She had done everything she could to defy the invaders. After the Bear Flaggers (an illegal militia that tried to seize California before regular American soldiers arrived) arrested her husband, four Americans tried to rob her family's Sonoma storehouse. She physically blocked the entrance and only stepped aside after the men threatened to shoot her. In another incident, Captain John Frémont demanded that de Leese personally bring a seventeen-year-old Indian servant girl to the officers' quarters at a camp near the Vallejos' rancho to be used for their sexual pleasure. De Leese refused. Frémont later punished her for this defiance by blackmailing her, while she was pregnant, into writing a letter to the Californios' leader, Captain Padilla, begging him not to attack Sonoma. The fact that her first husband was an American who abandoned her and their children after losing all of the family's money probably intensified her anger. As women, de la Guerra and de Leese were vulnerable to the invading American forces, but both refused to accept the situation passively.

Unique Opportunities for a Unique Woman

While some women negotiated changing legal systems that increasingly worked against them, other women profited from the new regimes. One such woman was María Gertrudis Barceló, a Santa Fe, New Mexico, businesswoman nicknamed *La Tules* (the Reed). Born in Mexico in 1800, she moved with her family to New Mexico around 1820 and married Manuel Antonio Sisneros in 1823. In the next two years she gave birth to two sons, each of whom died in infancy. She had no other children of her own but later adopted, formally and informally, many daughters, beginning with María del Refugio in 1826. In the mid-1820s she began to test her card-playing skills in the mining town of Real de Dolores, south of Santa Fe.

She and her family moved to Santa Fe in the early 1830s, and she quickly got involved in dealing the card game monte (named after the mountain of cards that piles up during a game). She also developed trading and investment interests in everything from mining and mules to gold and silver. Her husband disappeared suddenly in 1841, and during the next ten years Barceló had a succession of politically well-connected lovers, including a second lieutenant in the U.S. Army, August de Marle, and the governor of New Mexico, Manuel Armijo.

The Mexican community in Santa Fe both admired and criticized Barceló for not conforming to Mexican gender norms, which expected women to defer to their fathers, brothers, and husbands and spend most of their time at home. Many women challenged these norms in small ways, but Barceló did so publicly and proudly. Her gambling and her public visibility led her female neighbors to shun her. However, her wealth, political connections, and generosity toward her adopted daughters gave her the kind of independence and protection that few other women could dream of.

Barceló's relationship with the Anglo-Americans who assumed power in 1848 was even more complex than the one she had with her neighbors. Although the Americans were also critical of her behavior, they badly needed her help to make local connections and understand the new world in which they had to operate. The Americans justified their conquest in part by creating negative stereotypes about Barceló and the other women of Santa Fe. They believed that her unusual behavior proved that all Mexican women were immoral and immodest. Josiah Gregg, an American trader and doctor living in Santa Fe in the 1830s, repeatedly described her as a "loose" woman and a prostitute, even though he admired her wealth and said her generosity helped improve her moral character.

Anglo-American men were not Barceló's only critics. Susan Shelby Magoffin also had harsh words for Barceló and other Mexican women. In 1846 the eighteen-year-old Susan accompanied her husband, trader Samuel Magoffin, from St. Louis, Missouri, to Santa Fe, becoming the first Anglo-American woman in town. On August 31, 1846, she described herself in her diary as "the first American lady" to travel what would become the busy Santa Fe trail, "and some of our company seem disposed to make me the first under any circumstances that ever crossed the Plains." Although she herself stretched the bounds of acceptable femininity by accompanying her husband to such an "uncivilized" place, she criticized the local women's appearance and their failure to follow American fashion. She wrote that the women "dressed in the Mexican style; large sleeves, short waists, ruffled skirts, and no bustles—which latter looks exceedingly odd....All danced and smoked cigarillos, from the old woman with false hair and teeth [Barceló], to the little child." At the time Anglos considered smoking to be particularly distasteful and inappropriate for women. Magoffin added that Barceló was "a stately dame of a certain age, the possessor of a portion of that shrewd sense and fascinating manner necessary to allure the wayward, inexperienced youth to the hall of final ruin." From Magoffin's perspective, Barceló did not conform to Anglo-American standards of beauty or appropriate behavior; but given Magoffin's own very unusual place on the edge of American territory, she did not conform either.

In spite of their attacks on her reputation and behavior, the invading Americans needed Barceló. The town's social, political, and economic life revolved around her saloon. Politicians and military officers sought her opinions and information and gained access to important local politicians in her saloon. Barceló's loyalties tended to lie with the Americans, perhaps because she could see that they were going to dominate in the future. In 1846, shortly after the start of the American occupation, local American army officers had so little cash with which to pay their men that they came to Barceló for a loan. She gave them one thousand dollars in cash. At least two of her adopted daughters married American traders, and her will was one of the first by a Hispanic woman to be executed in English. Her sister and adopted daughters were the main beneficiaries. Barceló died in January 1852 and her funeral was one of the most ornate and expensive that Santa Fe had ever seen. At the time of her death, she was worth over ten thousand dollars, more than twice what most Spanish-Mexican men were worth and more than what most of the new Americans in town were worth.

New Roles for Spanish-Mexican Women

Barceló was able to use her atypical yet successful business pursuits to create unusual opportunities for herself as an influence broker and cultural mediator. A more common experience for elite Spanish-Mexican women in Texas, New Mexico, and California, was that after the Mexican-American War they acquired a new value as wives for the Anglo-American men. This situation brought the biggest change to their personal lives in the post-war period. Like Native American women across the West and like Barceló in her saloon, Spanish and Mexican women used their position to bridge the gap between their own culture and that of their Anglo-American husbands. In the 1840s and 1850s, elite Spanish-Mexican women occupied the role that Native American women had played in the sixteenth and seventeenth centuries, and they made the most of the opportunity.

There were significant differences, however, between the practical consequences of intermarriage in the Southwest and California. In the former, marrying an Anglo-American could bring status and wealth to Spanish-Mexican women and their families. In Texas, for example, marriages between American immigrants and leading Tejano families were central to the political and cultural alliances between the two communities. Intermarriage did not protect the Tejanos after the war with Mexico ended with the 1848 Treaty of Guadalupe Hidalgo, however; the tide of anti-Mexican sentiment promptly turned against them, and the Anglo-Americans uprooted and expelled entire communities In California in the early nineteenth century, in contrast, Anglo-American men gained more from marrying Spanish-Mexican women. By that time land ownership was the key marker of wealth and status, and Anglo-American men married into elite Californio families to gain access to and profit from that land.

Before the Mexican-American War, about two hundred Anglo- and Euro-American men had legally married Californianas, and that number grew in the wake of the war. The American immigrants to California before 1846 achieved their goals by marrying into elite families, as well as through military and economic infiltration, and their wives became important bridges between the two cultures. American merchants involved in the hide and tallow trade married into the leading cattle ranching families, or rancheros. These families belonged to an extravagant society that developed in California in the 1820s and 1830s when the Mexican government gave elite fami- lies the best land and stock after closing the missions. The ranchero families had little cash; their wealth was in their land and stock. They mortgaged their land to pay for expensive clothes, fiestas, and wed- dings, and they killed their cattle to sell the hides and tallow to the Boston traders. Guadalupe Vallejo, from the same elite Vallejo fam- ily as María Paula Rosalía Vallejo de Leese (discussed above), later wrote of the ranchero life, "It seems to me that there never was a more peaceful or happy people in the face of the earth."

The Anglo-American hide traders in California in the 1820s and 1830s knew that they would be there for a long time and had few marriage options. Marrying a Californiana, especially one from an elite ranchero family, gave them in one stroke a wife and better business connections in the ranchero community. The Americans had to convert to Catholicism to marry these elite daughters, and some became Mexican citizens to gain access to the government's generous land grants.

For example, two sisters from the elite de la Guerra family mar- ried British and American men in the early nineteenth century, bolstering their families' economic opportunities. Born in 1809, María Teresa de la Guerra y Noriega (known as Teresa) was a third- generation Californiana; her great-grandparents had immigrated to California in 1775. Her father, Don José Antonio Julián de la Guerra y Noriega, was a respected man of affairs and the richest in the Santa Barbara region, with thousands of cattle. The family had Native American women servants to do most of the household work, including cooking, sewing, laundry, ironing, baking bread, and making soap and candles. When Teresa was fourteen, a British-born trader, William E. P. Hartnell, wrote to her father proposing to marry her. They married three years later, when she was seventeen and Hartnell was twenty-seven, after he had converted to Catholicism. Teresa got pregnant nineteen times but only six of her children survived to adulthood. Hartnell did not achieve the prosperity he had hoped for, and his career as a trader ended in bankruptcy in 1829. Having become a naturalized Mexican citizen in 1830, he acquired a share in a ranch, but he knew little about ranching and had to rely heavily on Teresa's father for advice and connections. He never became as wealthy or important as he had hoped. When Teresa's father died, his will excluded her because he had already given her share of his estate to her in an effort to help Hartnell. As if economic difficulties were not bad enough, Hartnell cheated on Teresa often throughout their married life. After he died in 1854, she struggled to pay the increasing taxes on the family's three properties.

Teresa's sister Anita also married an American, Alfred Robinson. He was an agent for Bryant, Sturgis and Company, a Boston-based firm that dominated California's hide and tallow trade, and he and Don José did a lot of business with each other. Anita and Robinson married in 1836 when she was fifteen and he was twenty-nine. In both cases Don José could have refused the men's requests, but he had clear economic reasons to marry his daughters to men who seemed to be up-and-coming businessmen. He and other Californio fathers who supported similar marriages for their daughters also had another reason to grant permission: elite families wanted to maintain their supposed racial purity and although Anglo-Americans were not Spanish, they were at least white, which made them desirable sons-in-law.

Marriages between Spanish-Mexican women and Anglo-American men were fairly common at all levels of society in the Southwest and California, despite the fact that each side considered the other's gender norms and cultural practices inferior to its own. For some Hispanic women, marrying an American improved their social and economic status and started the process of assimilating the two groups. Some wives were determined to maintain traditional patterns of language, religious, and home life, because these practices gave them a great deal of power over household decisions. They educated their husbands about Hispanic life in the process. Others adopted Anglo-American patterns and became more truly bicultural by finding the points of connection between the two cultures. Marriages between Anglo-American women and Hispanic men were less common, but they did happen occasionally if both husband and wife were from elite families.

As the United States extended its reach over California and the Southwest, the Spanish-Mexican women who lived in these areas confronted new constraints and opportunities. They had fewer options within the American legal system, but they could exercise influence by marrying the American newcomers.

Anglo-American Women in Texas and New Mexico

While the imposition of Anglo-American racial and gender norms reshaped Native American, African American, and Spanish-Mexican women's lives in the 1830s and 1840s, a tiny minority of Anglo-American women found themselves at the top of the racial hierarchy in the Southwest. Some used this position to observe and judge the other people around them, and their opinions were rarely favorable. In Mary Austin Holley's widely read book *Texas* (1832), she described the Mexican settlers in Texas as "very ignorant and degraded, and generally speaking, timid and irresolute." In contrast, she thought that the Native Americans were a superior race, because "even the Comanches" (who had a reputation for being particularly fierce and barbaric) "were distinguished for two prominent virtues—fidelity and hospitality." Other Anglo-American women living in Texas in these decades were equally harsh in their remarks about Mexicans. Mary Helm had little personal contact with them, but nonetheless said that they were "the debris of several inferior and degraded races" and were characterized by "barbarism, butchery and cruelty."

A few Anglo-American women had more positive impressions, however. After living in San Antonio de Bexar, Texas, in the 1830s, Mary Maverick wrote that the Mexican women "dressed nicely and were graceful and gracious of manner." Also a Texas resident before the U.S. conquest, Jane Cazeneau wrote in her 1852 book *Eagle Pass or Life on the Border* that "filial love is a deep enduring trait in the Mexican character...and throws its light on some of its darker shades."

In contrast to her negative views of Mexican women, Mary Austin Holley had more complimentary things to say about the white women who lived in the colony on the Brazos river in Texas that her cousin, Stephen Austin, had settled. She stated that

> necessity has taught many of the more elevated rank in life, a hardihood and courage truly surprising in the gentle sex.... Living in a wild country under circumstances requiring constant exertion, forms the character to great and daring enterprise. Women thus situated are known to perform exploits, which the effeminate men of populous cities might tremble at.

Her choice of words echoes the nineteenth-century belief that urban life weakened men, while a rural life strengthened women and men both. She also expressed another popular sentiment, the idea that the harsh conditions of the West could benefit women and give them the opportunity to display a strength that they had been forced to hide in more refined eastern settings. According to Holley, "women have the capacity for greatness but they require occasions to bring it out....Many a wife in Texas has proved herself the better half, and many a widow's heart has prompted her to noble daring." Far from being too fragile to handle a less "civilized" way of life,

Anglo-American women found that the "wild country" of Texas encouraged them to show their strength and perseverance.

In the Southwest and California, some white women viewed Mexican women favorably even during the turbulent 1840s. Susan Shelby Magoffin (discussed above) was initially very critical of the Mexican women she encountered in Santa Fe in the 1840s, but she later learned Spanish and made many Mexican friends. Margaret Hecox, who arrived in California in October 1846, after the outbreak of hostilities between the United States and Mexico, was quite sympathetic toward the Mexicans. The people she had met "treated us most kindly....Never will I forget the kindness of the Spanish people....Particularly the Spanish women, who came to us as we traveled along...bringing us offers of homemade cheese, milk, and other appetizing food." Like Magoffin, she learned Spanish and was fond of her Mexican neighbors, "whom I learned to love like sisters." For Hecox, the gendered experiences she shared with Mexican women overcame the racial differences and privileges that divided them.

All women in the Southwest and California lived through significant political upheavals and regime changes in the early nineteenth century, and their place in the rapidly evolving race and class hierarchies determined the new constraints they faced or the opportunities they could seize. Anglo-American women were secure in their place at the top of a racial hierarchy that would be cemented by the U.S. conquest. That takeover demoted Spanish-Mexican women from the top spot, and they had to create new opportunities for themselves, usually by marrying Anglo-American men. Native American and African American women, meanwhile, found themselves firmly at the bottom of the new hierarchy with few available choices.

Suggested Readings

Bouvier, Virginia M. *Codes of Silence: Women and the Conquest of California, 1542–1840.* Tucson: University of Arizona Press, 2004.

Casas, María Raquél. *Married to a Daughter of the Land: Spanish-Mexican Women and Interethnic Marriage in California, 1820–1880.* Reno and Las Vegas: University of Nevada Press, 2007.

Chávez-García, Miroslava. *Negotiating Conquest: Gender and Power in California, 1770s to 1880s.* Tucson: University of Arizona Press, 2004.

Cook, Mary J. Straw. *Doña Tules: Santa Fe's Courtesan and Gambler.* Albuquerque: University of New Mexico Press, 2007.

González, Deena. "La Tules of Image and Reality: Euro-American Attitudes and Legend Formation on a Spanish-Mexican Frontier." In *Unequal Sisters: A Multi-Cultural Reader in U.S. Women's History,* 2nd ed., edited by Vicki L. Ruiz and Ellen Carol DuBois, pp. 57–69. New York: Routledge, 1994.

———. *Refusing the Favor: The Spanish-Mexican Women of Santa Fe, 1820–1880.* New York: Oxford University Press, 1999.

Gutiérrez, Ramón A. *When Jesus Came, the Corn Mothers Went Away: Marriage, Sexuality, and Power in New Mexico, 1500–1846.* Stanford, CA: Stanford University Press, 1991.

Hurtado, Albert L. *Intimate Frontiers: Sex, Gender, and Culture in Old California.* Albuquerque: University of New Mexico Press, 1999.

Layva, Yolanda Chávez. "'A Poor Widow Burdened with Children': Widows and Land in Colonial New Mexico." In *Writing the Range: Race, Class, and Culture in the Women's West,* edited by Elizabeth Jameson and Susan Armitage, pp. 85–96. Norman: University of Oklahoma Press, 1997.

McDonald, Dedra S. "To Be Black and Female in the Spanish Southwest: Toward a History of African Women on Spain's Far Northern Frontier." In *African American Women Confront the West, 1600–2000,* edited by Quintard Taylor and Shirley Ann Wilson Moore, pp. 32–52. Norman: University of Oklahoma Press, 2003.

Padilla, Genaro. "'Yo Sola Aprendí': Mexican Women's Personal Narratives from Nineteenth-Century California." In *Writing the Range: Race, Class, and Culture in the Women's West,* edited by Elizabeth Jameson and Susan Armitage, pp. 188–201. Norman: University of Oklahoma Press, 1997.

The remains of a pueblo in the Southwest. *Buffalo Bill Historical Center, Cody, Wyoming; North American Indian Photograph Collection, Gift of George D. Kolbe, P.35.155*

George Catlin painted this image of a Mandan village on the Missouri River sometime in the 1850s or 1860s, based on a village he had seen in the 1830s. *Buffalo Bill Historical Center, Cody, Wyoming; Gift of Paul Mellon, 25.86*

Woven-grass basket made by the Pomo sometime in the early 1800s. *Buffalo Bill Historical Center, Cody, Wyoming; NA.106.530*

This 9-inch doll is made of deerskin and canvas and decorated with shells and beads. It was made by the Sioux around 1890. *Buffalo Bill Historical Center, Cody, Wyoming; Chandler-Pohrt Collection, Gift of Mr. William D. Weiss, NA.507.64*

Alice Cooper's sculpture of Sacajawea, pointing westward, with her son on her back was unveiled in 1905 and stands in Washington Park in Portland, Oregon. *Image by EncMstr Photography, GFDL*

Three Navajo women working in front of two large looms, with a baby in a cradle board in the foreground. *Buffalo Bill Historical Center, Cody, Wyoming; Vincent Mercaldo Collection, P.71.1897*

Below: This 1879 Thomas Allen painting shows an early nineteenth century market plaza in San Antonio, Texas. *Courtesy of the Witte Museum, San Antonio, Texas, Accession # 1936-6518 P*

Hopi woman making a basket. *Buffalo Bill Historical Center, Cody, Wyoming; North American Indian Photograph Collection, Gift of George D. Kolbe, P.35.161*

This photo of Iron Teeth holding her hide scraper was taken by Thomas B. Marquis in the late 1920s. *Buffalo Bill Historical Center, Cody, Wyoming; Thomas Marquis Collection, PN. 165.1.77*

Mrs. Charging Twin using an elk horn scraper to remove hair from a bison hide. *Courtesy State Historical Society of North Dakota, 086-0060*

Iron Teeth in the late 1920s.
*Buffalo Bill Historical Center,
Cody, Wyoming; Thomas Marquis
Collection, PN. 165.1.92*

Girls of the Crow Boarding
School dressed in Anglo-American
clothing and standing in front of
their dormitory in the late 1800s.
*Buffalo Bill Historical Center, Cody,
Wyoming; Edward Becker Collec-
tion of Crow Indian Photographs,
Museum Purchase, P.32.84*

This 1921 W. H. D. Koerner painting titled 'Madonna of the Prairie' has come to symbolize popular perceptions of women's experiences of the overland trail. The woman is white, young, weary, and the covered wagon is creating a halo around her head. *Buffalo Bill Historical Center, Cody, Wyoming; Museum Purchase, 25.77*

There are no known images of Narcissa Whitman created during her lifetime, but artist Drury V. Haight painted this one in the twentieth century from sketches based on nineteenth-century descriptions. *U.S. National Park Service Collection, Whitman Mission National Historic Site*

CHAPTER FOUR

Native American Women in the Nineteenth Century

Of all the women in the West during the nineteenth century, Native American women undoubtedly faced the harshest constraints and had the fewest choices. By the end of the century, they hit their lowest point ever in population and status. The U.S. government forced some out of their homelands, confined others to reservations that were mere fractions of their former territories, and killed thousands in battles and massacres. Government officials, secular reformers, and Christian missionaries developed intense, invasive assimilation programs, many of which centered on making Native women behave more like white American women. Indigenous women had to deal with some well-intentioned but condescending white female allies, and others who were truly sympathetic but possessed limited influence. In short, all areas of their lives came under attack. Yet as this web of constraints tightened around them, Native American women continued to make as many choices as they could and seize whatever limited opportunities came their way. In doing so, they played key roles in ensuring that their peoples and their cultures survived.

The Trail of Tears

The U.S. government forced some Native American women to become westerners in the 1830s and 1840s by forcing them out of their traditional territory in northern Georgia, southeastern Tennessee, and western North Carolina. Tens of thousands of Cherokee women, men, and children had to leave their homes and move west of the Mississippi River because of white expansion and President Andrew Jackson's 1830 removal policy. This policy aimed to remove as many Native Americans as possible from their homelands in the Midwest and Southeast and contain them in a single "Indian Territory" (now Oklahoma). Removal freed their land to be settled by whites, and gathering them all in one place was supposed to make it easier to assimilate them to Anglo-American culture.

Cherokee women had been fighting land cessions for decades. Traditionally, they had a very high status in their culture, including a voice in government, and their society was both matrilineal and matrilocal. Contact with Europeans and Americans over the course of the eighteenth century had undermined women's power considerably because the newcomers would only deal with men. Even Cherokee inheritance practices, which had been very egalitarian, began to shift. Anglo-American pressure made the patriarchal family, which gave most of the formal and legal power to male heads of household, more common among the Cherokees by the early nineteenth century. In 1827 the Cherokees ratified a constitution that restricted voting and office-holding to free male citizens, just as the U.S. Constitution did. Excluding women from decision making did not cause the removal crisis of the 1830s, but their exclusion prevented them from opposing the land cessions and removal at the highest level of Cherokee politics.

Most members of the Cherokee nation did not support the small group of men who signed the 1835 Treaty of New Echota with the U.S. government. This agreement conceded that the Cherokee would leave their homelands voluntarily. Some headed west on their own, but most wanted to stay in their homes as long as they could. In the fall of 1838, 7,000 U.S. soldiers forcibly evicted the last 18,000 Cherokees from their traditional territory. At least 4,000 Cherokees died from cold, hunger, disease, and exhaustion during

Shaded areas indicate land areas recognized by the Indian Claims Commission (an independent tribunal established by Congress in 1946) as the "aboriginal territories" of several western tribes. Black areas represent the external boundaries of those reservations where members of those tribes currently reside. The aboriginal territories (and modern reservations) are as follows: California (Hoopa Valley, Round Valley, Tule River, and the Southern California Rancherias), Yakima (Yakima), Nez Perce (Nez Perce), Blackfeet and Gros Ventre (Blackfeet and Fort Belknap). Crow (Crow), Sioux (Pine Ridge, Rosebud, Yankton, Crow Creek, Lower Brule, Cheyenne River, Standing Rock, and Sisseton), Shoshone and Western Shoshone (Fort Hall, Wind River, Pyramid Lake, Walker Lake, and Duck Valley), Cheyenne and Arapaho (Northern Cheyenne, Cheyenne and Arapaho, Wind River), Pawnee (Pawnee), Kiowa Comanche and Apache (Kiowa), Jicarilla, Mescalero (San Carlos, and Fort Apache), and Navajo (Navajo). Note: Aboriginal areas were determined by the Indian Claims Commission on narrow legal grounds. In general they represent the boundaries of tribal habitation at the time treaties were negotiated with the United States; they do not reflect the precontact locations of tribes or account for seasonal migrations. In short, they are suggestive rather than definitive.

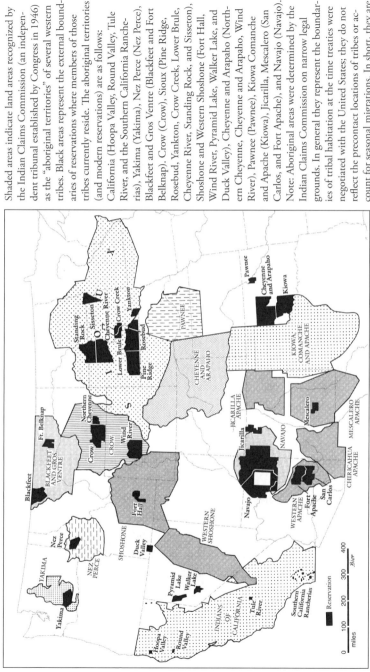

Aboriginal Territories and Modern Indian Reservations

the 1,000-mile forced march to Indian Territory. Numerous women gave birth along the trail, and many of them, along with many newborns and young children, died. This march became known as the Trail of Tears. It was not the only forced removal of eastern Native groups from their homelands to the West during the decade: the Choctaws, Chickasaws, Creeks, and Seminoles suffered the same fate. The Cherokees' exile had the highest death toll, however, and it marked the end of Cherokee women's traditional power.

The U.S. government repeated the process that led to the signing of the Treaty of New Echota many times across the West in subsequent decades. When the government signed the 1851 Treaty of Fort Laramie with the northern Great Plains tribes and the 1853 Treaty of Fort Atkinson with the southern Great Plains tribes, it dealt only with male Native American representatives. There is little record of what Native American women thought of these pieces of paper, which promised the tribes annual payments in exchange for allowing the United States to build army posts and railroads through their territory. Over the next several decades federal, state, and territorial governments and American citizens used treaties, military campaigns, and vigilante violence to force Native American peoples off their traditional territories and onto reservations. The result was a massive upheaval in women's lives, new constraints on their traditional roles, and unprecedented interference in their personal lives.

The removal crisis of the 1830s also sparked the first mass petition campaigns by white American women. After Connecticut activist and educator Catharine Beecher wrote a pamphlet opposing the removal, almost 1,500 women from several northern states sent petitions to Congress. This act marked the beginning of white women's political activism on Native American issues, and their involvement increased as the century progressed. The removal process could not be stopped, however, and over the next several decades treaties and more direct methods were used to force Native American peoples off their traditional territories and onto reservations.

Disease and Violence

As discussed in chapter two, most Native American communities suffered a dramatic decline in their population between the seventeenth and the nineteenth centuries because Europeans introduced diseases against which indigenous people had no immunity. The frequent violent clashes between Native Americans and the whites who wanted them out of the way worsened the death toll. Native American women saw their fathers, husbands, and sons killed by state and territorial militias as well as the U.S. Army. There were hundreds of battles and dozens of deliberate massacres, like the one at Sand Creek, Colorado, in November 1864, in which the Colorado militia killed approximately two hundred Cheyennes and Arapahos. During the 1870 Baker (or Marias) Massacre in northwestern Montana, the U.S. Army killed 173 Blackfeet in a dawn raid. In 1890 the army attacked a camp in the Dakota Territory, killing 146 people. In all of these massacres, and in dozens of similar attacks across the West, many of the dead were women and children. In contrast, Native American warfare usually avoided killing women and children.

The experiences of two Northern Cheyenne women, Buffalo Calf Road and Iron Teeth, illustrate the harsh constraints imposed on Native Americans, the difficult choices women had to make, and the chances they seized to resist. In the late nineteenth century, the Northern Cheyennes, whose key leaders included Little Wolf and Dull Knife, allied themselves closely with the Lakotas (one of the main tribal divisions of the Sioux). The two groups fought together in Red Cloud's War from 1866 to 1868, an effort to close the Bozeman Trail through their territories and stop American miners from getting to the gold strikes in Montana Territory. In 1876, some Northern Cheyennes helped the Sioux to defeat General George Custer and his men at Little Bighorn, just a few weeks after General George Crook and his soldiers had attacked a Cheyenne camp on the Rosebud River. In retaliation, the U.S. cavalry attacked the Northern Cheyennes' winter camp on the Powder River later that year.

Buffalo Calf Road was an important participant in both of the key battles in the summer of 1876. She was in her mid-twenties, married to a man named Black Coyote, and they had a four-year-old daughter. In June her people heard that General Crook and his soldiers were coming to attack the Cheyenne camp on the Rosebud River. Buffalo Calf Road accompanied the warriors when they rode out to stop the soldiers, and she made her reputation as a warrior that day by saving her brother when he was pinned down by enemy fire. One week later, she again rode out with the Cheyenne and Sioux warriors when General Custer attacked them at the Little Bighorn River. She fought so well that day that the Cheyenne gave her an honorary name, Brave Woman. When the U.S. Army attacked the Cheyennes' winter camp in November 1876, killing at least forty-five people and burning the winter village to the ground, the pregnant Buffalo Calf Road had to flee into the cold to survive. After another clash in January 1877, the army took four Cheyenne women and five children hostage. At that point, most of the Cheyennes decided to give up and move onto the reservation in Indian Territory. Thirty-four people refused, including Buffalo Calf Road and her husband. But a few months later, starvation drove them, by then the parents of a newborn son as well as a daughter, and others to surrender.

These battles also shaped the life of another Northern Cheyenne woman, Iron Teeth, who was born in 1834 in the Black Hills (in what was called Nebraska Territory at the time, now South Dakota). During the 1860s and 1870s, she was a member of Chief Dull Knife's band. She and her husband, Red Pipe, raised five children and prospered until the Great Sioux War in 1876. The U.S. cavalry killed Iron Teeth's husband Red Pipe when it attacked the Northern Cheyennes' winter camp in the Bighorn Mountains in November in that year. She recalled,

> They killed our men, women, and children, whichever ones might be hit by their bullets. We who could do so ran away. My husband and my two sons helped in fighting off the soldiers and enemy Indians. My husband was walking, leading his horse, and stop-

ping at times to shoot. Suddenly I saw him fall. I started to go back to him, but my sons made me go on with my three daughters. The last time I ever saw Red Pipe, he was lying there dead in the snow. From the hilltops we Cheyenne saw our lodges and everything in them burned.

She, too, had to flee into the cold, just like Buffalo Calf Road.

Iron Teeth was now a middle-aged widow with five children. She recalled that the survivors, "wallowed through the mountain snows for several days. Most of us were afoot. We had no lodges, only a few blankets, and there was only a little dry meat food among us. Men died of wounds; women and children froze to death." The survivors eventually made their way north into Montana and found refuge with the Lakotas. In the spring of 1877, emaciated and hungry, many surrendered to the U.S. Army at Camp Robinson.

The U.S. government's Bureau of Indian Affairs (the BIA, founded in 1824, and also called the Office of Indian Affairs or the Indian Bureau) ordered the Northern Cheyennes to move to the reservation in Indian Territory. The long trip south took more than two months. Once they arrived, they began to fall ill with diseases like malaria, which were unknown on the northern plains. Of the nearly 1,000 Northern Cheyennes registered with the agency (the local administrative branch of the BIA on the reservation), almost two-thirds became ill within two months of their arrival. The U.S. government eventually sent medical supplies, but these did not arrive until the middle of winter, and there was not enough food or winter clothing. By the spring of 1878, many of the Northern Cheyennes found their new lives in Indian Territory intolerable. That summer, Chiefs Little Wolf and Dull Knife asked agent John D. Miles (the local BIA employee responsible for the Northern Cheyennes) for permission to take their people north to their homelands. They told Miles that in 1877 General George Crook had promised them they could return to Montana if they did not like life in Indian Territory—a claim Crook denied. Miles and the BIA refused their request, so about three hundred Cheyennes escaped during the early morning hours of September 10, 1878, including Buffalo Calf Road, Iron Teeth, and their families.

The 1,500-mile journey north during the fall and winter of 1878–79 took the Northern Cheyennes through Kansas, Nebraska, Dakota Territory, and eventually to Montana Territory. They had to cross three major railroads, which the military used to mount troops quickly against them. Hungry and exhausted, the Cheyennes often traveled great distances at night to stay ahead of pursuit. Iron Teeth's oldest son, Gathering His Medicine, "kept saying we should go on toward the north unless we were killed, that it was better to be killed than to go back and die slowly." Iron Teeth and the other women had taken only what they could carry in small packs so that they could travel as quickly as possible. Iron Teeth had some clothes, pemmican (a combination of dried meat and berries pounded together to make a nutritious and long-lasting food), and a revolver that she later gave to Gathering His Medicine. She also carried her most treasured possession, a hide scraper that her husband had shaped from an elk antler and given her as a wedding gift. She cherished the tool as a symbol of honor and respect because she was a member of the prestigious hide-scraper society that prepared skins for lodges in Cheyenne villages.

The Cheyennes had to defend themselves against the pursuing soldiers more than once, and the group split up in October. Little Wolf's group included Buffalo Calf Road and her family. They hid in Nebraska's Sand Hills before making a run for the upper Powder River and Rosebud Country in northern Wyoming and southern Montana in the spring of 1879. Her husband, Black Coyote, grew increasingly bitter towards whites. The rest of Little Wolf's group began to perceive his attitude as a liability so they told him, Buffalo Calf Road, their children, and four others who shared his perspective to leave the group. In April 1879 U.S. soldiers captured Buffalo Calf Road's party and imprisoned them at Fort Keogh. She died of diphtheria in June 1879, and Black Coyote killed himself in his grief. Their daughter later married another Northern Cheyenne man. No further record exists of their son.

Chief Dull Knife led the other group of escaped Northern Cheyennes, which included Iron Teeth and her children. They decided to go to the old Red Cloud Agency (one of the BIA offices in what was then called Wyoming Territory, now the state of Nebraska) to join their Sioux friends. They did not know that the Indian Bureau had closed the old agency in 1877 and relocated the Lakotas to the new Pine Ridge Agency in Dakota Territory (now South Dakota). Along the way, the Northern Cheyennes encountered some American soldiers who insisted that the group go to the newly designated Fort Robinson in Nebraska while the government decided what would happen to them. Dull Knife's exhausted people agreed reluctantly.

U.S. government officials demanded that the military forcibly return the Northern Cheyennes to Indian Territory as an example to others. But the Cheyennes refused, stating that they would rather die than go back. In December 1878 the new commander of Fort Robinson, Captain Henry Wessells, decided to starve them into submission. He refused to give them any more food or water until they agreed to go back to Indian Territory. Once again the Northern Cheyennes decided they had to escape and try to get to the Pine Ridge Agency, even thought they knew many would die in the attempt.

On the night of January 9, 1879, about 125 of the Cheyennes were locked in the barracks, and of that number only forty-four were men of fighting age. They had a few rifles and revolvers—all that they had managed to hide when the soldiers searched them in October. Iron Teeth had her revolver hidden in her dress, and the women again had their small packs ready to go. Iron Teeth recalled, "The warriors decided to break out just after the soldiers had gone to bed for the night. I gave to my son the six-shooter I had…. He was my oldest child, then twenty-two years of age."

The breakout began around 10 p.m. at night, and the soldiers quickly gave chase. The Cheyennes scattered to minimize the number that would get caught. Those carrying heavy loads and smaller children, including Iron Teeth and her family, began to fall behind.

"My son took the younger of [my] two daughters upon his back. The older daughter and I each carried a little pack." They got separated and had not made "any agreed plan for meeting again." She and her daughter managed to find a cave to hide in and were not caught for more than a week. In the meantime, soldiers killed Gathering His Medicine while he was trying to protect his little sister and took the girl back to Fort Robinson. After the first few days of searching, only thirty-two of the fugitives were still at large, and troops found and killed some of those a few weeks later.

The Northern Cheyennes' determination not to go back to Indian Territory finally prompted the BIA to investigate Native American living conditions there. The bureau was forced to acknowledge the intolerable living conditions in the territory and then gave the Northern Cheyennes permission to stay in the north. Iron Teeth and the last of the survivors at Fort Robinson finally made it to Pine Ridge. By 1900 all Northern Cheyennes who wished to do so had relocated to the new Northern Cheyenne Reservation along Rosebud Creek and the Tongue River in Montana. Iron Teeth lived out the last of her days in poverty in an isolated log cabin in the hills above Lame Deer, Montana, and died in 1928. She kept her precious hide scraper until the end, because as she said, "Red Pipe was the only husband I ever had. I am the only wife he ever had. Through more than fifty years I have been his widow. When I die, this gift from my husband will be buried with me."

In the space of only three years, 1876–79, both Buffalo Calf Road and Iron Teeth suffered enormous losses and hardships, and yet their stories also demonstrate the choices that they made and the chances they seized. They refused to accept the U.S. government's plans for their people and did what they could to protect their families, communities, and cultures in the face of deliberate onslaughts.

Education

In addition to the forced removals, starvation, and warfare that the U.S. government used to get Native Americans out of the way of white settlement, it imposed a wide range of more subtle assimilative programs to make Native Americans behave more like whites. Along with religious and secular reformers, the government launched a massive push to re-educate Native Americans in the latter half of the nineteenth century. Education programs often focused on girls because government officials and reformers believed that if Native American girls could be taught to be like Anglo-American house-wives, they could then assimilate their husbands and children, just as Anglo-American housewives supposedly acted as the moral com-pass for their families. Even though most Native women had greater freedom to manage their own economic and marital lives than white women, nineteenth-century Anglo-Americans believed that Native American women were the overworked, exploited victims of their husbands' lusts and laziness. Federal officials and reformers thought that children had to be removed from their own homes and housed in boarding schools to "cure" them of the contaminating influences of their home environments.

The string of day and boarding schools that opened across the West was supposed to instill Anglo-American gender norms and work habits in Native children by emphasizing domestic chores and obedience. Reformers called these schools "industrial" because the curriculum aimed to teach the children how to do Euro-American-style work and participate in a modern industrial economy. By 1900 the U.S. government ran about a hundred fifty boarding schools and a hundred fifty day schools for some 21,500 Native American chil-dren. After 1892 the government did not even need to get parental consent before taking children away to school. Most of the teachers were white women; they constituted more than three hundred of the five hundred fifty teachers employed by Indian schools in the 1890s. The predominance of female teachers reflected the dominant society's belief that women were better teachers than men because women supposedly had an innate ability and desire to nurture chil-dren. The female teachers were also supposed to act as role models for the Native American girls. Finally, female teachers earned less than male teachers, lowering the cost of operating the schools.

The schools were often less concerned with giving the girls a formal education than instructing them in their supposedly "inferior" racial status and new "civilized" gender norms. The line between training the girls to do housework and exploiting them as laborers was blurred or erased. For example, many institutions expected the girls to do all the cooking and cleaning, thus saving the schools from having to pay staff to do this work. At Genoa, Nebraska, the superintendent reported that cleaning and sewing kept the few girls attending the school fully occupied, so the male students had to do the laundry. The superintendent of the Albuquerque, New Mexico, school had a similar problem and expressed relief when he finally got enough female students so that the boys no longer had to do feminized chores like cleaning and making the beds.

Some BIA employees recognized that these chores were not going to turn the girls into good housewives, because all they learned was how to keep an institution clean, not how to run a domestic household and keep a nuclear family happy. Josephine Mayo, the girls' matron at the Genoa, Nebraska, school, reported in 1886 that "making a dozen beds and cleaning a dormitory does not teach them to make a room attractive and homelike." Nor did cooking large quantities of a single dish to feed a school teach the girls how to "supply a family with a pleasant and healthy variety of food, nicely cooked." Some of the larger institutions did try to train the girls to be efficient housewives, at least according to Anglo-American standards, by teaching them how to set tables, cook, and care for children. By the end of the nineteenth century, a few schools also taught more employable skills like stenography and nursing.

The BIA envisioned the employment of Native girls as domestic servants in white households as a central component of its assimilation policy, so the schools developed what they called "outing" programs, which placed the children for part of each day and usually for the summer with local white families. Boys usually did farm labor, while girls did housework. These experiences taught the girls that they should be subservient to whites, at the same time that they learned how to clean an Anglo-American home the way an Anglo-

American housewife wanted it cleaned. Unlike other domestic servants in the West, who dealt directly with their employers, Native girls had to deal with the BIA as well as their employers. The bureau hired outing matrons to oversee the employment of Native American girls and young women in urban households, to protect them from possible sexual exploitation as well as ensure that their white employers provided the "civilizing" environment deemed necessary for assimilation. Outing matrons often kept detailed files on each young woman that they placed in service, indicating the intense scrutiny under which the women lived and worked. The young women themselves regularly challenged the BIA's many efforts to control them, however. They often refused to play their assigned roles as grateful servants and rejected attempts to "uplift" them. They also learned how to use the outing matron as a mediator in their conflicts with their employers.

Government officials and reformers also wanted to control the students' heterosexual relations, because they believed that Native American students came from homes in which adults allowed and even encouraged sexual promiscuity. For example, when the first boarding school opened on the Round Valley reservation in California in 1881, the local BIA agent wanted the teachers to keep the boys and girls apart to prevent what he deemed immoral contact. Native American students burned the school to the ground two years later to show how unhappy they were there. The government replaced it with a day school, so the children could live at home while attending school, but the local Indian agent kept lobbying for a boarding school to prevent sexual mischief. BIA officials and reformers believed that only constant, round-the-clock supervision at a boarding school could ensure "proper" behavior. The government finally built a new boarding school at Round Valley in 1897.

The industrial schools reached their peak between 1890 and 1910, when approximately twenty-five off-reservation schools operated. As many as 3,000 girls may have been enrolled each year in this period, and they generally made up 40 percent to 50 percent of the student body. Agents, superintendents, and teachers thought that the girls were easier to recruit, easier to hire out to the community as cheap domestic labor, and less likely to cause problems than the boys. Some of the girls were happy to be in school but most of them were not, and many resumed a traditional life when they moved back home. Although they might have learned a great deal at school about how to do laundry and sew, they rarely had the range of skills and knowledge they needed to thrive either on the reservation or in white society. The BIA represented their best chance at employment, and it reinforced the same racial and gendered lessons they learned at the schools: the Bureau paid many young Native women to cook, clean, and sew at its schools and Indian agencies, but it hired very few as teachers and none as administrators. In short, the schools often left the girls adrift between two worlds, lacking the skills to prosper in one or the other.

In 1891 the BIA developed another program to address what it saw as the irrational refusal of adult Native American women to abandon their traditional household practices. Anglo-American women's reform groups pressured the government into hiring field matrons for many reservations. The field matron was supposed to teach and model Anglo-American housekeeping and morals to Native American women, including everything from housekeeping, decorating, and gardening to "proper" sexual behavior.

Most Native Americans recognized that an Anglo-American education could be a useful tool in dealing with the rapid changes they were undergoing, but when they built their own schools, they often took a very different approach from the U.S. government. For example, the Cherokees had long valued formal education as a way to improve their relationship with whites, and some members of the tribe hoped that it would help them assimilate more quickly. A mere thirteen years after the Trail of Tears, the Cherokee Council opened its own Female Seminary in Indian Territory, modeling it as closely as possible on the Mount Holyoke Female Seminary (today Mount Holyoke College) in Massachusetts. The council hired the first two teachers from Mount Holyoke and based the Cherokee school's curriculum on that of the Massachusetts institution. The council was dominated by mixed-race Cherokees who wanted to get away from traditional ways, so the girls did not study any Cherokee history or culture. They did, however, get a rigorous education in math, science, Christian theology, philosophy, ancient and modern languages, literature, history, music, and many other subjects. The school also focused on teaching Anglo-American gender norms, and it required the girls to attend church. Instead of the physical discipline common at many of the white-run schools, the Cherokee Female Seminary disciplined misbehaving students by denying them privileges such as playing games or going on shopping trips.

In contrast to Native American girls in government-supported schools, the Cherokee girls received a formal education and did not have to help clean the school until 1900, when the BIA pressured the administration into teaching what the bureau considered more practical skills. Each grade maintained a garden plot, and the teachers taught household management and sewing to prepare the girls for their expected future roles as housewives, but these courses were part of a broader curriculum. The Cherokees designed the seminary to train Cherokee girls to blend into white, urban society. The parents who valued traditional Cherokee culture complained that the girls were not learning anything about Cherokee history, culture, or farming, and their daughters usually spent less time at the school than the daughters of the mixed-race, less traditional parents.

Although the Cherokee girls who stayed in their seminary likely received one of the best formal educations available at the time on any reservation, most Native American girls were not so lucky. At many schools the curriculum was limited and focused on training the girls to accept menial jobs on the margins of Anglo-American society.

White Female Reformers

The U.S. government's emphasis on education as the best way to assimilate Native Americans created new opportunities for middle-class, educated, white female reformers to get involved with shaping and implementing federal Indian policies. Many of these women were genuinely horrified by the violence and poverty experienced by Native Americans in the nineteenth century, and they felt that as educated white women they had a special ability and duty to help Native American women. White reformers assumed that their own gender norms, which they considered superior to those of Native peoples, would appeal to Native American women, whom the reformers believed to be exploited and oppressed by their own people. The activists were not able to understand or appreciate the rights and high status that many Native American women enjoyed; instead, the white women expected indigenous women to welcome such values as monogamy, chastity, domesticity, and dependence. As discussed in chapter one, Native Americans valued women's work and respected women for their contributions. However, white women believed that Native American women were overworked drudges, whereas white women whose dependence on male breadwinners "saved" them from hard work enjoyed more respect from their own society.

Individual white women had been trying to change Native American women's behavior and beliefs for years. For example, in the 1860s and 1870s Annie Bidwell of the Rancho Chico in California made it her personal mission to assimilate the Native American women who lived on her land. Her husband, General John Bidwell, had encouraged a community of Maidus to settle there in the 1860s when whites attacked them to force them onto the Round Valley Reservation. After Annie and John married in 1868, she believed that she had a mission to "civilize" the local Maidus. She made little progress until she bribed the women with free cloth to come to her house and sew American-style clothing that she considered more appropriate than the Maidus' traditional garb. Getting together to sew also gave her the opportunity to teach them about Christianity. The Bidwells built a school and church on their property and required the resident Maidus to attend. They also evicted any Maidus they caught doing any off-ranch work. Owning the land the Maidus lived on gave the Bidwells a powerful lever for forcing the

Native Americans to act, at least outwardly, the way Annie wanted them to. She tried to stop them from practicing their own religion and conducting their own social activities. She focused her efforts on the women because she believed their husbands degraded and enslaved them, and because it was more respectable for her to work with women than it would have been for her to work with men. The Maidus resisted as much as they could: church and school attendance were never perfect, and when people converted to Christianity, they often did so as a result of a traditional vision. Many retained other traditional practices, including dances, and combined them with the church attendance that Annie required.

Beginning in the 1880s, the BIA started funding similar female-dominated assimilation programs, prompted in part by a new generation of vocal and educated middle-class white female reformers. A group of Baptist women in Philadelphia founded the dominant organization, the Women's National Indian Association (WNIA), in 1879. By 1887 the group had eighty-three auxiliaries in twenty-eight states and territories. The women of the WNIA believed that the so-called "Indian Problem," the difficulty of assimilating Native Americans into mainstream society, could be solved with enough female, Christian influence and education. Two of the organization's founders and key leaders, Mary Lucinda Bonney and Amelia Stone Quinton, were experienced activists. During its first three years, the WNIA concentrated on lobbying the federal government to meet its treaty obligations and to prevent further white encroachment onto Indian land. After a group of men, inspired by the WNIA, founded a parallel men's organization called the Indian Rights Association in 1882, the WNIA decided to leave much of the public lobbying to the men and focus its own efforts on women's issues. Therefore, the WNIA highlighted the plight of women in a petition it sent to the BIA in 1882 criticizing the government's treatment of Native Americans. The petition emphasized that the WNIA members had a special duty to speak out on the issue, because "the plea of Indian women for the sacred shield of law is the plea of the sisters, wives, and mothers of this nation for them, the plea of all womanhood, indeed, on their behalf to you as legislators and as men."

The organization believed that Native American gender norms had to change if indigenous people were ever going to turn into "civilized" Christians. As Mary Dissette, a reformer who worked for decades among the Pueblos of New Mexico, phrased it, Native American women, "almost hopelessly dominated by the male animal, … are trained from infancy to consider themselves as created solely for his use." Dissette and her peers believed that Native American women both needed and deserved to be elevated to the same status that white, middle-class women believed they enjoyed. Together with the Quakers and other religious denominations, the WNIA encouraged the BIA to establish the field matron program, which it did in 1891. The federal government happily gave the WNIA access to the reservations because allowing activists to do the work was a low-cost way to achieve the government's assimilation goals.

As a result of the efforts of the WNIA and its allies, the number of white women employed on reservations increased significantly across the West. For example, Mary Dissette started working with the Zuni Pueblos in 1888. During the next forty years, she worked as a teacher, a school superintendent, a field matron, and a librarian. She became friends with another reformer, Clara True, who came to New Mexico in 1902 to convert and civilize the Pueblos after spending six years as principal of the boarding school at the Lower Brulé Agency on the Sioux Reservation. In 1908 True moved to the Morongo Reservation in California before returning to New Mexico. In addition to her educational work, she owned farms and ranches. Neither Dissette nor True embodied the submissive, domestic, marital ideal that they tried to teach to Native American women, but they did not doubt that the ideal needed to be taught anyway.

Few of these female reformers were as successful as Alice Fletcher at trying to convince the American public that Native Americans had rights, even if she believed for most of her career that those rights depended on their abandoning their traditional ways. An anthropologist, a WNIA member, and an employee of Yale University's Peabody Museum of Natural History, Fletcher traveled to Nebraska in 1881 when she was forty-two to study the life of Sioux women. At first she shared the mainstream belief that Native women were overworked, oppressed drudges who needed to be saved and civilized as quickly as possible. Soon after arriving, however, she had to admit that she had not realized "the power of woman's work and how she is indeed the mother of the race." Fletcher saw that the Sioux women owned their own horses, tents, and household items and that Sioux society praised and honored women because the family's survival depended on their work. Yet this realization did not shake her conviction that Native Americans had to be forced to adopt Anglo-American gender norms and that reservation land should be assigned (or allotted) to individual Indians, rather than communities, to encourage monogamy and private property. She went on to be one of the key figures who helped shape the 1887 General Allotment Act, commonly known as the Dawes Act (discussed below), which would transform the reservation system.

In May 1883 Fletcher went to the Omaha reservation in Nebraska as a special agent for the Bureau of Indian Affairs. There she met Francis La Flesche, who acted as her interpreter and would be her key informant in her fieldwork with the Omaha for the next thirty years. He even lived with her and her partner, Jane Gay, in Washington, D.C., between 1884 and Alice's death in 1923. Fletcher's task on the reservation in 1883 was to carry out a preliminary allotment experiment, and La Flesche's father, Chief Joseph La Flesche, was the first to take his assigned land. During her stay, Fletcher allotted nearly 76,000 acres of reservation land to almost 1,200 individuals. The federal government sold an additional 50,000 acres to white settlers and held a final 55,000 acres in trust for the next generation of Omaha children.

Although Fletcher was more willing to listen to Native Americans than most whites, she still portrayed herself as the "mother" of

Native American children who depended on her to make the right decisions for them and guide them towards a better future. Recognizing that Native American women faced unique challenges, she wrote in 1899 that "in the old time" a Native American woman "was an out door worker, she cultivated the fields, she was in the free fresh air from morning until night. Now her work is within doors...[and] she is taught to regard indoor employment, to cook, to wash and iron, to sew, to scrub as the sole avocation of women." In the past "women's industries were essential to the very life of the people and their value was publicly recognized. While she suffered many hardships and labored early and late, her work was exalted ceremonially and she had a part in tribal functions." Now, "there is no possible reward for her work" and when she gets married, she "finds herself under a domination that did not exist, and from which she cannot escape." Despite such insight and sympathy, Fletcher still continued to believe that her "children" had to adopt Anglo-American gender and property norms.

Just as Alice Fletcher held contradictory views of the Native American women she wanted to help, so too did Native American women make their own complex choices about the kind of help they wanted and would accept. Native women often rejected the field matrons' instructions if they increased the workload, but they used the matrons' ideas and resources if they eased Native women's domestic responsibilities. For example, Native women in California resisted using cook stoves because they needed pine wood, which had to be fetched from the mountains, while the traditional campfire could be fueled with sage bushes ready at hand. However, Native American women recognized the value of the ready-made clothes and medical care they could get from the matrons. Native American women developed a complicated relationship with the female reformers who wanted to "save" them, just as the white women had a contradictory relationship with the very gender norms they wanted to instill. Many of these reformers never married, at the same time that they tried to teach Native American women that their best future lay in submissive feminine domesticity.

The Dawes Act

The last significant government policy that dramatically affected Native American women in the nineteenth century was the Dawes Act of 1887. The act's sponsor, Massachusetts Senator Henry L. Dawes, was inspired by the work of the WNIA and women like Fletcher. By the 1880s the government realized that the reservation system had not encouraged or helped most Native Americans to assimilate into white American society. The reservations allowed many Native Americans to continue their traditional communal and egalitarian lifestyles instead of adopting American ways that emphasized private property and male dominance. The act launched the allotment program, which divided tribal lands into privately owned lots. Each "head of household" (assumed to be the father and husband) was supposed to receive 160 acres, whereas each single adult (wives and unmarried adult men and women) was to receive 80 acres and each minor child 40 acres. These numbers varied enormously depending on local conditions, the size of the reservation and its population, and so on. Women received smaller allotments than their husbands because the architects of the Dawes Act wanted Native American women to be economically dependent on men, just as Euro-American women were. The government was supposed to hold the allotments in trust for the first twenty-five years, meaning that the Native owners could not sell it. The land left over after allotment was sold to anyone, usually local whites, who wanted to buy it.

The Dawes Act discouraged Native American women from property ownership and decision-making just as the federal government had left them out of the treaty-making process. The irony of this exclusion was not lost on some of the more sympathetic white reformers who had been trying to build trusting relationships with the tribes. Jane Gay, who worked on the Nez Perce reservation during the 1880s, mocked the meeting at which government officials described the allotment process to the Nez Perce. Gay observed that "They are all men, the women staying at home in an exemplary manner, just like civilized white women when any matter particularly affecting their interests is being discussed by the men."

One of the communities where the allotments were far smaller than the Dawes Act intended and the gender bias more pronounced was the Round Valley Reservation in Mendocino County, California. In the 1850s federal troops rounded up the Pomos and marched them to the Mendocino and Round Valley reservations, where many became ill and malnourished and some fled in search of better conditions. By the late 1870s, the Pomos had pooled their limited resources to buy land and create their own small rancherías. In the early 1890s most people still lived in villages on the rancherías, not on individual family farms. The large dwellings were communal, and women owned the homes and domestic goods. The government began allotting the land in 1894, and within days the local Indian agent moved families out of their villages and onto their allotted tracts whether or not they wanted to go. Most of the adults and children at Round Valley received ten acres each, but married women got only five acres, and their husbands usually retained legal control of their wives' and children's land. As a result, because she was married Maggie Hoxie received less land than her husband, her three-year-old son, and her three-month-old daughter, whereas unmarried women like Sallie Haines and Martha Doan each got the full ten acres. Federal officials assumed that married women could and would rely on their husbands for financial support. The government tore down the last of the village houses in the fall of 1894, and shortly thereafter it stopped distributing rations to the reservation to force the Pomo to survive on their allotted land.

Native American women resisted these efforts to reshape their lives as often as they could. In 1894, for example, a Hopi community petitioned the federal government to stop the allotment process. In the petition the Hopi defended both the traditions that helped them cultivate corn in the arid climate of northern Arizona and their matrilineal social order:

> The family, the dwelling house and the field are inseparable
> because the woman is at the heart of these, and they rest with her.

Among us the family traces its kin from the mother, hence all its possessions are hers. The man builds the house but the woman is the owner, because she repairs and preserves it; the man cultivates the field, but he renders its harvests into the woman's keeping, because up on her it rests to prepare the food, and the surplus of stores for barter depends upon her thrift.

Their petition succeeded in freeing them from the Dawes Act, but few other tribes across the West were so lucky. For many Native American women, the act was another in a long series of attacks against them and their places as respected equals in their communities.

Reshaping Gender Roles

These deliberate assaults on the traditional ways of life dramatically reshaped most Native American women's gender roles over the course of the nineteenth century. The most significant changes took place in their marriages and in their economic contributions. In these two areas, above all others, the respect and egalitarianism they had enjoyed was gradually replaced by norms that devalued them and reduced the material sources of power and influence they had in their own communities and in their dealings with outsiders.

Women's ability to marry when and whom they wished and their status within marriage both declined over the course of the nineteenth century. Not only did the number of available marriage partners decline because of decades of warfare, but white missionaries and government officials also did everything they could to impose Anglo-American patriarchal marriages on Native American women. American reformers and policy makers saw the this kind of family as the linchpin of civilization, but it was very different from the egalitarian marriages common most Native American societies (see chapter one).

In the long run, one of the most disruptive aspects of the Dawes Act was the way it determined who counted as a wife. Officials modified the land provisions of the Dawes Act many times over the years, but they never gave up trying to force Native Americans to follow white customs when it came to marriage, divorce, gender, and sexuality. For example, in 1894 when allotment began, the Pomos on the Round Valley reservation in California typically married by tribal custom, and divorce traditionally had been very easy and frequent. The BIA decreed that all couples cohabiting at the time of allotment would be considered married under state law. This ruling eventually became a major source of tension on the reservation. Agents and superintendents tried to prosecute people who changed partners without obtaining formal divorce decrees from California courts, and the Pomos resisted this effort to interfere in their customary marriage and divorce practices.

Federal officials at the Round Valley Reservation viewed legal marriage as a key marker of "civilization," and they hoped that imposing it would stop a variety of Native Californian sexual practices that the officials considered immoral. The Pomo thought of courtship as a time of sexual enjoyment, and none of the tribes banned premarital sex. Girls often married in their early to mid-teens. They usually needed their family's approval, but there were no other religious or legal requirements for marriage or divorce. When white officials tried to interfere in the most intimate aspects of Native American life, Native Americans resisted strenuously. They avoided getting marriage licenses, would not stay in their first marriage if they did not want to, and refused to engage in formal divorce proceedings.

In addition to these intrusive attempts by the federal government and white reformers to remake Native American marriage and family norms, the nineteenth century also brought new economic roles for Native American women, including some opportunities not open to Native American men. Although the new options were not great, they became a way for Native American women to earn some money to supplement family incomes. For instance, women's domestic labor had a clear place in the new cash economy, just as the government's education programs envisioned. Native American women never made much money as servants, but domestic service did create an entirely new and unexpected opportunity for them to reclaim their older roles as cultural mediators. In California many Pomo women wound up supporting their families by working as domestics and gained social power in their communities because they were more familiar with Anglo-American households, goods, and habits than were Pomo men.

Just as Native American tribes had distinct economies based on local resources, regional differences also shaped the ways in which Native and Anglo-American economies interacted. For example, Southern Paiute women in the Great Basin, who suddenly had to share their limited resource base with whites in the 1840s, started working as domestics for Mormons or miners when these outsiders prevented the Paiutes from accessing their traditional food sources. Mormon men hired Paiute women to help their wives with laundry, and within a few years the women also got seasonal jobs, such as washing wool. The newcomers sometimes recognized Native American women's expertise in gathering plants, and Mormons occasionally hired them to harvest root crops with their own traditional digging sticks. In mining towns in Nevada, Paiute women began working for wages as early as the 1870s, primarily doing laundry and housecleaning. Paiute women also continued some traditional gathering and made baskets for their own use, and later some started selling the baskets to whites.

The Pomos of California also had to find work in the new cash economy when they lost their traditional land base to Anglo-Americans. Beginning in the late 1860s, Pomo women became hop pickers and servants in Anglo homes. They continued a few of their traditional activities, however; as late as 1900 the Pomos still ate their traditional diet of clover, bulbs, seeds, nuts, and acorns, all items that Pomo women had harvested for centuries. But by the 1920s the Pomo became almost entirely dependent on wage labor and purchased American foods.

For women of the northern Great Plains, the growing importance of the trade in buffalo hides in the nineteenth century increased the value of their economic contributions at the same time that it decreased their social and political status. The hide trade expanded significantly the amount of time that women spent tanning hides. Now that they hunted on horseback, men could provide the raw materials more quickly, but it still took a woman three to ten days to tan one hide, depending on how much other work she had to do. As noted in chapter two, the rise in demand for tanners resulted in more polygyny. Great Plains tribes began to calculate wealth almost exclusively in terms of the number of horses a person owned, so only successful raiders with a lot of horses could get and keep multiple wives. But even polygyny did not solve the labor shortage, so northern Great Plains hunters began to capture women from other tribes more often, and tribes began to punish women who committed adultery more harshly.

As these examples demonstrate, even gradual economic shifts often created significant changes in social norms. On the Great Plains women worked harder, got less recognition for their labor, and had less to trade. Men were increasingly free to pursue more wealth and other trading opportunities, whereas women's activities were increasingly limited to hide processing. Women who had to spend most of their time tanning their husbands' buffalo hides had less time to produce status-increasing goods for their own trade, and women's horses tended to be the less-valuable pack animals.

Before European contact, Native American women's economic contributions and family roles had garnered them respect in their communities. But over the course of the nineteenth century, the U.S. government and white reformers did their best to change those respected roles, to the lasting detriment of Native American women.

Resistance

While most Native American women resisted these intrusions into their lives in private, local ways, a few raised their voices loud enough for the nation to hear. By the end of the nineteenth century, an unintended and ironic result of the government's education programs emerged: a generation of Native American women who knew how to talk back to white Americans on their own terms. For example, the U.S. government employed Paiute activist Sarah Winnemuca (discussed in chapter two) as an interpreter, but she also devoted years of her life to trying to draw the nation's attention to the outrages being committed against her people in the Great Basin through public lectures.

In 1883 Winnemucca published *Life Among the Piutes: Their Wrongs and Claims,* describing her people's expulsion from their homes. At the time of their removal, she was working as an interpreter for the U.S. Army. When an officer told her about the government's plan, she replied, "My people have not done anything, and why should they be sent away from their own country?" She tried to imagine the sort of leader who would order such a thing:

> I have never seen a president in my life and I wanted to know whether he is made of wood or rock, for I cannot for once think that he can be a human being. No human being would do such a thing as that,—send people across a fearful mountain in midwinter.... Every night I imagined I could see the thing called President. He had long ears, he had big eyes and long legs, and a head like a bull-frog or something like that. I could not think of anything that could be so inhuman as to do such a thing,—send people across mountains with snow so deep.

She added,

> Yes, you, who call yourselves the great civilization; you who have knelt upon Plymouth Rock, covenanting with God to make this land the home of the free and the brave. Ah, then you rise from your bended knees and seizing the welcoming hands of those who are the owners of this land, which you are not.... Your so-called civilization sweeps inland from the ocean wave; but, oh, my God! Leaving its pathway marked by crimson lines of blood, and strewed by the bones of two races, the inheritor and the invader; and I am crying out to you for justice.

Winnemucca died in 1891 of tuberculosis, but her writing continued to call attention to the suffering of Paiutes and other Native Americans.

Similarly, although the white women who funded her education saw Omaha Susan La Flesche Picotte as completely "civilized," she used the status and skills she gained at school to criticize the BIA and white women activists. The daughter of the prominent Omaha chief Joseph La Flesche, she grew up in a frame house on an individual plot of land and attended Protestant missionary schools on the reservation until her parents sent her to a girls' boarding school in New Jersey when she was thirteen. She later enrolled at the Hampton Institute, an industrial school for blacks that was then in the midst of an experiment offering Native Americans an education. After she graduated from Hampton in 1889, the Connecticut Indian Association paid for her to attend the Women's Medical College in Philadelphia. She became the first Native American woman physician in the United States and was appointed as the government school physician on her reservation in Nebraska, the sort of position not usually given to a Native American or a woman of any race. For most of her adult life, La Flesche agreed with the white women's approach to changing Native American lives. But when her husband Henry Picotte died in 1905, the government initially gave control of his estate (and her sons' inheritance) to a male relative. She only won control after sending the BIA testimonials about her character from white friends. Her disillusionment grew when the WNIA promised to help her build a hospital on the reservation but abandoned the project in the 1890s. In 1909, when the federal government announced a new set of paternalistic policies for the Omaha without consulting them, La Flesche finally fought back against the government. She wanted Native Americans to have the right to control their own land, and that demand for autonomy extended into other areas. By 1910 she focused more on Native American forms of medical care and less on white medicine. She finally got her reservation hospital in 1913, just two years before her death, having raised the money herself by playing different missionary groups against each other.

Another vocal opponent of the government's policies was Zitkala-Sa (Red Bird), or Gertrude Simmons Bonnin, a Nakota (Yankton) Sioux who had been separated from her mother to attend a series of boarding schools. Between 1900 and 1902 she wrote articles for *The Atlantic Monthly* and *Harper's Magazine* criticizing the government's Indian schools. In 1901 she published *Old Indian Legends,* to preserve Nakota oral traditions. She later edited the *American Indian Magazine,* founded the Council of American Indians in 1926, and became a key leader in the early Native American rights movement of the 1920s, an effort that would lead to significant government policy changes in the 1930s.

Women like Winnemuca, La Flesche, and Bonnin found a few genuine allies among white women. The best-known supporter of Native American rights in the nineteenth century was Helen Hunt Jackson, who published *A Century of Dishonor* in 1881. Already a well-known speaker and writer about the government's poor treatment of Native Americans, she used the book to describe in detail several case studies revealing the government's dishonesty in its dealings with Native peoples. She publicly denounced Secretary of the Interior Carl Schurz (who was responsible for the BIA) and wrote letters about the desecrations committed against Native Americans during massacres, such as the one in Sand Creek, Colorado, in 1864. Similarly, novelist Constance Goddard DuBois wrote a scathing critique of a proposed compulsory education law in 1900, noting that white children would never be forcibly removed from their parents and kept against their will at school. These critics successfully drew some attention to the problems faced by Native Americans, occasionally stopped bigger problems from happening, and inspired many white reformers who genuinely wanted to help solve the problems. However, none of the critics of the government's policies and procedures were able to reverse the general downward trend in Native American women's lives over the course of the century.

Native American women faced an unprecedented range of personal and cultural assaults in the nineteenth century. Anglo-Americans attacked every aspect of their lives, from their most personal choices about sex and marriage to their economic and parenting roles. Some of those attacks came from racists who simply wanted the Native Americans out of the way, whereas others came from well-meaning reformers, officials, and missionaries who believed that Native Americans needed their help to survive in modern America. Sometimes Native American women found ways to resist and other times they did not, but there is no doubt that they helped their peoples and cultures to survive in spite of the enormous challenges and constraints they faced.

Suggested Readings

Abbott, Devon. "'Commendable Progress': Acculturation at the Cherokee Female Seminary." *American Indian Quarterly* 11, no. 3 (Summer 1987): 187–201.

Albers, Patricia, and Beatrice Medicine, eds. *The Hidden Half: Studies of Plains Indian Women.* Washington, D.C.: University Press of America, 1983.

Anderson, Karen. *Changing Woman: A History of Racial-Ethnic Women in Modern America.* New York: Oxford University Press, 1996.

Higham, C. L. *Noble, Wretched, and Redeemable: Protestant Missionaries to the Indians in Canada and the United States, 1820–1900.* Albuquerque: University of New Mexico Press; Calgary, AB: University of Calgary Press, 2000.

Jacobs, Margaret D. "Resistance to the Rescue: The Indians of Bahapki and Mrs. Annie E. K. Bidwell." In *Writing the Range: Race, Class, and Culture in the Women's West,* edited by Elizabeth Jameson and Susan Armitage, pp. 230–251. Norman: University of Oklahoma Press, 1997.

———. *Engendered Encounters: Feminism and Pueblo Cultures, 1879–1934.* Lincoln: University of Nebraska Press, 1999.

Jacox, Elizabeth. "'Cook, Photographer, and Friend': Jane Gay's Photographs, 1889–1892." *Idaho Yesterdays* 28 (Spring 1984): 18–23.

Klein, Alan M. "The Political-Economy of Gender: A Nineteenth-Century Plains Indian Case Study." In *The Hidden Half: Studies of Plains Indian Women,* edited by Patricia Albers and Beatrice Medicine, pp. 143–174. Washington, D.C.: University Press of America, 1983.

Lorini, Alessandra. "Alice Fletcher and the Search for Women's Public Recognition in Professionalizing American Anthropology." *Cromohs* 8 (2003): 1–25.

Mark, Joan. *A Stranger in Her Native Land: Alice Fletcher and the American Indians.* Lincoln: University of Nebraska Press, 1988.

Mathes, Valerie Sherer. "Nineteenth-Century Women and Reform: The Women's National Indian Association," *American Indian Quarterly* 14, no. 1 (Winter 1990): 1–18.

Mihesuah, Devon Abbott. *Indigenous American Women: Decolonization, Empowerment, Activism.* Lincoln and London: University of Nebraska Press, 2003.

Monnett, John H. "'My heart now has become changed to softer feelings': A Northern Cheyenne Woman and Her Family Remember the Long Journey Home." *Montana: The Magazine of Western History* 59, no. 2 (Summer 2009): 45–61.

Peters, Virginia Bergman. *Women of the Earth Lodges: Tribal Life on the Plains.* North Haven, CT: Archon Books, 1995.

Purdue, Theda. "Cherokee Women and the Trail of Tears." *Journal of Women's History* 1, no. 1 (Spring 1989): 14–30.

Tong, Benson. *Susan La Flesche Picotte M.D.: Omaha Indian Leader and Reformer.* Norman: University of Oklahoma Press, 1999.

Trennert, Robert A. "Educating Indian Girls at Nonreservation Boarding Schools, 1878–1920." *Western Historical Quarterly* 13 (July 1982): 271–290.

Wall, Wendy. "Gender and the 'Citizen Indian.'" In *Writing the Range: Race, Class, and Culture in the Women's West,* edited by Elizabeth Jameson and Susan Armitage, pp. 202–229. Norman: University of Oklahoma Press, 1997.

CHAPTER FIVE

The Overland Trails

Non-Native American women began to move west in large numbers in the mid-nineteenth century. Some made the decision themselves, hoping to escape old constraints and find new opportunities; others had no choice but to go along with their husbands once the men had made the decision. The overland trails opened less than a decade after the Trail of Tears in the 1830s and well before the first transcontinental railroad was completed in 1869. The trails brought the first massive wave of non-Natives west, and they changed the lives of all western women forever. More than 300,000 people migrated to the far West on the overland trails before the Civil War (1861–65), and the migration continued on an even more massive scale after the war was over, especially after the construction of the transcontinental railroad system. Except for the flood of male miners during and after the Gold Rush of 1849, most of the newcomers migrated in family groups, so women made up a significant minority of the total number of migrants.

Traveling the overland trail was incredibly difficult. Journeying on foot, in wagons, or on horseback, most groups took four to six months to make the dangerous 2,000-mile trip from starting points along the Missouri River to their final destinations in Oregon, Utah, or California. The trip entailed weeks on the open plains, crossing multiple rivers and traversing cliffs, and the migrants had to carry

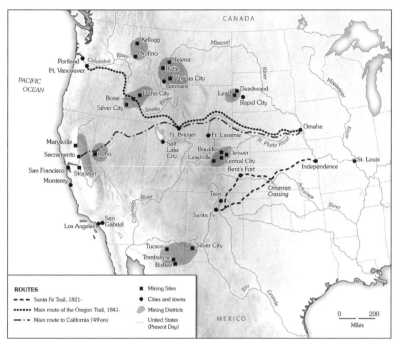

The main overland trails and mining areas.

all of their supplies with them. The newcomers had little regard for Native American communities whose lands they passed through or the resources those communities needed to survive. For the newcomer women who followed their hearts, souls, and families westward, the trails were a mix of great opportunities and great losses.

There were two main reasons why so many women headed west: religion and economics. The first white women in the Pacific Northwest were Protestant missionaries who went there in the 1830s to convert coastal and Columbia Plateau Native Americans to Christianity. These women traveled too early to be considered part of the overland trails migration, but their activities helped pave the way for the hundreds of thousands of migrants who came later. Protestant missionary groups valued married white women as missionaries because they were supposed to model appropriate female behavior as well as Christian piety to Native Americans. In the 1840s women of the Church of Jesus Christ of Latter-Day Saints (commonly known as the Mormons), both American-born and European converts, headed to the Great Basin to escape religious persecution in the Midwest and start building a new holy land. Women who migrated for economic reasons can also be divided into two groups. The single biggest group of migrants was farm families from the Midwest who left their homes because it was getting hard to make a good living east of the Mississippi River. Gold rush migrants followed dreams of instant wealth to California and subsequent mining strikes.

Religious Migrants

In 1836 two white women missionaries, Narcissa Whitman and Eliza Spalding, and their husbands, Marcus Whitman and Henry Spalding, migrated to Oregon Territory, which would later be divided into the states of Washington, Oregon, and Idaho. The couples did not get along and had very different approaches to converting and assimilating Native Americans, so they set up their missions a hundred miles apart.

The Whitmans settled among the Cayuse people near present-day Walla Walla, Washington, and the Spaldings settled among the Nez Perce near present-day Lewiston in Idaho. The Whitmans baptized very few Cayuses during their ten years in the Pacific Northwest because they were not particularly interested in or sympathetic to the Cayuse people or their culture. The missionaries did not make a real effort to learn the Cayuse language or understand the tribe's worldviews, and they wanted the Cayuse to have as much contact with whites as possible to assimilate them more quickly.

The Spaldings, on the other hand, tried to keep the Nez Perce isolated from whites to give them time to adapt. Eliza was a gifted teacher who eventually attracted some two hundred students to the mission school. She was the only one of the four missionaries to appreciate the Native cultures that they encountered. She eventually earned the respect and affection of the Nez Perce.

The Whitmans' inability to convert the Cayuses led them to shift their focus to the growing number of white settlers moving into the area. Marcus even went east to help promote Oregon Territory as a promised land for white settlement. More than 15,000 white migrants headed to the Pacific Northwest in the 1840s, and the newcomers brought more disease and disruption for the local Native Americans. After an epidemic nearly decimated the Cayuses in 1847, they retaliated against the encroaching whites. They killed Marcus, Narcissa, and eleven others in November 1847, after which the Spaldings fled to Oregon City, in what is now the northwest corner of the state of Oregon.

Whereas Narcissa Whitman and Eliza Spalding moved to the Northwest in the 1830s to convert Native Americans to Christianity, the Latter-Day Saints started moving to the Great Basin in present-day Utah in the late 1840s to try to escape the influence, harassment, and occasionally deadly violence of non-Mormon Americans. Driven out of all of their previous homes because of their belief in polygyny, these migrants sought a new home far away from other Americans. The harsh climate of the Great Basin also offered them the chance to test their skills and create a new promised land in the desert. By 1880 about 100,000 American and European Mormons lived in more than three hundred fifty communities scattered across the inland desert.

Swiss-born convert Mary Ann Stucki was six years old when her family made the trip to Utah by handcart in 1860. The Mormons who migrated in handcarts were an unusual minority. Most headed west in carts and wagons pulled by oxen, like everyone else on the overland trail. To reduce the costs of the huge migration, in 1856 the Mormon leadership told those making the journey to put their belongings in handcarts and push them westward themselves. The church abandoned the handcart experiment after more than two hundred people in a handcart party died when it did not make it to the Mormon settlements before winter set in. Stucki wrote, "Our company was the tenth and last to cross the Plain in handcarts. It contained 126 persons with twenty-two handcarts, and three provision wagons drawn by oxen." Her family began its 1,000-mile trip in July 1860. Her parents pulled the cart, she and her older brother walked, and her two younger siblings rode in the cart. Her mother's feet became so swollen from walking that she had to ride in the cart for about three weeks to let her feet heal. Mary Ann recalled that her mother "would get so discouraged and down-hearted," but her "father never lost courage. He would always cheer her up by telling her that we were going to Zion, that the Lord would take care of us, and that better times were coming."

White Mormon women were not the only ones to follow their souls westward. One of the first African American converts to Mormonism was Jane Elizabeth Manning James. Born in Connecticut in 1813, she converted in 1842 after hearing a traveling Mormon missionary. She started working for the church's founder, Joseph Smith, in 1843 in Nauvoo, Illinois, and then for the Latter-day Saints' new leader, Brigham Young, after Smith was murdered in 1844. She married one of the few other African American Mormons, Isaac James, and in 1847 they and their two young sons began the trip to Utah. They made it to Salt Lake City only two months after Brigham Young's own party had arrived, and they were the first free blacks to settle in Utah. A year later, more than forty black slaves lived in the territory, most brought by Southern converts, and only a handful of free blacks. The church would not treat African Americans as full and equal members until the mid-twentieth century, and Jane spent the last years of her life struggling to get the same rights as white Mormons had. She died in 1908.

The communal nature of the Mormon migration and early settlement meant that Mormon women could count on far more community support than other women who took the trails westward. British widow and Mormon convert Jean Rio Baker came to Utah in 1851 with her seven children. As they neared the end of their journey, they "were met by several men with teams, ready to assist those who needed help....[T]he descent of the mountain was awfully steep and dangerous, for about four miles." Her daughter and another young woman had given birth on the trail, and they remained in the wagons as the men helped them descend. Baker carried her new grandson in her arms. Three days later, they arrived in Salt Lake City. On September 29, Baker wrote in her diary that after arriving in the city, she had made her way "to Mrs. Wallace's house, having a letter of introduction to her from her husband, whom I left in England fulfilling his mission. She received me most kindly and desired me to have my wagons brought inside her inclosure, at the same time offering me, any convenience her house afforded."

Women who moved west for religious reasons were in the minority, but they helped pave the way for the hundreds of thousands of migrants who followed over the next few decades. Many of the religious migrants thought that they would find a promised land in the West because it was so far away from the rest of American society, but that society caught up with them in record time.

Economic Migrants

Most women traveled the overland trails for economic reasons: they (or their husbands) believed that moving west would free them from the economic constraints of their current lives and give them new opportunities that would lead to better lives for themselves and their families. Most of these migrants were farm families from the Midwest who wanted to start farming again, while a minority headed to the mining districts of the Rocky Mountains and west coast. Most of the women who made the trip were between the ages of sixteen and thirty-five. Some migrants were newlyweds looking for a better place to start their married lives. At least one-fifth of the women were pregnant and many had young children, for whom they were hoping to find better opportunities. Another group of women had adult children who were ready to leave home to find better prospects, and their parents wanted to keep the family together.

Most women did not make the decision to move west; instead, their husbands or fathers made the decision. Many women did not want to leave their homes for a long, risky journey. Lucy Henderson

Deady, whose family moved to Oregon in 1846, recalled that her mother knew "nothing of this move until father had decided to go." Margaret Hereford Wilson told her mother in 1850 that her husband had decided "to go to California. I am going with him, as there is no other alternative." Mary A. Jones' husband also made the decision unilaterally, after a neighbor loaned him a copy of a common travel guide of the day. Jones begged him, "O let us not go…but it made no difference." Eighteen-year-old Illinois newlywed Miriam Thompson was one of the exceptions; she was eager to make the trip. In 1845, just a few months after their wedding, she and her husband headed to Oregon, and she wrote that she "was possessed with a spirit of adventure and a desire to see what was new and strange."

In 1849 Louisiana Strentzel accompanied her husband, a Texas physician, to Southern California, with their young children. Instead of sailing around South America (the canal through Panama would not open until 1914), the couple took what they hoped would be a shorter and easier route across the deserts of the Southwest. Instead, the heat and lack of water made the trip very dangerous. When the Strentzels finally arrived in San Diego in December 1849, Louisiana warned others not to take the overland route, writing that they traveled

> through a wilderness of eighteen hundred miles; underwent many hardships and privations; passed through many dangers and difficulties; crossed garden and desert; landed safely in California and are enjoying very best health at present…. I know not what to say to you about coming, but…. I cannot advise any family to come the overland route, but if they should let them prepare well for the journey and travel in small consolidated companies, say about ten wagons and twenty or twenty-five men, to each family I would say one light strong carriage for women and children to ride in (with two mules) and a woman can drive it anywhere; one strong wagon with six mules.

Only families with better than average resources could have followed Louisiana's advice. Few of the overland migrants could afford a separate carriage just for women and children. Another part of her advice was more practical: the family had brought a cow with them, and Louisiana wrote, "She has been worth thousands of dollars to us, yes, I may say millions, for she has been the means of preserving the lives of our children." Instead of having to drink water from suspect sources along the trail, her children had been able to drink milk and thus avoided many of the waterborne ailments that migrants often suffered. The myth that the West promised an easy new life was already firmly entrenched in American minds, but the hard realities of life on the trail and a new start on the other end meant that the people with the most resources were most likely to survive and prosper.

The Raymond family of Missouri was unusual compared to most migrant families because it consisted of a widowed mother and her four children. Delilah Raymond's husband had died in the 1840s, and she raised her three sons and one daughter on her own. Her daughter, Sarah, became a teacher. As the Civil War drew to a close, the family decided to head west to better its fortunes. Delilah was fifty-two and Sarah twenty-four when the family left Missouri in May 1865 in two covered wagons. At first they traveled with another family from their home town, the Kerfoots, and both families later joined a bigger group. Sarah and her friend Cash Kerfoot had their own horses and preferred to ride alongside the wagons. The two families parted in present-day southwestern Wyoming, as the Kerfoots headed to California and the Raymonds to the mining town of Virginia City, Montana.

Both Sarah and her mother eagerly embraced the idea of a new life in a new land. When one of Sarah's brothers suggested that she and her mother head for California while the men went to Montana, her mother responded, "Well, if he is going to Montana, we are going too. How many women are on their way there in these [wagon] trains? I reckon it will not be any worse for us that it will be for them." Sarah and her mother believed that women were just as capable as men of handling the rigors of the journey, and the younger woman also thought that the trip had real benefits for women. On August 20, 1865, Sarah wrote in her diary about an old lady ninety-three years old in a train camping near us to-night. She is cheerful as a lark, sings sometimes, and is an incessant talker. She says she is going to Oregon, where she expects to renew her youth. She looks very old and wrinkled in the face, but is very active in her movements, and not at all stooped. The people she is with are not at all refined or cultured, but I do like to talk to the old lady, she is so quaint.

Sarah's own mother seemed happier and healthier than she had been since the Civil War began. When Delilah turned fifty-three at the end of August, Sarah wrote, "We have been now four months on this journey. Have lived out of doors, in all sorts of weather. It has been very beneficial to mother. She was looking frail and delicate when we started, but seems to be in perfect health now, and looks at least ten years younger."

Sarah and Delilah had plenty of female traveling companions. In June they joined a bigger wagon train and met the Walker family: "Joe has his wife with him. Milt is a bachelor; their sister, Miss Lyde, and a younger brother, De, are with them. They are going to Montana." A few weeks later, Sarah admitted that the trip was harder for the women who had to ride in the uncomfortable and crowded wagons, not on horseback as she did. She wrote, "I would not enjoy taking this trip without a saddle-horse or pony [to ride]. I must be more generous hereafter and let Lyde and Mrs. Kennedy and other ladies that have no horse ride [my horse] Dick oftener than I have been doing. I have not fully realized how very tiresome it is to ride in the wagon all day, and day after day." Sadly, she later had to sell her horse for $125 in gold dust when the family started to run out cash at the end of August.

Sarah criticized women who complained about the trail and the often disappointing results at the end of it. For example, in the first week of September her party camped near a large group of people who were leaving Virginia City and heading back east. Sarah noted that the returning group stressed "the disadvantages and disagreeable things with regard to life in Montana," but she was not discouraged because she recognized that they were homesick. "Everyone knows," she wrote, "that when that disease is fairly developed, everything is colored with a deep dark blue, and even pleasant things seem extremely disagreeable to the afflicted person. The ladies seem to have the disease in its worst form, and of course they make the gentlemen do as they wish, which is to take them home to mother and other dear ones."

The Raymonds reached Virginia City in September 1865 and rented a two-room log cabin for eight dollars a month. By the spring of 1866, twenty-five-year-old Sarah was the lone teacher working at the only school in town. She taught for only one term before quitting to marry thirty-four-year-old James Herndon, another Missourian, who had been in Virginia City for two years. After their marriage in the spring of 1867, they opened the first Protestant Sunday school in the state. They ran the school for nearly forty years and had five children.

The vast majority of migrants on the overland trail headed west in search of better economic opportunities, and in doing so they helped cement a key facet of the myth of the West: the deeply held belief that somehow, just by moving there, life would get better. In reality, migrants' new lives on the other end of the trail were often more difficult than they expected, but the West was fundamentally transformed by their presence and their hopes.

Other Reasons for Heading West

As Sarah Raymond's diary indicates, some women hoped for more than religious and economic opportunities in the West. Some hoped that the huge disparity between the number of white men and white women during the early decades of western settlement would make it easier to find a husband. On July 27, 1865, Sarah wrote that they had met

> a family of four young ladies and their father—a widower—named Ryan.... Mr. Ryan told some of the young men that he was taking his daughters to the west, where there are more men and fewer

women, so they could have a better chance to get good husbands than in Missouri. It has been a good joke among the boys, and some of them have tried to be very gallant to the young ladies—as they are on the market.

A month later, after encountering a family heading back to Missouri after giving up on Montana, Sarah complained that the woman assumed that she was "going to Montana husband-hunting, and volunteered a deal of advice on the subject, especially I must not tell that I am from Missouri, as Missourians are below par in Montana. She is from New York. Oh, dear, it makes one tired to see a full-grown woman so frivolous." Although Sarah married within two years of arriving in Montana, perhaps it was no coincidence that her husband was also from Missouri.

For black women, the West represented a chance at an even more basic opportunity: the chance to be free. In 1860 the roughly 1,500 African American women who lived in California represented the majority of all free black women in the West, and they had worked hard to get there. In August 1850 while traveling from Indiana to California with her husband, Margaret Frink wrote, "Among the crowds on foot, a negro woman came tramping along through the heat and dust, carrying a cast-iron bake oven on her head, with her provisions and blanket piled on top—all she possessed in the world—bravely pushing on for California." The fact that the woman was black and apparently traveling alone must have surprised many of the white women who watched her go by.

Not every black woman made the trip as a free woman, however. Biddy Mason traveled west as the property of Robert Smith and his family, Mississippi slave owners who had converted to Mormonism in the 1840s. In 1848 the family and their slaves joined an expedition headed for Utah. Not only did Mason have to care for the Smith's children as well as her own during the trip, but also she had to perform her usual domestic chores, guard the family's cattle, and take on any new task the Smiths gave her. She had some experience as a midwife and helped deliver more than one baby along the way.

The Smiths and their slaves stayed in Salt Lake City for about three years but then moved on to San Bernardino, California, to found a new settlement as a rest stop for Mormons travelling to Utah by sailing around South America.

Other black women migrants were members of families who used western laws to gain their freedom. Mary Jane Holmes was born in 1841 in Missouri, to a family of slaves owned by Nathaniel Ford. In 1844 Ford moved to Oregon Territory and took the Holmes family with him, promising to free them once they had helped him establish his farm. After arriving in December 1844, Ford gave the Holmes family some space to grow its own vegetables, and the family worked hard to get Ford's farm going. The Territory's provisional government outlawed slavery in 1844, and in 1849 Mary Jane's father Robin asked Ford for their freedom. Ford said that Robin and his sons had to accompany Ford to the California gold fields first. When Robin came back in the spring of 1850 with $900 in gold, Ford freed him, his wife Polly, and their youngest son, but kept their other four children, including nine-year-old Mary Jane. Robin and Polly started saving money to buy the children. In 1852 they took Ford to court because one of the girls had died and Ford still would not release the other three (eleven-year-old Mary Jane, seven-year-old James, and five-year-old Roxanne). In early 1853 a judge ruled that Ford could keep Roxanne, James would go to his parents, and Mary Jane (now twelve) could choose where to live. She did not want to leave Roxanne alone with Ford, so she stayed with him, too.

A few months later a different judge finally ruled that since slavery was illegal in Oregon Territory, all of the Holmes children were to be awarded to their parents and Ford was to pay the court costs. Roxanne and James went home to their parents, but Mary Jane stayed with Ford for reasons that remain unclear. She was still living at Ford's house when she was sixteen and met her husband, fifty-year-old Reuben Shipley. When Reuben asked Ford for permission to marry her, Ford demanded $750 for her release. This demand was illegal, and the couple probably would have won if they had taken him to court, but neither wanted another long court battle, so Shipley paid the money. After they married, they moved to an 80-acre farm near Corvallis, Oregon, and had six children before Reuben died in 1873. Mary Jane was only thirty-two when he died, and she remarried two years later. When her second husband, R. G. Drake, died in 1880, she left her farm and moved to Salem with her two youngest children. In 1889 she went to Portland to live with her only remaining son. She died in 1925.

As Mary Jane Holmes's case illustrates, moving west did not automatically confer freedom on enslaved women. The West's patch-work of laws and local practices meant that slavery left a complex legacy of constraints and opportunities in the region.

Common Experiences

In spite of the many reasons women had for heading west, they faced many common challenges. Births and deaths were common because there were hundreds of people in each wagon train, most of the migrants were families in their childbearing years, and the trip was long and dangerous. Another common feature of women's lives on the overland trail was that they still had to fulfill many of their usual responsibilities. Their families had to be fed and clothed, for example, even when housecleaning was not necessary. Many of these chores required new techniques, such as learning to cook using dried buffalo dung rather than wood. And many women, some for the first time, encountered other women whose lives were very different from theirs.

Women often had to give birth with no one to help except their husbands. In March 1837, less than a year after arriving in the Oregon Territory, missionary Narcissa Whitman gave birth to a daughter. Unlike most migrant women, she had a great deal of help from her physician husband and a local métis woman named Katie Pambrun. Narcissa wrote to her family that "Mrs. P" and her husband "dressed the babe. It would have made you smile to see them work over the little creature. Mrs. P. never saw one dressed before as we dress them, having been accustomed to dress her own in the native style. I was able to lend a helping hand and arrange the clothes for them, etc. Between us all, it was done very well." Later in the letter, she erased the value of Mrs. Pambrun's help by complaining that she had "no mother, no sister, to relieve me of a single care—only an affectionate husband, who, as a physician and nurse, exceeds all I ever knew. He was excessively pressed with care and labor during the whole time of my confinement. I received all the attention I required of him. He had my washing and the cooking to do for the family."

Two months later, Narcissa revealed that Mrs. Pambrun had stayed with her for the first two weeks after her daughter's birth, and then the midwife's twelve-year-old daughter stayed to help the Whitmans and to learn how to read and write. Knowing that the arrangement was not permanent and considering the girl's help insufficient, Narcissa had her husband contact a man he knew in Vancouver and ask him to send them "an orphan girl" to be their domestic servant. Narcissa wrote to her family that their Vancou-ver contact sent a girl "by express. She arrived the first of April. Is entirely unacquainted with every kind of work, neither can she speak the English language. Said to be sixteen, but she is not larger than a girl of twelve years. You have no idea how difficult it is to realize any benefit from those who do not understand you. During the winter, husband had two men only to assist him." Later in the letter she complained, "To be a mother in heathen lands, among savages, gives feeling that can be known only to those who are such." In spite of living with her husband in the midst of a Cay-use community, Narcissa considered her infant daughter "pleasant company for me, here alone." Sadly for the Whitmans, the little girl drowned when she was two.

Women who lived near missions and army posts had better chances of getting help during delivery than women on the overland trails. Mary Richardson Walker had her baby at the Whitmans' mis-sion in December 1838. Ellen McGowan Biddle survived a difficult childbirth because of the help of an army doctor at Camp Halleck in Nevada, but the baby died.

Mormon women on the trail and in their first settlements often had the assistance of a midwife selected and paid by church authorities. Some of the midwives were largely self-taught, whereas others had formal medical training. For example, Mormon midwife Janet Downie Hardie had studied obstetrics in Edinburgh. Midwives provided a wide range of prenatal and postnatal care for women, in addition to sometimes providing other health-care services for their neighbors. After a baby was delivered, the midwife might stay for up to ten days helping the new mother and infant. Yet even the Mormons faced a health-care crisis in the 1860s, because their high birthrate far outpaced the availability of midwives.

Death was another frequent companion for women on the trail. All members of the wagon trains were at risk from accidents and disease, which caused the vast majority of migrant deaths, and maternal and infant mortality rates were high. After arriving in Oregon in 1845, for example, Anna Maria King wrote to her family listing the people she knew who had died along the way: "But listen to the deaths: Sally Chambers, John King and his wife, their little daughter Electa and their babe, a son 9 months old, and Dulancy C. Norton's sister are gone." Abigail Malick watched her teenaged son Hiram drown while he was swimming in the Platte River in the summer of 1848, as the Malick family journeyed from Illinois to Oregon Territory. Writing to her daughter two years later, Malick said that her son's death "has Almost kild Me but I have to bear it. And if we Are good perhapes then we can meete him in heven." On August 20, 1865, Sarah Raymond wrote in her diary that her party had "passed a grave this morning that was made yesterday for a young mother and her newborn babe. Oh, how sad. With what an aching heart must that husband and father go on his weary way, leaving his loved ones by the roadside."

One unfortunate family experienced a birth and a death only a few days apart. Lucy Henderson Deady was eleven years old in 1846 when her family made the trip to Oregon. She wrote, "Three days after my little sister Lettie drank the laudanum [a strong opium-based medicine that was used for many ailments in the nineteenth century] and died we stopped for a few hours, and my sister Olivia was born. We were so late that the men of the party decided we could not tarry a day, so we had to press on. The going was terribly rough....The men walked beside the wagons and tried to ease the wheels down into the rough places, but in spite of this it was a very rough ride for my mother and her new born babe." Deaths usually entailed lengthy mourning periods in mid-nineteenth-century America, but the practical demands of the overland trail made familiar cultural rituals like these impossible.

One of the most striking tragedies that occurred on the overland trails was the fate of the Donner-Reed party. Two families named Donner and one named Reed, totaling more than eighty people, were traveling from Illinois to California in the fall of 1846 when they got caught in the snow in the Sierra Nevada Mountains. Half of the party members died before they were rescued, and many others only survived by eating the bodies of the people who had died. Thirteen-year-old survivor Virginia Reed wrote a letter in May 1847 to tell her cousin Mary in Illinois about "our trubles getting to California." The party got stuck in November, and the last of the survivors were not rescued until March. At one point her family had to kill and eat their pet dog to survive. Near the end of her letter, she wrote, "O Mary I have not wrote you half of the truble we have had but I hav Wrote you anuf to let you now that you dont now what trubel is but thank the Good god we have all got throw and the onely family that did not eat human flesh we have left every thing but i dont cair for that." Oddly enough, young Virginia did not want to discourage any other would-be western travelers, but she did stress "never take no cutofs [i.e., short cuts] and hury along as fast as you can."

Births, deaths, and other challenges did not change the fact that the migrants had to be fed and clothed, and women's traditional gender roles changed little on the trail. Women were still responsible for the cooking, sewing, and childcare, and their work did not stop when the sun went down. Some chores, like cooking and washing clothes, were more difficult because of the lack of clean water and firewood. Many emigrant families started their journey with a cook stove, only to have to abandon it along the way to reduce the weight. The lack of a stove did not stop a few women from producing remarkable meals, however. In 1853, eight-year-old Henrietta Catherine McDaniel Furniss' mother managed to produce "a big plate of cookies made in the shape of animals—the surprise and delight of the dinner," which was celebrating Henrietta's father's thirty-first birthday. Three years later, Mary Powers managed to create strawberry dumplings by stewing up the last of her dried strawberries. Many women regretted bringing white sheets and pillowcases because they were impossible to keep clean, and they advised future emigrants to bring dark calico. Others brought things like bedsteads and chinaware for their new homes in the West, only to have to burn or abandon them along the way.

Some of women's traditional chores disappeared completely along the trail: there were no floors to scrub, for example, and the rocking of the wagon churned butter all by itself. At the start of the journey, novelty made the work easier. Shortly after setting out, Sarah Raymond wrote in her diary on May 4, 1865,

> Mother prepares breakfast, while I roll up the beds and cover closely to protect them from the dust; one of the boys milks the cows, while I assist mother, and when breakfast…is over, I strain the milk into an old-fashioned churn that is big at the bottom and little at the top, cover closely and fix it in the front of the freight wagon, where it will be churned by the motion of the wagon, and we have a pat of the sweetest, most delicious butter when we stop in the evening that anyone ever tasted. Mother washes the dishes, we prepare lunch for our noon meal, I stow it in the grub-box under the seat in the spring wagon [which they rode in], the boys take the pipe off the little sheet-iron stove, empty the fire out and leave it to cool, while I am putting things away in the places where they belong. It is wonderful how soon we have learned to live in a wagon, and we seem to have an abundance of room.

An additional challenge was keeping up religious obligations on the trail. Keeping the Sabbath, which meant stopping for the day, listening to sermons, singing hymns, and praying, proved particularly difficult. Most groups wanted to reach their destinations as soon as possible, and not everyone was willing to stop one day out of every seven. In addition, very few groups included a minister to lead services. Some women's diaries only mention prayers and hymns when a party member died, not any kind of observance or halt on Sundays. Others mention the Sabbath in their diaries, but circumstances usually prevented them from observing it. For instance, in 1851 newlywed Amelia Hadley wrote one Sunday that it "does not seem much like" the Sabbath because the group had to keep moving "to where we could get timber." Eighteen-year-old Eugenia Zieber wrote one Sunday, "We are traveling to day. I regret doing so, but the company generally are not willing to lie by, and we of course who would like to, being the smaller number, must comply with the other's wishes." To her frustration, the group was willing to stop the very next day to rest. The next week she wrote, "I do wish the company could be prevailed upon to rest on Sunday. It would be better in every respect, both in regard to *duty*, and the welfare of our teams." Parthenia Blank noted in her diary that she actually had "more time for reading and meditation when we are traveling than...when we stop and spend a day we have so much to do when we stop it keeps us busy all day." Mormons and other groups that had a preacher with them stopped much more regularly on Sunday, although even those groups tended to keep moving seven days a week the closer they got to the end of the trail.

In addition to the practical necessities that forced women and other overlanders to adapt familiar household and cultural routines, the journey brought several groups of women together for the first time. White women had not entered Native American women's territory in large numbers before, and most of the former feared even the possibility that they might encounter Native Americans because all they had heard about Indians were rumors of unpredictable, violent attacks. When encounters did occur, they tended to be harmless, at least for the whites. Far more Native Americans died at the hand of migrants than the other way around.

Many white women on the trail noted in their diaries when they had seen a Native American for the first time. Mary Jane Caples wrote, "They were the first Indians I had ever seen, and to my frightened vision, dressed in their long macinaw blankets with eagle feathers in their hair—my thought was that they would kill us all, and take my baby in captivity." In fact, it was far more common for white women to trade with Native Americans. Women on the trail eagerly traded for fresh food to supplement the migrants' monotonous diet of beans, bread, and bacon. Many also admired the clothing Native American women made and the skill that went into making it. Lodisa Frizzell, for example, wrote, "I must say that nicer work with a needle I never saw...or anything more beautiful, it [the leather] looked like satin, and was finely ornamented with various colored beads." White women were not always so admiring, however. For example, Sarah Raymond wrote in her diary on July 6, 1865,

> As we were passing another Native American town I peeped into two or three of their dwelling-places. They are desolate-looking homes; no sleeping-places, no tables, chairs, nor any furniture, just some rolls of blankets and buffalo robes, some camp-kettles, and that was all. There were squaws and papooses innumerable squatted around on the outside of their teepees, the squaws making moccasins, or decorating them with beads. When we said 'How,' they grinned and held up two fingers, indicating they wanted two dollars for a pair. We did not purchase.

Raymond also had a low opinion of Mormons, so when they passed a Mormon community in August, she wrote, "The women appeared sad and sorrowful enough to be the wives of Mormons. I did not see one of them smile. Our wagons were thronged with women and children selling butter, eggs, cheese and vegetables. They sold eggs at seventy-five cents per dozen, butter seventy cents per pound, cheese fifty cents, potatoes twenty-five cents, and everything else in proportion." Raymond thought the prices were a little high, but noted that her party would have paid even more because they were so short of fresh food.

The West might not have been the promised land that the religious and economic migrants sought, but it did represent a fresh start. Far away from old constraints and confronted by new ones, every western woman was affected by the trails and the changes they wrought. Some of the changes resulted from practical necessity, and sometimes they were the opportunities women had sought. Many women worked hard to bring familiar ways with them, such as keeping a proper "civilized" household and keeping the Sabbath, and they worked even harder to make new lives once they arrived at their destination. While Native women had to contend with hundreds of thousands of newcomers, the migrants started new lives with high expectations for the opportunities the West was supposed to deliver.

Suggested Readings

Coleman, Ronald G. "'Is There No Blessing for Me?': Jane Elizabeth Manning James, A Mormon African American Woman." In *African American Women Confront the West, 1600–2000,* edited by Quintard Taylor and Shirley Ann Wilson Moore, pp. 144–162. Norman: University of Oklahoma Press, 2003.

De León, Arnoldo. *Racial Frontiers: Africans, Chinese, and Mexicans in Western America, 1848–1890.* Albuquerque: University of New Mexico Press, 2002.

Faragher, John Mack. *Men and Women on the Overland Trail.* New Haven, CT: Yale University Press, 1979.

Hoffert, Sylvia D. "Childbearing on the Trans-Mississippi Frontier, 1830–1900." *Western Historical Quarterly* 22, no. 3 (August 1991): 272–288.

Holmes, Kenneth L., ed. *Covered Wagon Women: Diaries from the Western Trails, 1840–1890.* 11 vols. Glendale, CA: Arthur H. Clark Company, 1983–1993.

Hurtado, Albert L. *Intimate Frontiers: Sex, Gender, and Culture in Old California.* Albuquerque: University of New Mexico Press, 1999.

Myres, Sandra L. *Westering Women and the Frontier Experience, 1800–1915.* Albuquerque: University of New Mexico Press, 1982.

Palmer, Rosemary G. "The Sabbath According to Female Diarists on the Trail." *Overland Journal* 22:4 (Winter 2004–2005): 160–170.

Riley, Glenda. "Sesquicentennial Reflections: A Comparative View of Mormon and Gentile Women on the Westward Trail." *Journal of Mormon History* 24, no. 1 (Jan. 1998): 29–53.

Schlissel, Lillian, ed. *Women's Diaries of the Westward Journey.* New York: Schocken, 1982.

Schlissel, Lillian, Byrd Gibbens, and Elizabeth Hampsten, eds. *Far From Home: Families on the Westward Journey.* New York: Schocken, 1989.

Voeller, Carey R. "'I have not told half we suffered': Overland Trail Women's Narratives and the Genre of Suppressed Textual Mourning." *Legacy* 23, no. 2 (2006): 148–162.

Wagner, Tricia Martineau. *African American Women of the Old West.* Guilford, CT: Globe Pequot Press, 2007.

Watson, Jeanne H. "'A Laughing, Merry Group': Women Triumphant Over Travail on the Overland Trails." *The Californians* 12, no. 2 (1995): 10–19.

Williams, Carol. "'My First Indian': Interaction Between Women and Indians on the Trail, 1845–1865." *Overland Journal* 4, no. 3 (Summer 1986): 13–18.

CHAPTER SIX

Women and Mining

Women in California had little time to adjust to the discovery of gold in California's Sacramento Valley in the summer of 1848, which occurred on the heels of the rapid American conquest in the late 1840s. The 1849 gold rush and subsequent mining booms across the West produced significant changes and new constraints for some women and unexpected opportunities for others. The Native American population in California dropped from 150,000 in 1848 to only 30,000 in 1860, a decrease unprecedented in American history, and more women died than men because of sexually transmitted diseases the women caught from newcomer men. Meanwhile, the non-Native population grew from less than 15,000 in 1848 to more than 220,000 in 1852, of which fewer than five percent were women and children. The arrival of thousands of male miners (often called the forty-niners) made displacement and sexual assault all too common occurrences for Native American women in California, as they would be again during later mining booms. At the same time, many of the newly arrived women seized the chance to carve out interesting and sometimes lucrative careers for themselves, including prospecting for precious metals. Men outnumbered women significantly in the mining camps and towns of the West, and some women turned that unusual situation to their advantage, as men would pay high prices for domestic and sexual services. In the mobile, unstable world of mining camps and towns, women also helped create communities that could stand together in the face of low wages and labor unrest.

Women in California's Gold Rush

After the discovery of gold in California in 1848 but before the arrival of the forty-niners, some Native Americans briefly turned mining into a family and community enterprise. One miner reported seeing a group of Miwoks panning for gold by a stream. The men scooped the mud out of the stream bed and the children carried it to the women, who dug through for the gold. However, the huge, rapid influx of non-Native miners that started in the spring of 1849 drove them off their lands and away from the streams. In the subsequent decade, the tribes north of San Francisco Bay suffered some of the most brutal treatment experienced by any Native American group on the continent. White miners and settlers hunted Native American men, raped Native American women, and kidnapped adults and children to sell them into indentured servitude. Whites drove Native Americans into the mountains, where they had to raid ranchers' cattle for food to survive. The ranchers retaliated harshly. In the 1850s miners, ranchers, and vigilante groups murdered thousands of Native Americans. More women died than men because women caught sexually transmitted diseases from the immigrant men. The low number of women made it harder for Native communities to recover and created more competition among men for wives.

The fever for quick riches meant disaster for Native Americans everywhere that a prospector struck gold or silver. Luckily, the miners did not usually stay for more than a few months or years. Most took off after each new rumor of gold or silver, leaving Native American communities to try to rebuild in their wake.

In California, gold rush society was multicultural, multinational, and multilingual. It included people from South America and Polynesia as well as the United States, Europe, Canada, and China. Despite this diversity, it was not gender-balanced. The most extreme gender imbalance occurred in the Chinese community, because most young

Chinese men who came to California only intended to stay just long enough to make enough money that they could go home and marry. In 1852 the first California census showed only seven Chinese women in the state out of a total of approximately 25,000 Chinese residents. By the 1870s there were fewer than 4,000 Chinese women in the state out of a total population of approximately 60,000.

The small number of wives who insisted on accompanying their husbands to California during the Gold Rush did so out of a sense of duty or adventure. When Luzena Wilson's husband headed to California from Missouri in 1849, she decided that she "would not be left behind…. I thought where he could go, I could, and where I went I could take my two little toddling babies." Newlywed Margaret DeWitt arrived in San Francisco in the summer of 1848 with her husband Alfred. She had to manage a large household that included her husband's bachelor brothers, and so she promptly hired help. She was grateful that she was able to hire "a nice Irish woman" almost immediately. The woman had already lived in the United States for ten years "and came out [to California] with her husband who is going to the mines—and she wanted a good home was willing to come for Sixty dollars a month." As an added bonus, she noted, the woman "is a good washer and ironer." DeWitt was particularly glad that the woman would work for so little: within a few years domestic servants could charge up to $150 a month.

These women sometimes regretted their choice, though. Martha Hitchcock wrote home in 1851 to say that from her perspective California's Gold Rush seemed like "the Paradise of men, I wonder if a paradise for poor *Women* will ever be discovered." Gold Rush society revolved around the needs and interests of men, and it could often seem very difficult for a woman to find her place in that society.

Women Prospectors

A small number of women found their own personal paradise by becoming prospectors. Sometimes they helped their husbands, lovers, fathers, or brothers, but many prospected on their own or with another woman. A significant proportion of female prospectors were widows. A few Spanish-speaking women from Mexico and South America show up in the census as gold panners (miners who used large pans to sift gold out of river sediments) in nineteenth-century New Mexico and California. The number of female prospectors rose dramatically by the end of the nineteenth century, especially during gold rushes in Alaska and Nevada, but they remained a tiny minority of all prospectors.

The women who caught "gold fever" often preferred the freedom and wide open spaces over being cooped up in town. Most female miners thought that "normal" society was boring and unpleasant compared to their lives of challenge and discovery, and that mining towns seemed dirty and crowded compared to the clean, open spaces where they prospected. Some of the women who became prospectors had already pursued other unusual jobs; very few had ever worked as domestics or factory workers, which were typical jobs for working women in the mid-nineteenth century. Even their clothes made them stand out. They usually wore pants because skirts were impractical, yet in many states it was against the law for a woman to wear pants. French-born prospector Marie Pantalon (who deliberately chose that name when she started prospecting in the United States) had special permission from the municipal government of Virginia City, Nevada, to wear pants, but San Francisco's authorities were not so understanding. While she was visiting there in 1871, they arrested and fined her and forced her to wear "proper" women's clothes. Elizabeth Gunn sailed around the tip of South America with four young children to join her prospecting husband in California. Once there, she wrote to her family that "a Frenchman and his wife live in the nearest tent, and they dig gold together. She dresses exactly like her husband—red shirt and pants and hat." Some women chose to pass for men when they could, to take advantage of the greater range of economic and social opportunities available to men and to avoid the sexual harassment to which women in public places were subjected.

Women prospectors faced challenges and constraints that their male counterparts did not. For example, a woman who wanted or needed to sell her claim could not sit in the local saloon or men's club talking about its value, so it was harder for her to find a buyer. Few women could make a full-time living out of mining, and most had to combine their prospecting with other work available to women in mining towns. Unlike men, they also had to balance prospecting against their family responsibilities.

Irish-born Nellie Cashman is a good example of the diverse experiences and difficult choices of female prospectors. She ran boardinghouses in mining towns before and during her years as a prospector. After moving from Ireland to Boston when she was a child, her family headed to San Francisco in the 1860s. In the early 1870s Nellie and her mother opened a boardinghouse in Virginia City, Nevada, where Nellie apparently caught gold fever. Over the next few decades, she moved all over the West and the world, mining and running other businesses on the side. She prospected for gold, silver, and diamonds in locations as far-flung as British Columbia, Canada; South Africa; and Arizona, California, and Alaska. She also operated boardinghouses and restaurants, alone or with her mother and sister. For a while, she ran a boot and shoe store in Arizona with a woman named Kate O'Hara and then a groceries and provisions store with Jennie Swift. When Cashman stayed long enough in one location, she devoted a lot of her time and money to charitable work. She donated money for a hospital in Victoria, British Columbia, and later raised money in Tombstone, Arizona, for a hospital, a new Catholic church, and the town's first school. After her sister died in 1884, Nellie had to raise her five nieces and nephews. Cashman brought the children with her on her travels when she could and put them in boarding schools when she could not. She died in a Victoria, British Columbia, hospital in 1925.

In contrast to Cashman, whose ability to move frequently was perhaps possible because she did not have children of her own, Nicaraguan-born prospector Ferminia Sarras made a permanent home base in Nevada. The thirty-six year old immigrated to the United States in 1876 with four daughters but no husband. By 1880 the family was in Nevada, and in 1881 Sarras gave birth to a son. She placed her two youngest daughters in an orphanage in Virginia City while she prospected in the southwest corner of Nevada. Although she staked many claims in the 1880s and 1890s, she never made any real money from mining them herself. After 1900, however, a central Nevada mining boom allowed her to sell many of her claims at a good price. In 1905 a mining town was even named "Mina" in her honor, when a railroad was built through a region where many of her mines were located. When Sarras had enough cash in her pocket after a big sale, she headed to San Francisco for good meals, new clothes, and time with one of her many younger lovers. In 1910 the census recorded her chosen occupation: miner. She died in 1915.

Another prospecting woman was Lillian Malcolm, who did not catch gold fever until 1898, when she was thirty. The former New York actress did not get rich in the Klondike gold rush in northern Canada or in Alaska, her next stop. After losing several claims to male claim jumpers (people who forced others off their claims), Malcolm headed to central Nevada just after the turn of the twentieth century. She prospected around the state for several years, but usually had to earn money for room and board with her storytelling skills.

Other western women tried mining once or twice on a whim, but the hard work soon discouraged them, as it did some men. California schoolteacher Lucena Parsons recorded in her journal that she had not been able to resist trying her hand at panning for gold. She started in May 1850 by observing male panners for a few days before giving it a try herself. She spent a few days actively searching for "that bewitching ore" but soon gave up. Louisa Clapp, the wife of a doctor at Rich Bar, California, also gave it a try. She found $3.25 in gold dust, which she thought qualified her to be a "mineress," but she had no intention of doing it again. She complained to her sister, "I wet my feet, tore my dress, spoilt a pair of new gloves, nearly froze my fingers, got an awful headache, took cold and lost a valuable breast-pin, in this my labor of love."

These women had no previous mining experience but felt compelled to try it; in contrast, women who had grown up in mining towns had a better idea of both the opportunities and the challenges. Ellen Clifford was born in 1879 in a central Nevada mining camp. Her father had been a coal miner in the east and a silver miner in the West before moving the family to a sheep ranch. She married Joseph Brigham Nay in 1899 when she was twenty. They were caught up in the 1900 silver rush in Tonopah, Nevada, and then the 1904 gold rush in Goldfield, Nevada. Mining was a family affair, as their children, Ellen's father, and her in-laws came along both times. After Joe was disabled in a 1902 shootout, Ellen took in laundry and Joe did whatever mine work he could manage. In 1905 Ellen staked her first claim in Gold Reed, just before giving birth to their second daughter. Three years later she and Joe decided to get serious about mining. Settling southwest of her father's ranch, they ran a roadhouse and prospected in their free time. In March 1909 they discovered gold on one of Ellen's claims. The family kept it quiet for as long as it could, but by June the rush was on in the brand-new town of Ellendale in the mining district of Ellen. The Clifford and Nay families profited nicely from land sales before the rush ended a month later. Ellen and Joe spent that winter in California but came back in the spring. They bought a rundown ranch and kept working the Ellendale claim off and on. It produced just enough gold over the years to keep Ellen's hopes up. She sold the ranch after Joe died suddenly in 1939, and she died in 1947.

Very few women worked as prospectors, but even fewer developed careers as mine owners, operators, and investors. Mrs. E. C. Atwood of Denver promoted mining as a career for intelligent women at the International Mining Congress at Milwaukee in 1900. She had already pursued several unconventional careers, including blacksmithing and carpentry, before getting into mining. After losing a lot of money on a bad mining investment, she educated herself about the industry. She became president and general manager of the Bonaccord Gold Mining and Milling Company with interests in Colorado and California. She managed all of the operations herself. She and the other women who followed their dreams into the hills may not have gotten rich, but they did get a lot of personal satisfaction from their work.

The Sex Trade in Mining Towns

Historians and contemporary observers have paid much less attention to the small number of western female prospectors than they have to another small group of women workers in mining regions: those in the sex trade. Prostitution was illegal, but it took place in every mining camp and town across the West. Most "respectable" women in mining towns were horrified at the visibility and pervasiveness of the sex trade. For instance, on October 4, 1863, Idaho schoolteacher Louisa Cook wrote to her mother and sisters in Ohio, "I have but two or three Lady acquaintances in this country. *Ladies* are not plenty. There are a great many in all the mining towns who wear the form of a woman, but o so fallen and vile, a living, burning shame to the sex they have so disgraced." As mentioned at the start of this chapter, mining camps were heavily male dominated; in 1850 in California, there were approximately twelve white men for every white woman, and the number of local Native American women was already dropping sharply. By 1860 this ratio had dropped to two to one, yet men's demand for women's sexual services did not decline.

Mining-camp sex trade workers were as diverse as the mining camps themselves. In Gold Rush California most miners were white men, but most of the prostitutes were women of color, including Native Americans, Chinese, African Americans, South Americans, and Polynesians. Typically, Native women were the first sex trade workers in the mining districts because in the early 1850s they comprised the single biggest group of women in California. Hundreds of women from Latin America, primarily Chile, quickly joined them. Pimps often bought these women right off the boat to work in the "fandango houses" or brothels for poor men. Later in the century in one small mining camp in Montana, a census taker found a brothel with six prostitutes ranging in age from seventeen to thirty and hailing from Canada, Ireland, Chile, Mexico, and New York. By 1900, half the prostitutes in Helena, Montana, were Chinese.

Most women who worked in the sex trade did so out of tiny rooms called "cribs," which lined the streets and alleys of red-light districts in mining towns. A few had the resources to own their own shacks or run-down brothels. Wealthier brothels, like the elaborately furnished Windsor and the Irish World in Butte, Montana, were also important social centers. In these houses, madams hired women, usually white, who could dress and act like ladies, to be social companions as well as a sexual partners for male customers. Businesses like these were the exceptions, though.

Some women earned more money in a mining town's sex trade than the men could make mining or than women could in any other paid employment. One woman in Helena, Montana, earned an average monthly income of over $200, more than twice what a miner could make. In Cripple Creek, Colorado, a young woman who had made $2.50 a week in a Denver department store had to turn to prostitution, in which she could earn far more, to help support her family when her father got sick from working in the mine. Another young woman, Lillian Powers, made $2.00 a week as a domestic servant but discovered that she could charge a dollar per sexual transaction.

Women's Work in Mining Towns

Female prospectors and sex trade workers were a tiny minority of the women who lived and worked in mining towns, and they only stood out in a town's early years when the population and the number of women were both small. Most women earned more money and kept their respectable reputations intact by turning their existing domestic skills into full-time occupations: cooking, doing laundry, and running boardinghouses.

For most women, these jobs started when they began cooking or cleaning for male miners in addition to their own male family members. Women with more money, entrepreneurial instincts, and energy turned that informal work into a flourishing business such as a boardinghouse or restaurant. Mary Jane Megquier opened a boardinghouse in San Francisco in 1849 and did an enormous amount of work to keep it going. Every day she broiled three pounds each of steak and liver to serve at breakfast; baked six loaves of bread and four pies or a pudding; prepared another three kinds of meat and vegetables for dinner; and made six beds, as well as doing all the washing and ironing for her boarders. As she described it in a letter, "If I had not the constitution of six horses I should [have] been dead long ago but I am going to give up in the fall whether or no, as I am sick and tired of work." Jeshua Merrill ran a much larger boardinghouse in California in 1849. Her house had eleven rooms on the first floor and nine on the second, and it held on average sixty boarders. She charged eighteen dollars a week for room and board, and fourteen dollars a week for board alone. Sometimes she had as many as seven servants to help, but on other occasions she only had one. By the end of 1849 she rented the boardinghouse to someone else, and in 1850 she and her husband started farming outside of San Francisco.

As Merrill knew, owning a boarding house and restaurant meant hiring help, and women entrepreneurs had to deal with the same problem that had created their opportunities in the first place: the scarcity of women. Even as the number of white women rose in a developing mining town, there still were not enough to fill the demand for female servants. Finding and keeping them was difficult because they could earn upward of one ounce of gold dust a day or anywhere from $50 to $150 a month, very high wages for the mid-nineteenth century.

One mining town in the West that had a higher proportion of white women than many others was Anaconda, Montana. The Irish were the biggest ethnic group in this copper-mining and smelting (the process of heating the mined rocks to extract the valuable metal) town, and Irish women left Ireland in huge numbers in the nineteenth century because there were so few economic opportunities for them at home and so many overseas. Unlike other immigrant women, most of the Irish were unmarried, so they had the freedom to pursue a wider range of economic possibilities in the United States. This unique pattern meant that Anaconda had a higher proportion of white women than most towns across the West. From the 1880s to the 1920s, Irish women owned and operated most of the boardinghouses in Anaconda. Yet even here there were never enough women to fill all the available jobs as housekeepers, waitresses, chambermaids, seamstresses, laundresses, and dishwashers.

Women elsewhere faced similar constraints and had to find their own solutions. In 1856, when Mrs. Lee Whipple-Haslam was a child in the mining town of Cherokee, California, her father was killed in a bar brawl. Her mother decided to open a boardinghouse in the large, comfortable home that her father had built before he died. Her mother needed a cook and was going to hire a Chinese man, Haslam recalled, but the men who lived in the boardinghouse "all refused a China cook. As she could not get a white cook she told them it was a China cook or move boarding houses, they consented. With the new help mother took on more boarders."

The lack of domestic servants in mining towns undermined many marriages, as wives simply refused to do so much work without help but could not afford the going rate. Margaret DeWitt noted many separations among the couples who came to California in 1849: the men usually stayed in California to keep hunting gold, and the wives generally headed back east because "it was so very expensive and difficult to get along without several servants and that besides the high wages cost a great deal." One couple who reversed that trend was Emeline Day and her husband. They came to California in 1853, but for some reason he soon went back to Ohio without her. She managed a rooming house in Sacramento, earning $184 in three months, a very good income at the time. Lucy Stoddard Wakefield and her husband, whose marriage had been troubled long before they left New Haven, Connecticut, in the spring of 1849, divorced shortly after arriving in California. Once happily divorced, Wakefield headed for the mining town of Placerville, California, and started a pie business. Two-and-a-half years later she wrote to friends that she made and sold an average of 240 pies a week all by herself. She sold them for a dollar each, earning an excellent income in return for fourteen-hour days.

The mining West also created new, albeit rare, business opportunities for a handful of African American and Chinese women. Black women generally opened laundries because washing clothes was one of the few respectable jobs available to them in the nineteenth century, and being self-employed let them avoid employers' racism. Unlike white women, who could diversify their operations, African American women tended to get stuck in this sector of the mining economy. Nevertheless, some made significant profits and significant changes to their lives and communities.

For example, Clara Brown had been a slave in Kentucky before being freed in 1856. She immediately started searching for her children, who had been sold away from her. While in Kansas in 1858 looking for her daughter, Eliza Jane, she heard rumors about gold in Colorado. She decided to head west, open a laundry business, and use her earnings to keep looking for Eliza Jane. She got a job as a cook for a wagon train and arrived in the Denver region in June 1859. She stayed there for a few months before moving to a mining town in the mountains, where a more lucrative laundry business seemed possible. There was plenty of demand for her services. She charged fifty cents per shirt, or about two pinches of gold dust. She worked from a two-room cabin and saved as much as she could, while simultaneously giving food and shelter to anyone who needed it and donating generously to local churches. By 1865 Brown had saved more than $10,000 and still hoped to find her daughter. After the Civil War she could travel more safely, so at the age of sixty-two she headed back east. Although she did not find Eliza Jane, she returned to Colorado with about thirty former slaves, friends, and orphans. In 1879, as thousands of "Exodusters" (African Americans who were making their own exodus out of the deep South in search of a better life in a new promised land) made their way to Kansas (see chapter seven), Brown served as an official representative of the governor of Colorado to try to convince some to move to that state.

She was finally reunited with her daughter in 1882. In 1884 the Colorado Pioneer Association chose Clara as its first woman member. She died in the fall of 1885.

Like Brown, Chinese American Polly Bemis was determined to make her own opportunities during a difficult life. Born in northern China in 1853, she eventually became one of Idaho's most famous early residents. Her parents were poor and sold her, like many Chinese daughters at the time, to a woman who smuggled her into Oregon. She was eighteen in 1872, when a Chinese businessman paid $2,500 for her to be his concubine and took her to the gold mining town of Warren, Idaho. In 1880, the census listed her as the widowed housekeeper of Charlie Bemis, who owned and operated a saloon in town. There is no record of what happened to the Chinese businessman. In the 1880s Polly ran a laundry and a boardinghouse that Bemis had built next door to his saloon. According to one account, she once silenced a boarder's complaints about her coffee by waving a butcher knife and demanding, "Who no like my coffee?" Polly and Charles finally married in 1894, preventing her deportation in 1896 when officials discovered that she was not a legal resident of the United States. Shortly after their marriage, the two left Warren and took up a mining claim outside of town. Charlie was very lazy and did little mining, so it was Polly's hard work that helped them develop a busy and self-sufficient ranch. Bemis died in 1922, Polly in 1933.

The scarcity of women in a mining town's early years created a surprising number of opportunities for women of diverse backgrounds. Male miners were willing to pay a good price for a homemade pie, a clean shirt, or a place to sleep at night, and women were able to capitalize on those desires.

Family Strategies

If a mining town lasted long enough to diversify its economy, the opportunities and challenges for women's waged work increased. Men who worked in mines and smelters rarely made enough money to support their families, so the paid and unpaid labor of girls and women was critical to family survival. Girls worked as domestic servants, cared for their siblings and other people's children, and helped their mothers with whatever cleaning, sewing, or cooking they did to make money. Although married women rarely worked outside the home, inside it they ran boardinghouses, rented rooms, took in laundry, raised chickens, and sold the produce from their gardens. For example, Delia Vaughan of Anaconda, Montana, helped a neighbor woman wash the smelter superintendents' laundry for twenty-five years; in exchange, Vaughan got a discount on the groceries she bought from the woman's small store.

A miner's wife was only one accident away from becoming the head of her household. Widows had to do whatever they could to support themselves and their children. Some had enough money or skills to open small stores or boardinghouses, but most had to find other ways to earn an income at home so that they could continue to care for their children. For example, when Anne Ellis's husband died in a mine accident in Cripple Creek, Colorado, his fraternal organization paid for the funeral. The mining company gave her $600 in exchange for her promise not to seek any further compensation, and each man who had worked with her husband donated one day's wages to her. After that, she had to support her two young children on her own. At first she made money by selling her baked goods to local sex trade workers, and later she took in boarders. In Anaconda, Montana, Mary McNelis lost two husbands in the 1920s, one to a mining accident and the other to emphysema caused by the polluted air in the smelter. She worked as a midwife but sometimes had to leave her two sons at an orphanage for short periods of time when she did not have enough money to support them. After Mary Jane Walton's father died, her mother supported the children by raising chickens and washing clothes for the men who worked at the smelter. When Walton's own husband died in the 1920s she used his life insurance to open a store.

Women also played important roles as community builders once mining camps became permanent towns. They created and maintained the social networks and institutions that made the growing towns at least a little more family-friendly. Women taught school, cared for sick neighbors, and looked out for each other's children in the dangerous environment typical of mining towns. They raised money for churches, schools, and their husbands' unions. In addition, women participated actively in ethnic organizations to preserve their heritage, particularly in Irish-dominated towns like Anaconda, Montana. In 1886, working-class Irish women in that town founded the Daughters of Erin, the women's auxiliary to the men's group, the Ancient Order of Hibernians.

Perhaps the most famous and scandalous mining wife was Elizabeth McCourt, better known as Baby Doe Tabor. She was born in Oshkosh, Wisconsin, in 1854, although she would later shave a few years off by telling people she was born in 1860. She pursued her first husband, William Harvey Doe, largely because he came from a wealthy family that owned shares in some Colorado gold mines. They married in June 1877, much to his family's disapproval, and headed to Colorado that fall. When she realized that he did not have the drive and determination to make her dreams of being a wealthy mine owner's wife come true, she divorced him in 1880. That year she met the man who would become her second husband, politician and mine investor Horace A. W. Tabor. He was twenty-four years older than she was and married, but he quickly took her on as his mistress and set her up in a luxurious suite at Denver, Colorado's Windsor Hotel.

Tabor's wife Augusta assumed that Horace would tire of Baby Doe quickly, as he had with previous mistresses, but instead he moved out of their home in 1881 and asked Augusta for a divorce. She refused and continued to do so for two years. In the meantime, Horace and Baby Doe married in St. Louis in the summer of 1882. They were both bigamists: the final papers on her 1880 divorce were not filed until 1886, and he had failed to get a hasty, illegal divorce in 1882 from a Colorado judge who owed him a favor. Augusta finally sued for divorce in January 1883, and the public's view of her as the victim of Baby Doe's gold digging ended Horace's political career. Horace and Baby Doe married again on March 1, 1883, in a lavish ceremony in Washington, D.C. After their return to Denver, the city's elite women snubbed Baby Doe completely, in spite of her large donations to charity. She had three children: daughters in July 1884 and December 1889, and a son who only lived in a few hours in October 1888. She stuck with Horace even as their fortune began to disappear thanks to his bad investments. He died in April 1899. Baby Doe was only thirty-eight years old and was still considered a beautiful woman, but she never remarried and never regained any wealth. She died alone in March 1935 in a crude cabin near a mine that Horace used to own.

Most women chose safer and more respectable paths than Baby Doe Tabor. They turned their domestic skills into profitable businesses during the early years in a mining town and used those skills to help their families and communities survive as towns became more established. A woman's cooking, cleaning, and sewing skills could make the difference between a family's being able to survive in a town and having to move on in search of something else.

Unions and Strikes

Life in a mining town was incredibly harsh for the miners and their families, so they joined unions and participated in strikes to try to improve their working and living conditions. In Cripple Creek, Colorado, during the 1890s and early 1900s, for example, the presence of a strong union meant that miners got paid in cash and could shop where they liked, instead of being paid in "scrip," or company-issued money that could only be spent at company-run stores. The union meant that miners and their families could rent or own their own homes rather than living in company-owned housing. Women also knew they could rely on the union for some support if their husbands or fathers got sick, injured, or killed. Women played key roles in the unions and the often violent strikes of the era; their auxiliaries raised money, hosted consciousness-raising picnics and socials, provided the refreshments for meetings, and sometimes took direct action against the mine companies.

Some tactics, like boycotts against the mining companies and their stores, involved women exercising their power as consumers. Women did the shopping, so they determined the success or failure of a boycott. Other tactics, like strikes, depended on women's support and often took an even higher toll on them than on the striking men. For example, women had to figure out how to feed and clothe their families when the main wage disappeared. Women had to make sure that the men on the picket lines got fed and that the community maintained its social bonds. During a 1903–04 strike in Cripple Creek, the women's auxiliary organized social events to raise money for the strikers' relief fund, and gave free tickets to women whose husbands were on strike.

Strikes also created opportunities for women to act in far less traditional roles. During the Cripple Creek strike, for example, women distributed strike relief and harassed the Colorado National Guard soldiers (sent in by the governor to support the mine owners and break up the strike) and "scabs" (workers who crossed picket lines to work during a strike), knowing that these men would not attack women. When local authorities arrested some of the striking men, women raised money for bail, fed the imprisoned miners and their supporters, and distributed strike relief despite company and state efforts to stop them. When soldiers arrested the editor and printers of the local newspaper, the Victor *Record*, in September 1904 because it had criticized the soldiers and published official union statements, Emma Langdon, a linotype operator whose husband edited the *Record*, sneaked into the office, barricaded herself inside, and got the next edition out. In recognition of her actions she became the first woman to be elected an honorary member of the Western Federation of Miners and was hailed as a "Colorado Heroine" by the *Miners' Magazine*.

Women were not always safer than men from the violence that marked so many western strikes. During one lengthy strike in Ludlow, Colorado, in 1913–14, many of the striking workers and their families had to live in tents after being evicted from their company-owned homes. In April 1914, when the Colorado National Guard and the company's hired thugs attacked their tent community, thirteen women and children hid in a pit. They were burned to death after the National Guard set fire to the tents to force the strikers to leave. Quickly dubbed the "Ludlow Massacre," the incident prompted President Woodrow Wilson to send in federal troops to restore order.

One of the best-known female labor leaders of the day, Mary "Mother" Jones, actively participated in the 1903–04 Cripple Creek strike. Born in Ireland in 1830, Jones immigrated to Toronto, Canada, with her family when she was young. She moved to the United States and in 1861 married a member of the Iron Molders' Union in Memphis, Tennessee. After her husband died, she and her four young children moved to Chicago, Illinois, where she began to attend meetings of the newly formed Knights of Labor and came to see the labor movement as a woman's cause. She traveled around the United States to lend whatever support she could to striking workers. When she arrived in Colorado during the strike, she went to the coal camps, "eating in the homes of the miners, [and] staying all night with their families. I found the conditions under which they lived deplorable....I felt, after listening to their stories, after witnessing their long patience that the time was ripe for revolt against such brutal conditions." In her autobiography, Jones described the violence and intimidation she witnessed first-hand, and stated that her support of the miners led Colorado's governor to try to throw her out of the state.

Prominent female union activists and organizers like Mother Jones were extremely rare because most people considered unions and leadership to be male domains. Women could play supportive roles but were not supposed to be leaders. Exceptions were made during strikes, however; in Cripple Creek, after many of the striking men were imprisoned or deported, Emma Langdon served as vice-president of the Trades Assembly (the umbrella organization for the different trades operating in town) and chaired the executive board of the Typographical Union, in addition to being the secretary of the local women's auxiliary.

A mining town with a strong union also sometimes offered unusual opportunities for working women to organize on their own behalf. For example, in Butte, Montana, women formed a Women's Protective Union local in the first decade of the twentieth century. The local welcomed women of any race and included women who worked as waitresses, cooks, dishwashers, and janitors in many of the town's restaurants and boardinghouses. Its biggest achievement was reducing its members' workday to eight hours a day from fourteen to sixteen hours, which was the average at the time.

Although mining is often considered one of the most male-dominated aspects of the history of the West, women were actively involved in every facet of life and work in the mining West, and they did what they could to survive and even challenge the constraints of life in a mining town. For Native American women, the onslaught of miners during the second half of the nineteenth century brought violence, death, and dispossession, compounding the constraints they already faced. Black women sometimes found ways to use the one respectable business they were allowed to enter, laundry, to carve out small but lucrative opportunities for themselves in mining camps. White women's racial privilege allowed them to play a wider range of roles and seize more opportunities. Some women followed their dreams into the hills and made a living by combining prospecting with other jobs. Others performed the typical paid and unpaid labor of women, making life more bearable for the men who mined and helping turn temporary mining camps into real communities. Although women were not as central to the mining West as they had been to the fur trade, they nevertheless played a critical role in developing the relationships, communities, and institutions that shaped (and sometimes softened) life for everyone in a mining town.

Suggested Readings

Butler, Anne. *Daughters of Joy, Sisters of Misery: Prostitutes in the American West, 1865–90.* Urbana and Chicago: University of Illinois Press, 1985.

Jameson, Elizabeth. *All That Glitters: Class, Conflict, and Community in Cripple Creek.* Urbana and Chicago: University of Illinois Press, 1998.

Jensen, Billie Barnes. "Woodrow Wilson's Intervention in the Coal Strike of 1914." *Labor History* 15, no. 2 (1974): 63–77.

Jones, Mary "Mother." Excerpt from *The Autobiography of Mother Jones.* In *The Western Women's Reader: The Remarkable Writings of Women Who Shaped the American West, spanning 300 Years,* edited by Lillian Schlissel and Catherine Lavender, pp. 393–406. New York: Harper Perennial, 2000.

McCunn, Ruthanne Lum. "Reclaiming Polly Bemis: China's Daughter, Idaho's Legendary Pioneer." *Portraits of Women in the American West,* edited by Dee Garceau-Hagen, pp. 156–177. New York: Routledge, 2005.

Mercier, Laurie. "'We Are Women Irish': Gender, Class, Religious, and Ethnic Identity in Anaconda, Montana." In *Writing the Range: Race, Class, and Culture in the Women's West,* edited by Elizabeth Jameson and Susan Armitage, pp. 311–333. Norman: University of Oklahoma Press, 1997.

———. *Anaconda: Labor, Community and Culture in Montana's Smelter City.* Urbana and Chicago: University of Illinois Press, 2001.

Moynihan, Ruth B., Susan Armitage, and Christiane Fischer Dichamp, eds. *So Much To Be Done: Women Settlers on the Mining and Ranching Frontier.* Lincoln: University of Nebraska Press, 1990.

Murphy, Mary. *Mining Cultures: Men, Women, and Leisure in Butte, 1914–41.* Urbana and Chicago: University of Illinois Press, 1997.

Riley, Glenda. "Baby Doe Tabor: The Culture of Beauty." In *Wild Women of the Old West,* edited by Glenda Riley and Richard W. Etulain, pp. 2–28. Golden, CO: Fulcrum Publishing, 2003.

Wegars, Priscilla. "Polly Bemis: Lurid Life or Literary Legend?" *Wild Women of the Old West,* edited by Glenda Riley and Richard W. Etulain, pp. 45–68. Golden, CO: Fulcrum Publishing, 2003.

West, Elliott. "Beyond Baby Doe: Child Rearing on the Mining Frontier." In *The Women's West,* edited by Susan Armitage and Elizabeth Jameson, pp. 179–192. Norman: University of Oklahoma Press, 1987.

Zanjani, Sally. *A Mine of Her Own: Women Prospectors in the American West, 1850–1950.* Lincoln: University of Nebraska Press, 1997.

COPYRIGHT 1909 ELLEN E. JACK
THE MINER'S DREAM.

This unusual image shows Colorado miner and business owner Ellen E. Jack, who was also known as 'Captain' Jack. Later in her life she led mine tours for tourists and self-published an autobiography called 'The Fate of A Fairy.' Here Jack chose to show herself with wings on her back, a pickaxe in her hand, and a pistol tucked into her skirt. *Buffalo Bill Historical Center, Cody, Wyoming; Vincent Mercaldo Collection, P.71.558*

E. Rinehart photo of Elizabeth 'Baby Doe' Tabor as a young woman. *Buffalo Bill Historical Center, Cody, Wyoming; Vincent Mercaldo Collection, P.71.1512.1*

Photo taken in 1913 or 1914 during the Ludlow Colorado strike, showing women preparing food for the striking coal miners. *Denver Public Library, Western History Collection, Z-215*

Clara Brown, between 1875–1880. *Denver Public Library, Western History Collection, Z-275*

This 1909 photo shows a woman and two children in front of the farm house at the B.E. Smith Ranch in Minidoka, Idaho. Only the more prosperous ranchers could have lived in a house of this type. *National Archives (115-J-O391), Record Group 115: Records of the Bureau of Reclamation, 1889–2008*

The men and women of the Moses Speese family on their homestead in Custer County, Nebraska in 1888. Photo by Solomon Butcher. *Nebraska State Historical Society, [Digital ID: nbhips 10963]* RG2608,PH:01345

A rare photograph of women working on a ranch. Shown are the Becker sisters branding cattle on a ranch in the San Luis Valley in Colorado in 1894. *Denver Public Library, Western History Collection, O. T. Davis, Z-338*

African American teacher and activist Elizabeth Piper Ensley. *Denver Public Library, Western History Collection, F-45641*

This 1901 photo shows Carrie Nation in her favorite pose, holding a Bible in one hand and her hatchet in the other. *Kansas State Historical Society/ kansasmemory.org, Item #207581*

The interior of a saloon in Enterprise, Kansas, after Carrie Nation and her supporters destroyed it, 1901. *Kansas State Historical Society/kansasmemory.org, Item #1925*

Sharpshooter Annie Oakley in 1908. *Buffalo Bill Historical Center, Cody, Wyoming; Gift of Dorothy Stone Collins in memory of her father, Fred Stone, actor and friend of Annie Oakley and Frank Butler, P.69.61*

Populist speaker Mary Elizabeth Lease of Kansas. *Kansas State Historical Society/kansasmemory.org, Item #690*

Oregon's suffrage activist Abigail Scott Duniway in 1885. *Oregon Historical Society Research Library, OrHi 47215*

Arizona suffrage activist and senator Frances Lillian Willard Munds, in Prescott Arizona ca. 1910. *Photo courtesy of Sharlot Hall Museum Library and Archives, Prescott, Arizona, SHM Photographs Collection; ID: 15383, Call Nbr: PB-129,F-001,I-006P*

Arizona Governor George W. P. Hunt signing the Women's Minimum Wage Law in
Phoenix, Arizona, in 1923. *Arizona State Library, Archives and Public Records, History and
Archives Division,Phoenix, #01-2119.jpg*

1917 photo of Representative
Jeannette Rankin of Montana.
*Courtesy of the Senate
Historical Office*

Adelina Otero Warren in 1918 when she was elected School Superintendent. *New Mexico State Records Center and Archives, Bergere Family Photograph Collection, ID #21703*

An African American teacher and her adult students at a night class in Marshall, Texas, 1939. *National Archives (69-N-21531D); Record Group 69: Records of the Work Projects Administration, 1922–1944*

CHAPTER SEVEN

Rural Women

Homesteading and ranching are more central to popular images of the West than any other facets of its history. As with mining, most people associate white men, particularly cowboys, with western ranching. Popular culture portrayals of homesteading in the West do include white women, however, usually as the hardworking wife and mother in a sod or frame house. The powerful Euro-American association of men with land ownership and development placed significant constraints on women's participation; nevertheless, women of many different backgrounds were actively involved in facing the challenges and seizing the opportunities that homesteading and ranching involved. Some women took advantage of nineteenth-century land legislation to claim their own homesteads, and many more helped their families and communities expand their landholdings. Very few women ranched by themselves, but the hard work of wives and daughters was critical to the success of any ranching operation. A few of those daughters became the first female rodeo competitors and in so doing added the word "cowgirl" to the American vocabulary. Other women worked for the U.S. government's Agricultural Extension Service (AES) to try to make rural women's lives easier, and many took advantage of what the AES had to offer. In all these ways women helped create, modify, and sometimes challenge the myths that still shape how much of America sees the West today.

A Home of Her Own: The Homestead Act

In 1862, in the midst of the Civil War, a Republican-dominated Congress passed the Homestead Act to ensure that nonslaveholding white farm families would settle western lands, rather than slaveholders from the South. Congress also hoped that the highly anticipated flood of white homesteaders would speed up the dispossession of Native Americans across the West. The legislation created a simple process by which an individual could claim up to 160 acres of land at a very low cost. After filing a homestead claim on a particular site, the claimant had to cultivate the land, build a house or barn, and live on it for five years, after which he or she would receive the title (proof of ownership), all for a ten dollar fee. Tens of thousands of unmarried women took advantage of the Homestead Act to claim land in their own names, sometimes to satisfy personal ambitions and sometimes to expand their families' landholdings. Legislators never specifically intended the act to help unmarried women gain access to land; the goal was to help single men acquire farms so that they could settle down, marry, have children, and contribute to the growth of the nation's economy. Yet the act did not bar unmarried women from staking their claim to a piece of the West, and many seized the chance for economic independence and the pride of landownership.

Unmarried women not only filed for homesteads in surprising numbers, but they also often completed the process more successfully than men. Before 1900 women made up anywhere from 5 to 30 percent of all homestead claimants, and they "proved up" (that is, they received the final patent, or deed of title, for their land) as often or more often than men. The numbers varied according to region, time period, and ethnicity. In late nineteenth-century Cochise County, Arizona, about 13 percent of the successful Anglo-American homesteaders were women; that percentage rose after 1900, peaking in 1918 at 21 percent. Before 1900, women represented 12 percent of the claimants in Logan, Colorado. In North Dakota between the 1870s and 1910, women claimed about 10 percent of the homesteads, and in some areas that rose to 22 percent. In several Wyoming counties between 1888 and 1943, nearly 12 percent of patents went to women. In northeastern Colorado women made as many as 18 percent of the homestead claims after 1900, with a roughly 55 percent success rate. Across the West at least 30,000 women got title to land in their own names in the late nineteenth and early twentieth centuries, and the number may have been as high as 40,000. Most, but certainly not all, of these women were Anglo-Americans. Claiming their own land allowed these women to improve their futures and those of their families.

A wave of positive advertising at the turn of the twentieth century created a publically accepted image of an independent woman living on her own land, which helped to produce a dramatic rise in the number of women homesteaders in the first decades of the twentieth century. The image did not reflect the complex realities that women homesteaders faced, but it did provide an inspiring model for thousands of urban and rural women. Western women themselves were some of the biggest promoters of the personal and economic benefits of homesteading for women. In 1914, for example, New York transplant Lortah Stanbery wrote in a Cochise County, Arizona, newspaper called the *Artesian Belt Homeseeker Edition,* that women and men both wanted to have their own homes and be self-sufficient land owners. The only difference was that men were fussier about the land they chose, while women were just thankful to have their own piece. She published "Impressions by a New Arrival" in the Arizona paper on March 21, 1914. In it she wrote:

> After years of living in other people's houses the prospect of sitting down and getting up, sleeping and waking, working or idling on MY land was a new and seriously absorbing sensation. Men who come to the valley homeseeking go about in critical attitude, disdaining this, discarding that, objecting to something else, but not I. I took the first claim I found, and sat down on it at once.

Stanbery did not survive solely on homesteading, however; she also worked as a teacher and principal. For her, land ownership had more to do with individual freedom than economic independence. She and most of the other promoters of homesteads for women knew that most women would still have to work for wages because they could not get by on farming alone, but she did not believe that this necessity diminished the symbolic importance of women's owning their own homes and land.

The symbolic importance of land ownership is also evident in the life and writing of the best-known promoter of homesteads for women, Elinore Pruitt Stewart. She went from being a washer-woman to a Wyoming homesteader, and she wanted every working woman to have the same chance. She published testimonials in the *Atlantic Monthly* and later in a single volume, *Letters of a Woman Homesteader* (1914). She was born in 1876 in either Arkansas or Oklahoma and was the oldest of nine children. She was only seven-teen when her parents' death left her to raise her younger brothers and sisters. When Pruitt was twenty-six, she married engineer Harry Rupert, and they filed on a homestead in Oklahoma. Sometime after giving birth to her daughter Jerrine in 1906, she and Rupert separated. After moving to Denver for her health, she worked as a housekeeper, nurse, and laundress and wrote occasional pieces for the local papers. She did not like "the rattle and bang…, the glare and the soot, the smells and the hurry" of life in a city and longed to get out of it. In the spring of 1909 she accepted a job as housekeeper for Wyoming rancher Clyde Stewart. She applied for a homestead adjacent to Stewart's land, and the two got married a week later. By applying while she was still single, she was not technically break-ing laws that barred most married women from homesteading. She never met the Homestead Act's residency requirements, however, because she lived in Stewart's cabin on his land, although she would have preferred to have her own place; as late as 1911 she still signed her letters to her friend as Elinore Rupert. In 1912 she finally relin-quished her claim to Clyde's mother, Ruth, who gained the title in 1915 and later sold the land back to Clyde. Elinore bore another daughter and four sons, but only the three younger boys lived to adulthood. She died in 1933.

Stewart's book consisted of the letters she wrote to a former employer, Juliet Coney, after moving to Wyoming in 1909. She was very excited about homesteading for women, especially urban working women, because, she said, it "requires less strength and labor to raise plenty to satisfy a large family than it does to go out to wash, with the added satisfaction of knowing that [women's] job [on the homestead] will not be lost to them if they care to keep it." Stewart touted her experiences as typical for independent women homesteaders and did not reveal until late in the book that she was married. She was determined to emphasize her independence and did not want her readers to discount her accomplishments by assuming her husband had done everything. In her view, "any woman who can stand her own company, can see the beauty of the sunset, loves growing things, and is willing to put in as much time and careful labor as she does over the washtub, will certainly succeed; will have independence, plenty to eat all the time, and a home of her own in the end."

As the number of women who claimed homesteads indicates, many women heeded this call. In 1886 Mary Anderson and her friend Bee Randolph homesteaded adjoining quarter sections (160 acres or one-quarter of a square mile, a square mile being a full section of surveyed land) in Colorado and shared a shack built over the property line. In May 1902, thirty-year-old Jessie de Prado Mac-Millan of Scotland arrived in Alamogordo, New Mexico. She had dreamed of homesteading in the American West since she was a child. Her older brother Eben was going to inherit their family's considerable wealth, so there was little to keep her in Scotland. When she turned twenty-one, she enrolled in England's Leaton Colonial Training School in 1892 to learn how to become a nanny on a western ranch. MacMillan had to quit because of her health and instead went to work on an English farm, learning to ride, make butter, dress poultry, and work in the fields, until she was strong enough to emigrate. Her favorite aunt made her promise to stay in England until she was thirty, assuming that Jessie would be married by then and give up the idea of emigrating to the United States. Unmarried and undeterred, the young woman left for New Mexico as soon as she could. She bought a quarter section for $300 and named it Glen-Eben after her brother. It had a one-room log cabin in poor condition, partially raised walls for a new cabin, and more than 20 acres of crops. It also had a rundown barn, outbuildings, fencing, and a good spring. MacMillan paid a crew to finish the new cabin and adapted the agricultural techniques she had learned in England to the New Mexico land. She kept the crops that were already growing on the land and experimented with new ones. She managed her money carefully and only hired help for work that she could not do herself. After a bad accident she had to go back to England for knee surgery, but she returned in 1908 with a heavy metal brace. In 1909 she married Loftus Farrington, a British man who was farming in Kansas, and gave up her New Mexico property to join him there.

Homesteading was not just a strategy for unmarried or soon to be married Anglo-American women like the ones described above; unmarried and widowed women of other racial and ethnic groups used it as well, for similar reasons as well as some culturally specific ones. For example, Arizona's legal system was a unique hybrid of Spanish civil law and Anglo-American common law that gave married women some significant legal advantages. Women in Arizona retained control over their own property and earnings after they got married, and this right created opportunities for women, especially when combined with the Homestead Act. Jesús Maldonado de Mejia of Arizona began acquiring land in the early 1890s with a 40-acre claim on the San Pedro River. When she died in 1907, her estate included 200 acres, five horses, and 200 cattle. Her daughter Rafaela inherited it all. Another relative, Francisca Comadurán de Mejia, also had her own homestead by 1890. In an 1889 lawsuit over water rights on the San Pedro River, male property owners stated specifically that the widow Maria Ruíz de Montgomery farmed her own land except for two years when she had rented it to Chinese farmers. Although she hired men to do the labor (as many male landowners also did), she owned the land and decided what it would be used for. Some women, such as Tres Alamos rancher Guadalupe Saenz de Pacheco, even held cattle brands in their own name.

Some unmarried women used their homesteading success as a springboard into other areas of individual achievement. For example, in Cochise County, Arizona, in 1916 unmarried landowner Helen Benedict ran for assistant superintendent of schools. Her claim was far from her parents' land, and she identified herself as a homesteader even as she supported herself as a teacher. While campaigning, Benedict bragged that "she could plow more acres of a dry farm in one hour than any other female homesteader in the valley."

Although Congress passed the Homestead Act with the stereotypical independent male farmer in mind, the act gave unmarried women an unprecedented opportunity to become landowners. For some women this law meant a chance at economic independence, and for many more it meant that they could have the same pride and self-confidence that landownership usually gave to men.

Land Strategies for Women, Their Families, and Their Communities

As the examples of Elinore Pruitt Stewart and Jessie de Prado MacMillan demonstrate, many unmarried women homesteaders did not stay that way for long. Single women homesteaders were not common or always completely independent, but few male homesteaders were truly independent, either. They, too, depended on the work of their siblings, spouses, and children, on and sometimes off the farm. Many women filed claims on land near sites being claimed by their fiancés, fathers, and brothers. By doing so, women helped their families expand their landholdings quickly. Congress eased the land laws in the early twentieth century, allowing homesteaders to prove up their claims more quickly, eliminating restrictions, and permitting claimants to live off the homestead for longer periods of time. The new laws also enabled women to keep their own claims after marriage as long as they had filed on the land at least one year before they married.

The legal changes made it easier for women to help their families acquire more land more quickly. In Arizona the number of Mexican American women who homesteaded doubled after 1900, until they made up about one-third of homesteaders of Mexican descent in Cochise County alone. By comparison, only about 15 percent of Anglo-American homesteaders in the county were women. Very few Mexican American women headed households, so the high number of female homesteaders likely reflected a community strategy of encouraging daughters to claim homesteads before they married to bolster the community's landholdings in the face of the rising population of Anglo-American homesteaders in the area.

Three other groups of women also used the acquisition of western land as a critical family and community survival strategy: African American "Exodusters," European immigrants, and Mormons. Black women played key roles in organizing and inspiring African Americans to go to Kansas, the state closest to the South that allowed African Americans to homestead, in the 1870s, because they were frustrated with racist violence in the post–Civil War South. The migrants became known as the Exodusters because, like the Jews leaving Egypt in the Biblical Book of Exodus, they fled persecution and looked for a promised land. At an emigration meeting in New Orleans in 1875, the women declared "that even if their husbands did not leave, they would." Many were widows and single mothers with families to support. Thousands began to leave the South in 1875, and their numbers peaked at more than 10,000 in 1879. The move was not necessarily an easy transition, however. Willianna Hickman, who homesteaded 14 miles west of the African American town of Nicodemus, Kansas, recalled of her first glimpse of the area: "The scenery to me was not at all inviting and I began to cry." Nevertheless, she and her husband raised three daughters on their farm and lived there for nearly twenty years.

Norwegian immigrants Louise Jakobsen and Tinus Anderson completed an even longer journey when they arrived in Buffalo County, in eastern South Dakota in 1897. They had met in Norway and married soon after they settled in the United States. In 1904, the Andersons and three of Louise's nephews, who had just come from Norway, moved 120 miles west across the Missouri River to Lyman County, South Dakota. Soon after, the oldest of the nephews, James Jenson, married another recently arrived immigrant, Maggie Amundson. The Andersons and Jensons homesteaded adjoining quarter sections, and for the next seventeen years, the lives of the two families paralleled and overlapped. The women helped each other with the cooking, cleaning, canning fruit and vegetables, childbirth and childcare.

Mormon women also used land legislation to support their extended families. In the early twentieth-century Mormon settlement of Pomerene, Arizona, nearly 20 percent of the Mormon women headed households and about 16 percent filed homestead claims in their own names. U.S. law did not recognize plural wives as married, so these wives could legally claim to be unmarried when they filed their claims. Like their Mexican American neighbors, Mormon homesteading women chose to live in close-knit settlements and used land claims to help advance family and community economic strategies. Mormon women's experiences were unique, however. Plural wives often had to be highly autonomous because they did not live with their husbands full time, but they also faced the prospect of being left with nothing when their husbands died, because the law would give his entire estate to his first wife and her children. Living on their own homesteads close to their husbands helped them to hide their polygamous marriages from government officials, and it was also a critical economic survival strategy. Lucy Fenn, for example, lived on her own homestead claim with her four grown sons. Her husband, John Fenn, lived nearby with his first wife, Matilda.

However, just because the Homestead Act said women had the legal right to homestead does not mean that others took them seriously as homesteaders. Nor could they count on the laws being interpreted in their favor if someone challenged their land claims. The most common legal challenge that women faced was the issue of whether a woman who filed a claim when she was single could keep it after she married. The General Land Office (GLO), a division of the Department of the Interior from 1849 to 1946, adjudicated such challenges, and its decisions could only be appealed to the Secretary of the Interior. Maria Good of Kansas had to appeal to the secretary when the GLO ruled that she was not entitled to her homestead. She had filed a claim in Kansas in 1880 and then married a man in a nearby town. She lived in town in the winter and on her homestead in the summer, and she met all the improvement requirements. When she applied for the final title in 1885, the GLO said she was not entitled to the land because she was married and not an actual settler (someone who lived on his or her claim year-round). Luckily for Good, the secretary disagreed, finding that she had clearly met all the legal requirements. Her case set a precedent, so that in the future women who married after filing a claim could be confident that they would not lose it automatically. Not all women were so lucky, though; many did lose their land after they got married. Montana was a particularly favorable jurisdiction for women homesteaders, who won more cases than they lost from 1881 to 1920.

Just as unmarried women used the Homestead Act to forge an independent economic future, so too did many other women use it to bolster the fortunes of their families and communities. The act gave them a way to make a direct contribution to family and community property in their own name, an unusual circumstance in Anglo-American property law.

Women and Ranching

No promoters encouraged women to become ranchers, because most Americans considered ranching a fundamentally male activity and not something that women could do. The popular image of farming featured a family farm that included a wife, but the image of ranching was all about cowboys. Although few women could ranch on their own, some women wound up in charge of ranches when their husbands or fathers died. Some ranch women helped bring their herds to sales centers like Abilene, Kansas, and negotiated their own sales. Most helped their husbands tend cattle and sheep and managed the ranch when the men were away, on top of the time they spent cooking, cleaning, canning, tending children and chickens, and growing a small garden.

Ranching could be a more solitary life than farming for women because their husbands, unlike farmers, often spent long periods away from the ranch buying or selling stock. Some women had a hard time adjusting to the solitude, especially during difficult times like childbirth when they needed help. Mrs. E. A. Van Court, who ranched in California between 1856 and 1864, wrote, "I had never lived on a ranch before, having been born and raised in a country village" in New York. In the fall of 1856 she was pregnant and felt as if she was living "in a foreign land, seven thousand miles from home among strangers." A friend was supposed to come to her ranch from San Francisco before she gave birth in October, but the woman did not arrive until a few days after her son was born. Van Court was terrified of being left alone and would not let her husband ride for help. She recalled, "My boy was born at three o'clock in the morning. The nearest neighbors came to me, brought a Spanish midwife with her who could not speak a word of English. I could not speak Spanish, but my neighbor could, and so we managed to get along." The family did not stay in ranching. They moved several times over the next few years before finally settling in San Francisco, where Van Court ran a boardinghouse.

By contrast, Sadie Martin ranched near Palomas, Arizona, from 1888 to 1897 and loved the life. She and her husband John had been married for about a year when they moved from Iowa to Arizona in 1888. At first they lived with her husband's family and a handful of Yuma Apache hired hands. Martin wrote, "There were few settlers in the valley at that time and it would be two of three months at a time that Mother [her mother-in-law] and I would not see another white woman." It took her a while to adjust to local Native American women "appearing without a sound" and peeking in her windows, but they were quite friendly and meant no harm and really were just as curious about us and our methods of living as we were about them. After a few years, they moved their tepees nearer us, as the men worked on the ranches and the women washed for us. What a boon that was for the boys, who up to this time, had insisted on doing the rubbing [the step where the heavy, wet clothes are rubbed against the washboard] for us, which John said was the hardest work a woman could do.

Both a doctor and a nurse came from a nearby settlement to help when Martin's first son was born in November 1889. This child died as a toddler, and she gave birth to daughters in 1893 and 1895. In 1897, financial problems and her husband's health caused her and the children to move in with relatives in Los Angeles while her husband and his brothers headed to the gold mines. She and the girls moved back to Arizona within two years, but the family wound up living in town.

Ranch wives, like farm wives, did whatever work needed to be done. On the Texas Panhandle in the early 1890s, Sarah Leon Coleman tended the cattle when her husband was away, often not getting back to the house until after dark. Susie Mann Ellis Ivy fed the cattle and baled hay. Sammie Barks married Ed Harrell in 1898 when she was fifteen, and she did all the cooking for him and the cowboys, even when they were out on the range. Barks wrote,

> Ed Harrell said he wanted a wife who could cook with nothing and that's exactly what I done. He and the cowboys wanted the food on the table in a hurry. While they were putting up the horses, I got dinner or supper. Then as soon as dinner was over, the cowboys helped me with the dishes and we were riding again till supper. After supper the cowboys did the dishes themselves.

Evalena Farmer Black enjoyed working the cattle with her husband and the cowboys. She said, "I did my big riding on that ranch of 42 sections." She "made a hand, right with a man," meaning she did as much work and did it as well as any of the other male ranch "hands" (employees, most of whom were cowboys). "I used to pick up a calf and put it on my horse and ride with it as easy as some women pick a bouquet." She could ride all day, help with two roundups, and still make dinner. Some ranch women had lighter workloads. While she was living on a ranch between 1886 and 1898, Anna Exum Masterson sent her laundry fifteen miles away to be done by another woman because her husband did not want to see his wife doing the hard work that dominated many rural women's lives.

Being a rancher did not always mean living on a ranch full-time and dealing directly with the cattle, the cowboys, and the rough living conditions. South Texas rancher Mattie B. Morris Miller was born in 1874, the oldest of six children. When she was fourteen, her family bought the ranch that became the Rafter-3 in Coleman County in south Texas. Miller did not work on the ranch as a young woman, though. Instead, she got a teaching degree, married, and had seven children. After her husband died in 1915, her father gave her a job in the ranch office. Upon retiring in 1920, her father took the unusual step of dividing the ranch equally among his six sons and daughters. Each got 12,000 acres and a share of the cattle. In an even less common move, her father gave Miller the original ranch and the use of the Rafter-3 brand because she was the oldest, even though ranchers usually passed such assets to sons, not daughters. Miller and her two brothers formed the Morris Cattle Company, pooling their resources for a total of 36,000 acres of land and 3,800 cattle. One brother lived on the original ranch and the other brother on an adjoining property. Miller lived nearby in the town of Coleman and ran the ranch's business office. She did everything from hiring and paying the ranch hands to planning the breeding program.

Girls who grew up on ranches sometimes spent even more time outside than their mothers did and often grew up doing the same chores that male ranch hands might. For example, sixteen-year-old Martha Farnsworth, who had one sister but no brothers, wrote in her diary on March 2, 1884, "In the morning, Belle and I hitched up ole Barney and Prince to the wagon and hauled two barrels of water, about ¹/₂ mile from a nice Spring." With no brothers, she and her sister were "Pa's 'boys.'"

At least one woman rancher, already straying from respectable gender norms, went a bit further and became a cattle rustler. Ellen Liddy Watson was born in Ontario, Canada, in 1860 and moved with her family to a homestead in Smith County, Kansas, in 1877. In 1879 Ellen married William Pickell, a local farm laborer who owned some land, but she left him in 1883 after four years of abuse. She found a job as a cook and housecleaner at a hotel in Rawlins, Wyoming. There she met widower and fellow Canadian James Averill, who was in town to file the paperwork for a homestead near the main trail people used to get to Oregon, Utah, and California. Averill offered Ellen a job at the roadhouse he planned to set up. He also wanted to become a rancher, but his application for a brand, the only way to indicate who owned an animal, was rejected. Although he and Ellen married in 1886, they tried to keep it quiet, and she did not take his name, to make it easier for her to file on her own homestead, thus doubling their land holdings.

At first their economic prospects looked good. Averill got a job as postmaster at the Sweetwater Post Office, and Ellen used her maiden name to file for a homestead as an unmarried woman. Ellen and James decided to file on adjacent pieces of land to get one big ranch. Ellen's claim annoyed a local cattleman, Albert J. Bothwell, who had been using the land that she filed on as open range for his own cattle. He offered to buy the land from them outright, but they refused. In the fall of 1888 Ellen supposedly bought a small herd of twenty-eight cattle, but she had no paperwork to prove the sale had happened. She applied for several different brands in December 1888, but none of them were approved, so she bought a brand from another rancher in March 1889 and branded all the cattle she had. She almost certainly had some "mavericks" (unbranded calves) in her herd, and normally ranchers did not brand mavericks until after the spring roundup, when they would be proportionally divided among local ranchers. Those with big herds, like Bothwell, would have received most of the animals, and those with small herds, like Ellen, would have gotten very few. On July 20, Bothwell and some of his men confronted Ellen, accused her of cattle theft, and lynched her and Averill. No charges were ever brought against the men who killed the couple.

Perhaps it is not too surprising that Ellen, already involved in an activity far outside the typical feminine role, took it one step further. Popular images of farming and homesteading included women in ways that images of ranching did not, and ranching itself had a much rougher image than that of the family farm. Women ranchers had to be that much more independent and fight for their place in an even more male-dominated world, but the penalties for cattle rustling made little allowance for gender.

Ranch Daughters Become the West's First Cowgirls

The first generation of "cowgirls," many of whom grew up on ranches, created one of the most unusual opportunities for western women in the early twentieth century. Rodeo events started as informal competitions at the end of the workday or during ranch owners' social gatherings. The cowboys competed to see who was better at all the day-to-day skills they used in their jobs. Rodeos evolved into organized shows for a nonranch audience in the 1870s. Women participated in the informal contests from the beginning, experiences that gave some of them the skills and confidence to compete in the public rodeos. Three women, Bertha Kaepernick, Lucille Mulhall, and Fanny Sperry, took some of the first steps for women into rodeo competitions and the wild west shows, which showcased western experiences and skills and were becoming popular forms of entertainment in the late nineteenth century. These western women followed in the footsteps of the well-known Ohio-born sharpshooter Annie Oakley, who starred in William "Buffalo Bill" Cody's Wild West show in the late 1880s and 1890s.

Bertha Kaepernick was born in Germany in 1883 and moved to Colorado with her family in 1886. The youngest of seven children, she learned how to ride and handle cattle while working alongside her father. In her free time, she competed against local cowboys at the informal competitions held during roundups. Her first official competition occurred in Wyoming at the 1904 Cheyenne Frontier Days. Cheyenne had started the annual event in 1897, and it would become the oldest continuous rodeo in North America. Kaepernick entered the bronco riding competition, in which a rider had to stay on a bucking horse for a certain length of time. She borrowed an unbroken horse named Tombstone from a local rancher before starting the hundred-mile trip from her home to Cheyenne. The local paper wrote that she was the first woman "ever to enter the championship bucking and pitching contest." Kaepernick only stayed on Tombstone for a few seconds before she had to "pull leather" or grab some part of the saddle to stay on, an action that automatically disqualified her. The horse threw her anyway. Even though she was already disqualified, Kaepernick got back on Tombstone and rode him until he stopped bucking. She then rode him home instead of her saddle horse. After competing in other shows in 1904 and 1905, she joined the Pawnee Bill Wild West show in 1906, then left it a year later to perform in the Miller Brothers' 101 Ranch Wild West Show. In 1909 Kaepernick married Dell Blancett, and they worked in Los Angeles as trick riders in the movies. In 1911, 1912, and 1914 she won the women's bucking horse championship at the Pendleton, Oregon Round-Up and won money in other women's and mixed events. She competed and rode in exhibitions until she retired in 1934. In 1975, at the age of ninety-two, she was inducted into the Rodeo Hall of Fame.

Lucille Mulhall was born in 1885 in Missouri, one of four girls and two boys born to Colonel Zack Mulhall and his wife, Mary Agnes. Only Lucille and one of her sisters survived to adulthood, and she was more like a son than a daughter to her father. In 1889 her father moved the family to a homestead in Oklahoma, before becoming a rancher. From a young age she showed her skill with livestock, learning how to ride, rope, train horses, brand and doctor cattle, and shoot. She grew up challenging the cowboys from neighboring ranches during the open-range roundups.

When she was fourteen, Mulhall's father started a wild west show called the Congress of Rough Riders and Ropers, and she became the show's star. She performed at the 1901 presidential inauguration and in Madison Square Garden in New York in 1905. As early as 1903 she had set a world record for roping a steer in thirty seconds at a competition in Texas, and in 1913 she was crowned the Champion Lady Steer Roper of the World at the Winnipeg, Manitoba, stampede. Newspaper reports of Mulhall's accomplishments were the first to use the word "cowgirl" regularly and brought the word into common usage. She told a reporter,

> I ride because I like to and I rope cattle because it is fun. I like to do things as well as I can, and it makes me feel nice to know that I can take care of myself in the country. I ride astride because it is the safest and most comfortable way. I don't know that I can explain how a rider sticks on a pitching horse. I suppose it is by having perfect control of the muscles of the body and limbs, and in knowing more than the horse does—that is, knowing what he is going to do just a little before he knows he is going to try do to.

Married and divorced twice, Lucille continued to compete through the 1920s and 1930s. She died in a car accident in 1940 at the age of fifty-five, and the Rodeo Hall of Fame and the National Cowboy Hall of Fame inducted her in 1975.

Fanny Sperry was born in 1887 on a ranch in the Beartooth Mountains of Montana. Her parents molded her into an expert rider. She used her skill at breaking horses as a performer with Buffalo Bill's Wild West show. When she joined the show in 1916, she already had an impressive resume, having won the Women's Bucking Horse Championship of Montana and earned the title of Lady

Bucking Horse Champion of the World. In 1913 she married rodeo clown Bill Steele. In the show she demonstrated her marksmanship by shooting china eggs out of her husband's fingers and a cigar out of his mouth. They both worked for the Miller Brothers 101 Ranch Show for a few years before creating their own show. She competed until 1925, when she and Bill moved to a ranch near Lincoln, Montana. Sperry later worked as a guide and outfitter and was sharply critical of trophy hunters who shot animals purely for sport.

These three women were not the only ones competing in the earliest rodeos and wild west shows, but they helped popularize women's events in the early twentieth century. During those years, women entered rodeo contests around the country in increasing numbers. Two of the best-known rodeos aside from the one in Cheyenne were the Pendleton, Oregon, event, which started in 1909, and the Calgary, Alberta, Stampede, which started in 1912. Both of these rodeos scheduled competitions for women from the early years. Many smaller rodeos also existed, and women and men became "circuit riders," moving from one rodeo to another. The best women riders often challenged each other to special contests to claim the title of world champion.

The popularity of the many women's events generated a surprising amount of positive coverage of the cowgirls and what they could do. For example, the *Cheyenne Leader* newspaper, in its August 1901 coverage of the Cheyenne Frontier Days, reported that the half-mile "Ladies' Cow Pony Race was one of the most enjoyable features of the program and was as exciting as the most exacting could desire. Nowhere else in the world do women display the fearless horsemanship to be found on the prairies of Wyoming, and as the ladies came under the wire at break neck speed they were wildly cheered." The winner also got to call herself the champion of the world. A Ladies' Relay Race, first organized in 1906, was so popular that it remained on the program until 1946. The prize money was greater for this race than for any other women's events, and the winner also got a silver cup donated by the *Denver Post.* As the *Wyoming Tribune* explained in 1906,

In this event each contestant is provided with three horses. When the word is given she mounts one of the animals, dashes around the half mile track, dismounts, leaps onto another cow pony and is off again. The race is one and one-half miles long, so that each lady must dismount and remount twice. As much time is either lost or gained according to the dexterity of the fair competitor to leap from a horse, often with the animal in full gallop, and spring on to her next mount, it can well be imagined that the contest is such as to excite the greatest possible enthusiasm and excitement in the spectators.

After Kaepernick's outstanding performance in the 1904 rodeo, a women's bronco riding competition became a regular event at the Cheyenne Frontier Days. In 1914 the organizing committee added a World Championship Ladies' Bronco Riding contest to the regular program. The rules were the same for women as for men: they had to stay on for eight seconds, spur the horse at the beginning, and could not grab the saddle or horn for assistance. Women did have the option of competing with "hobbled" stirrups, which were hooked together by a cinch under the horse to prevent them from flapping wildly when the horse bucked. Public interest in women's bronco riding waned in the 1920s, and the event was canceled completely in 1928.

Instead of scorning these early cowgirls for their unfeminine skills and appearance, the media praised them and held them up as positive role models. The *Cheyenne State Leader* stated in 1909 that the cowgirls might not have "drugstore complexions [that is, so fair that they were likely produced by using products that came from drugstores], but they have bounding health." They wear their "divided skirts, high topped boots, spurs, and sombreros with quite as much grace as the ennuied lady of the city mansion wears her *directoire* gown and her Paris headgear. And the odds are all in favor of the cowgirls when it comes to a question of the comparative amount of real happiness which the two types get out of life." Although such praise did not directly challenge cultural norms for respectable women, it did perhaps reflect the potential for western women to push the boundaries of these norms. Likewise, even though cowgirls were not typical of the western women who lived and worked on ranches and farms, they did represent some of the more unusual opportunities that women had in the West.

The Agricultural Extension Service

This surprisingly positive publicity for some very untraditional women could not, however, change the fact that rural life was not easy, nor could it stem the tide of rural depopulation that was well underway in the early twentieth century. To try to improve the lives of America's farm families, in 1914 the federal government created the Agricultural Extension Service (AES). Its purpose was to share the expertise of the U.S. Department of Agriculture (USDA) with local agents, who would convey it to farm families. There were almost twice as many male agricultural agents, who worked with men on improving farming techniques and other outdoor tasks, than female home demonstration agents, who focused on improving women's housekeeping and childcare. This difference in focus did not reflect the true division of labor on most farms, in which women did whatever tasks were necessary, indoors and out. Rather, it reflected an urban middle-class gender norm that the AES struggled to apply to farm families.

Reacting to a widespread belief that farm life was drudgery, especially for farm women, the USDA surveyed farm women in 1921. The final report indicated that "farm women on the whole are more contented than the people at large think they are." This finding did not stop the AES, whose leaders believed that people would stay on the farm if life there was more like living in a city, with all of its services and conveniences. The home demonstration agents wanted to show rural women how to do more with their existing resources by teaching such things as more efficient canning techniques or better hygiene practices, and to help create better homes and farms, healthier families, and reduce rural women's isolation. In 1925 Edna Durand, the extension agent for Curry County, New Mexico, stated in her annual report that the major obstacle facing home extension agents in New Mexico was not farm women's lack of education, because "there are plenty of college-trained women in these prairie shacks, but she must pay the price of pioneering and do much on very little. The mission of the extension worker is helping her make that little do as much as possible—perhaps just a little more than either of them thought possible—that is achievement."

The poverty, isolation, and ethnic diversity that characterized much of the rural West forced AES agents to discard the service's rigid gender and ethnic guidelines and adapt their work and attitudes to local situations. After the AES assigned a home demonstration agent like Durand, she met with a group of farm women to discuss what they needed and wanted from the extension service. The agent appointed a woman as a local leader in each community. Several women might attend a day-long meeting with the home demonstration agent and then pass along the techniques they had learned to women in their own communities. Adherence to strict gender prescriptions frequently hampered this extension work, however. For example, many counties lacked female home demonstration agents, and few male agricultural agents were willing to talk to women about "women's work." Similarly, AES agents mistakenly promoted poultry raising as a male activity because the chickens were outdoors and the agents believed that men did the outdoor work while women stayed indoors. In reality, on most farms women were responsible for the flocks.

Crossing the gender line sometimes happened in counties or on reservations where there were no home demonstration agents. When extension work began on Indian reservations in the early 1930s, male AES agents conducted canning and drying demonstrations for women and tried to encourage food preservation. Agents soon learned that they could be more effective when they discarded the rigid gender rules about who did what and adapted their programs to local conditions. In Santa Fe, New Mexico, agent Juan Ramirez handled canning demonstrations but did not feel qualified to teach sewing. In these cases, men arranged and publicized the meetings but then hired local women to teach the classes. The AES never hired women to teach farming methods or soil conservation, however.

Extension work also floundered when the agent did not speak the dominant local language. Fabiola Cabeza de Baca Gilbert was the home demonstration agent in two New Mexico counties from 1929 to 1940. She recognized how important it was to have agents who understood the language, social customs, and food preferences of the Hispanic farmers. In her first five years she reported great progress in improving the diets and food preparation among Hispanic farm families. But she was also able to work successfully with Anglo-American groups and in organizing children's clubs. She also ignored the gender separation that was so common in extension work, encouraging girls to expand beyond the usual food and clothing projects to work with the boys in the agricultural clubs. Her success with Hispanic and Anglo-American farmers demonstrated what could be done when rules were more flexible.

Extension work among minority racial and ethnic groups was limited and uneven until agriculture became a major focus of New Deal policies (government programs intended to ease the impact of the Great Depression) in the 1930s. In many western states rural families spoke a variety of languages. In New Mexico in 1920, nearly half of the state's population spoke only Spanish, and there were pockets of German, Russian, Polish, and Native American people who spoke little or no English. Western AES members made little effort to reach out to black farmers, and they did not regularly reach out to Native American communities until the Bureau of Indian Affairs (BIA) created the Indian Extension Service (IES) in 1929. The IES grew slowly, largely because of the Anglo agents' ethnocentricity. For example, Henriette Burton, supervisor of home demonstration work, toured New Mexico's northern pueblos in 1931. The women's pottery impressed her, and she considered it a way for the women to make more money, but she nevertheless wondered if their "primitive methods" should be encouraged "or should modern methods be taught and modern equipment provided?" Burton failed to appreciate their centuries-old method of pottery making, which required a lot of hand polishing and several firings, and she did not understand that a faster method would produce an inferior result. When the agents were more understanding of local culture and the projects more appropriate, however, Pueblo and Navajo people responded enthusiastically. More than twelve hundred group meetings were held for Native Americans in New Mexico in 1934 and just over 2,000 in 1935. Unlike Hispanic and Anglo-American men, Pueblo and Navajo men often attended the meetings in equal numbers to the women.

Although ethnic differences were an important challenge for extension work, the sheer poverty of many western farm families was another. Many farm women were desperately poor by the AES' middle-class standards, so agents focused on projects like canning vegetables, which was labor intensive but produced large amounts of food and could be done with simple equipment (a large pot, tin can sealers, and glass jars) that could be purchased collectively and used cooperatively. For example, in 1932 agent Olive B. Cruse reported from the southwestern cattle-ranching region of New Mexico that "Mr. and Mrs. McCant had cans and equipment. Mr. and Mrs. Weatherby had meat and potatoes. They got together and had a 'canning bee' and divided the products." Elsewhere in the state in the summer of 1932, residents cooperatively canned 1,200 quarts of tomatoes, beets, and beans. A woman named Mrs. Lee contributed all of the tomatoes, so she was allowed to keep one-quarter of the total amount of canned food; the other workers received ten cans of vegetables for each day's work.

The AES started out as a well-intentioned but not always well-informed effort to improve the lives of rural families. The agents' abilities to adapt to local conditions often determined the service's success or failure in specific regions. Undoubtedly, the agents' efforts provided a great deal of useful information to farm women and men who could use it.

Rodeo cowgirls were the best-known image of rural women in the early twentieth century, but their experiences were certainly not typical. Most farm and ranch women spent their days keeping their families fed and clothed and did enough unpaid labor to keep their family's business going. In popular images of the West, white men are usually at the center of this story, but most farms and ranches thrived because of the labor of women. Tens of thousands of women also seized legal opportunities to have their own land. As a result, women in the West balanced a new kind of female independence with traditional gender roles, and the opportunities at hand with the very real economic constraints they faced as they entered the twentieth century. Many homesteading and ranching women were grateful for the opportunities and experiences they found in the West. As Katherine Fitzgerald Wetzel recalled of her years on the Frying Pan Ranch in Texas in the 1880s, "Those days on the ranch were busy ones, filled with labor, but also filled with that happiness that comes from an honest effort to make a living." And in 1887 Sarah Gatch wrote to her brother-in-law in Ohio from her home in Nebraska, "This is beautiful country, all I ask is good health and good crops and I am sure I can make myself satisfied."

Suggested Readings

Becker, Jack. "Mattie B. Morris Miller: Matriarch, Ranch Woman, and Benefactor." *West Texas Historical Association Year Book 2004* 80 (2004): 126–136.

Benton-Cohen, Katherine. "Common Purposes, Worlds Apart: Mexican-American, Mormon, and Midwestern Women Homesteaders in Cochise County, Arizona." *Western Historical Quarterly* 36, no. 4 (2005): 428–452.

Dykstra, Natalie A. "The Curative Space of the American West in the Life and Letters of Elinore Pruitt Stewart." *Portraits of Women in the American West,* edited by Dee Garceau-Hagen, pp. 208–230. New York: Routledge, 2005.

Harris, Katherine. "Homesteading in Northeastern Colorado, 1873–1920: Sex Roles and Women's Experience." In *The Women's West,* edited by Susan Armitage and Elizabeth Jameson, pp. 165–178. Norman: University of Oklahoma Press, 1987.

Katz, William Loren. *The Black West: A Documentary and Pictorial History of the African American Role in the Westward Expansion of the United States,* Rev. ed. New York: Harlem Moon, 2005.

MacMahon, Sandra Varney. "Fine Hands for Sowing: The Homesteading Experiences of Remittance Woman Jessie De Prado MacMillan." *New Mexico Historical Review* 74, no. 3 (July 1999): 271–294.

Montrie, Chad. "'Men Alone Cannot Settle a Country': Domesticating Nature in the Kansas-Nebraska Grasslands." *Great Plains Quarterly* 25 (Fall 2005): 245–258.

Moynihan, Ruth B., Susan Armitage, Christiane Fischer Dichamp, eds. *So Much To Be Done: Women Settlers on the Mining and Ranching Frontier.* Lincoln: University of Nebraska Press, 1990.

Riley, Glenda, and Richard W. Etulain, eds. *Wild Women of the Old West.* Golden, CO: Fulcrum Publishing, 2003.

Schackel, Sandra. *Social Housekeepers: Women Shaping Public Policy in New Mexico, 1920 to 1940.* Albuquerque: University of New Mexico Press, 1992.

Schweider, Dorothy, and Deborah Fink. "U.S. Prairie and Plains Women in the 1920s: A Comparison of Women, Family and Environment." *Agricultural History* 73, no. 2 (Spring 1999): 183–200.

Smith, Sherry L. "Single Women Homesteaders: The Perplexing Case of Elinore Pruitt Stewart." *Western Historical Quarterly* 22, no. 2 (May 1991): 163–183.

Taniguchi, Nancy. "Lands, Laws, and Women: Decisions of the General Land Office, 1881–1920, A Preliminary Report." *Great Plains Quarterly* 13 (Fall 1993): 223–236.

CHAPTER EIGHT

Women and Politics

Historians have paid a lot of attention to a single facet of western women's experiences: western states started giving women the right to vote in the late nineteenth century, while most women in the East had to wait until after the First World War. But western women's politics extended far beyond the suffrage campaign. Women were involved in all of the major national political issues of the day because those issues gave them a chance to try to change the world and free themselves from the common belief that women should have a limited place in public life and no role in formal politics. For example, the Women's National Indian Association (WNIA), discussed in chapter four, played a key role in national debates over the so-called "Indian Problem" in the late nineteenth century, and white women opposed to slavery moved to Kansas in the 1850s to help support the abolition movement in that key state. In the late nineteenth century western temperance activists campaigned to ban the production and sale of alcohol, and women brought their own unique spin to the fledgling conservation movement.

In addition to their involvement in these national issues, western women also participated in the club movement, in which tens of thousands of rural and urban women of all racial and ethnic groups organized around a wide range of local issues. A highly visible but very small minority of politically active western women got involved in populism and suffrage because they were frustrated with the constraints they faced in effecting all the other changes they wanted to see. In a world in which the word "politics" referred to the things that white male voters and politicians did, many western women insisted that they had a right to be heard on the local and national issues that mattered deeply to them.

Abolition

One of the first national political campaigns in which western women participated was the movement against slavery in the years before the Civil War. Some white women from the east became westerners in the 1850s and 1860s as a political statement, moving to Kansas to show their support for the "free soil" movement, which sought to prevent the extension of slavery into new states like Kansas. Slavery should have been illegal in Kansas because the 1820 Missouri Compromise had banned the institution in states west of the Mississippi River and north of Arkansas. But in 1854 the Kansas-Nebraska Act (an effort to defuse the growing tension between the North and the South) turned the question of whether Kansas would be a slave or free state over to the territory's voters, meaning that property-owning white males would make the decision. Violence erupted in Kansas as a result, and proslavery and antislavery supporters rushed to the territory in an effort to sway the outcome.

Many white female abolitionists (people who wanted to abolish slavery) from the East were among the newcomers. Ellen Goodnow wrote to her sister-in-law Harriet, who had refused to join her husband in Kansas, that the Goodnows' land was far enough from the Missouri state line to avoid the violence concentrated in that area. Ellen scolded Harriet for refusing to leave Rhode Island: "One thing I do believe I should not stand acquitted in the great day [of judgment], had I not been willing to join my husband in laboring for the freedom of this territory." Sara Robinson was another active supporter of the movement against slavery in Kansas. Proslavery militias arrested her husband Charles, one of the leaders of the antislavery forces, as he tried to leave Kansas in the summer of 1856 with a report on the violence in the territory. After his arrest, she carried the report east, toured New England to speak on the issue, and appeared at the Republican Party's state convention in Illinois. Her husband became the first governor of Kansas in 1861 when it became a state.

Kansas represented a battleground for both slavery and women's suffrage as early as the 1850s, because many of the same politically active women cared about both issues. Clarina I. H. Nichols, a journalist and speaker who was keenly interested in the suffrage movement, willingly subordinated that goal to the effort to keep slavery out of Kansas. She wrote that the "strong-minded" women of Kansas

> will be content to run bullets, transfer ammunition, and inspire their husbands and sons with hope, faith and courage, until public offices of honor and trust are redolent of domestic peace and quiet before they ask a share in their responsibilities. Yes, woman, self-denying now as in the past, is forgetting herself and her wrongs in the great national wrong that threatens to deprive the manhood of the nation of the right and the power to protect the altars and the hearths consecrated to God and humanity.

In 1859 Nichols presented a series of petitions to the Kansas constitutional convention demanding equal political and civil rights for women. The convention rejected the suffrage provision to avoid the possibility that Congress might use it to deny Kansas' application for statehood, but Nichols convinced delegates to let women vote in school elections, and she helped to secure legal protection for women's property rights and equal guardianship of children.

Temperance

The temperance movement, which wanted to stop the production and sale of alcohol, was also a national political campaign, like abolition, but it garnered the support of far more women. Temperance activists were one of the largest groups of politically active women in the nineteenth century, nationwide and in the West. The movement gave women a legitimate way to enter the male-dominated national political arena by arguing that a wasteful, violent, drunken husband and father directly affected them, their children, and their homes. As the respectable defenders of the home and family, they had to speak publicly. Alcohol abuse was a real problem across the West, to a much greater extent than in other parts of the nation. In 1888 California had roughly one saloon for every sixteen white men, and San Francisco was estimated to have at least thirty saloons for every church. The city had more than twice as many saloons per capita than New York or Chicago, and nine times as many as Boston and Philadelphia.

The key national organization was the Woman's Christian Temperance Union (WCTU), which was founded in New York in 1873. The first western chapter was established six years later in California and another in Oregon in 1881, reflecting the concentration of white women in those two states. National WCTU President Frances Willard encouraged many influential western women to get involved, including the Reverend Alice Barnes, who was the state treasurer, editor, and president of the Montana chapter. The WCTU spread rapidly across the West between 1880 and 1900, and members debated a range of issues in addition to temperance, including improving marriage and divorce laws for women, giving married women legal control of their own earnings, and higher salaries for teachers, most of whom were female.

WCTU tactics ranged from aggressive confrontation to public speeches and petitions. In cities like San Jose, California, and Portland, Oregon, temperance activists organized large numbers of women to sing and pray outside saloons. In the early years of the twentieth century, Carrie Nation of Kansas invaded taverns with a hatchet to destroy mirrors, glasses, bottles, and furniture. She attacked saloons in Topeka with help from other women, and often spent time in jail as a result. She also founded the Topeka temperance newspaper, the aptly named *Smashers Mail.*

Although WCTU president Willard wanted to reach out to women from all backgrounds, local chapters usually organized along racial, ethnic, and religious lines. In general, the organization was dominated by Anglo-Saxon, Protestant, middle-class women who lived in cities and towns. Some rural women took their own action against alcohol, however. For example, in January 1890, about a dozen Norwegian farm women attacked saloons in the town of Hatton, North Dakota. They used axes, hammers, and sticks to smash tables, windows, mirrors, bottles, and kegs. For immigrant women like these, preventing an alcoholic husband from losing their land was even more important than it was for Americans, because the immigrants had given up everything at home to come to the United States.

Most temperance activists in the West used less aggressive tactics. They attended meetings; read and wrote speeches, books, and pamphlets; and sang temperance songs. The women in Bismarck, North Dakota, who founded a WCTU local in 1882, concentrated their efforts on giving lectures, setting up reading rooms with material describing the horrors of alcohol, holding annual state conventions, and paying for a lobbyist at the state legislature. The Grand Forks, North Dakota, Scandinavian WCTU circulated petitions and pamphlets, put booklets in local jails, sponsored school essay contests, organized an enforcement league, and sent Christmas baskets to the families of alcoholics.

The WCTU did more than try to get men to stop drinking and lobby government authorities to stop the sale of alcohol; many locals also cared for working-class women and children. In Portland, Oregon, in the late 1880s, WCTU groups established a baby home, a women's exchange to sell goods made by women, and (as the women of the WNIA did for Native American women and girls; see chapter four) it founded an industrial home for women and girls that included a kindergarten, day nursery, and sewing school. Western WCTU activists were more successful in these areas than they were at stopping the sale and consumption of alcohol. That key failure highlighted the fact that women had no formal political power:

although western women were gradually gaining the right to vote at the state level, they would not gain the federal franchise until the nineteenth amendment was ratified in 1920. The political limitations of the temperance movement compelled many women to fight for the vote.

The Environment

A smaller number of women supported a third national movement, conservation, which originated in the West in the late nineteenth century. In many ways the modern American environmental movement began with the efforts to preserve the West's beauty; it is no accident that Yellowstone, which includes parts of Wyoming, Montana, and Idaho and was established in 1872, was the first national park created in the United States. Western women added a distinctive voice to that early effort in their roles as artists, scientists, and outdoorswomen. Some female conservationists used the widely shared belief that women were innately nurturing to justify their political activism on behalf of the environment. In 1911, the Mesquite Club formed in Las Vegas, Nevada, and started an ambitious tree-planting program. The club planted more than two thousand trees in one day through its "Town Beautiful" project. A year later the club's president, Mrs. Omer Maris, stated that "conservation is particularly a woman's job."

This way of thinking was particularly common among the women who wrote about and produced visual images of the West. For example, between 1901 and 1909, Sharlot Mabridth Hall wrote a series of articles, poems, and essays for the literary journal *Out West,* while also working as its associate editor. She called for the careful use of Arizona's mineral, water, and timber wealth, while simultaneously arguing that the territory was worthy of admission as a state because it had so many resources to offer. In a September 1910 letter to a friend, she described a three-month trip she had taken through northern and central Arizona: "

> I do enjoy everything—just the sunshine on the sand is beautiful enough to keep on giving thanks for eyes to see with. And all day long I'm so glad, so glad, so glad that God let me be an out-door woman and love the big things. I couldn't be a tame house cat woman…. I'm not unwomanly…but God meant woman to joy in his great, clean, beautiful world—and I thank Him that He lets me see some of it not through a window pane.

From 1909 to 1912 Hall was Arizona's territorial historian, a post that gave her more time and resources to research and write about Arizona's history. New Mexico's Mary Hunter Austin wrote frequently about the Southwest and published her first book, *The Land of Little Rain,* in 1903. She believed that the West gave women the chance to learn about Mother Earth and become keepers of the land. In her view, white women were sympathetic caretakers of the land, but white men were materialist and exploitative.

Female visual artists, such as photographers Maude Wilson, Annie W. Brigman, and Imogen Cunningham and painters Else Jemne, Mary Colton, and Mary Morgan, were even more influential than writers. Many Americans saw their photographs, paintings, and drawings in books, journals, newspapers, greeting cards, garden books, arts and crafts exhibits, stage shows, and commercial art like railroad company brochures. Female photographers needed the strength and stamina to deal with the large, heavy, awkward photography equipment of the era. And, like the women miners described in chapter six, these artists usually traded their long, impractical skirts for split skirts, bloomers (loose knee-length pants), or even men's trousers.

The handful of women scientists who studied the plants, animals, and geography of the West made up a second, very small group of women who actively participated in the early conservation movement. For example, Alice Eastwood was a botanist who moved from Denver to San Francisco in 1892 to join herbarium curator Katharine Brandegee at the California Academy of Sciences. In San Francisco, Eastwood pursued extensive field work, published her research, climbed Mount Whitney, and joined the Sierra Club, which had been founded in 1892 "to do something for wilderness and make the mountains glad." She was particularly keen to encourage Californians to plant native species.

Outdoorswomen were a third group of conservationists, and they usually focused on tree planting, preserving natural resources and animal species, promoting careful water use, and stopping industrial pollution. Virginia Donaghe McClurg, for instance, had explored the Mesa Verde, Colorado, cliff dwellings in the 1880s. In 1900, she approached the Colorado Federation of Women's Clubs to help her preserve this important archaeological site. After six years of lobbying, the clubwomen convinced Congress to pass legislation creating Mesa Verde National Park. During the early 1900s, rancher and rodeo performer Fanny Sperry Steele (see chapter seven) also worked as a hunter, outfitter, and guide in Montana's Blackfoot Valley. She developed an intense dislike of the male trophy hunters who just wanted animal heads for their walls.

Whether they had any other political goals, a lot of western women were attracted to the early conservation movement because they could often see the fragility of nature and the consequences of the rapid expansion of mining, farming, and ranching all around them. Additionally, many believed that they had a special awareness of that fragility and a special duty to help protect it because they were women.

The Club Movement

That same sense of duty drew even more women into the local clubs that were the main venues that most women used to try to change their worlds. Whereas thousands of women actively participated in highly visible campaigns like temperance, tens of thousands more were club members. Women's clubs focused on improving the lives of their members and their communities. They gave many women their first chance to step into the world of organized social and

political action and their first opportunity to change the world outside their own homes.

In 1838 the Protestant missionary Narcissa Whitman founded
what can be considered the first club for women in the Northwest,
the Columbia Maternal Association, which brought together a small
number of missionaries' wives to share reading material. They also
promised to care for each other's children if one of them died, a
provision that Narcissa's own murder showed to be a real concern.
Women founded two other early clubs in California and Idaho. The
San Francisco Ladies' Protection and Relief society was founded
in 1853 to "render protection and assistance to strangers, to sick
and dependent women and children." Within a year the society
had decided to open a home for "all respectable women in want of
protection, employment in families or as needlewomen." In 1864
women in Idaho City founded the Ladies' Mite Society, a benevo-
lent organization meant to help the poor in a booming mining town
north of what would become Boise.

Urban, Protestant white women founded most of the women's
clubs across the West, but rural white women had their own clubs,
which focused on issues relevant to their communities. For example,
the Ladies' Aid Society of Wichita, Kansas, struggled in the 1870s
to ease the widespread rural destitution caused by a combination of
factors ranging from drought to locusts. Male community leaders
opposed the club because they did not want the women to publicize
the area's problems, but the women still managed to get food, clothing, and money to the most destitute families. Seven newly arrived
women founded the Rupert Culture Club in Rupert, Idaho, in the
fall of 1905, and agreed that immigrant and Catholic women were
not welcome to join. The club committed itself to the cultural and
artistic advancement of Rupert, and one of its first accomplishments
was to get the state's traveling library to add Rupert to its schedule. The club organized a lecture series and an art exhibit, lobbied
for women's public restrooms, and sparked several other clubs in
the area. Broadening their focus, members also tried to eliminate

alcohol consumption and the sex trade, attacking the latter by personally informing all the women in the red light district that they had twenty-four hours to leave town or be arrested and fined. In 1909, Rupert and two neighboring towns passed legislation banning the sale of alcohol within town limits.

Like rural white women, black women also tended to form separate organizations, but this had more to do with the racism of the day than location. Black women were not welcome in most white women's clubs, and they often had different concerns. They, too, held raffles and bake sales to raise money for deserving causes, but they usually focused on providing services to black communities. Kansas was the first state to have a statewide federation of black women's clubs, formed in 1900. In 1904 women in Cheyenne, Wyoming, formed the Searchlight Club after white vigilantes lynched an African American man.

Denver, Colorado, had a particularly active group of black clubwomen, because it had one of the largest black communities in the West. A key leader in the late nineteenth century was Elizabeth Piper Ensley. She had taught at Howard University in Washington, D.C., and at Acorn University in Mississippi before she and her husband moved to Denver in the early 1890s. She was one of the founding members of the Woman's League of Denver, which local black women organized around 1894, and Denver's correspondent to the *Woman's Era,* the official journal of the National Association of Colored Women. In the June 9, 1894, issue of the *Woman's Era,* Ensley described the active role that black women had played in an election earlier that spring—the first time that women in Colorado had been allowed to vote. She noted the "special part…colored women have taken in the election. Most of them have done admirable work in the interest of the Republican party. They also formed clubs on their own and heroically helped their brothers to elect a representative to the legislature, although the majority of those brothers voted against women's enfranchisement." In 1904 Ensley founded the Colorado Association of Colored Women's Clubs.

Denver's African American clubwomen formed at least twenty-two clubs between 1900 and 1925, and four of them lasted until the end of the twentieth century. Sixteen-year-old Augustavia Young Stewart founded one such organization, the Pond Lily Art and Literary Club, in 1902. Angered by racist comments published in the local newspaper, she formed the young women's club to dispel racist stereotypes. The members focused on developing their talents to help create a better public opinion of African Americans. Seven of the Denver clubs joined to create the Negro Woman's Club Home Association, and they opened a new building in December 1916. Its original purpose was to be a dormitory and nursery for young black women and children, and it was run by a matron who enforced strict rules about behavior and cleanliness. In 1921 the Home had thirty children in the nursery and nine girls in the dorm, and it had added a health clinic. When the Young Women's Christian Association (YWCA) sponsored the construction of a dorm for black women in the 1920s, the Negro Woman's Club Home Association decided to close its dorm and turn the whole building into a nursery.

African American communities outside of Denver were typically a lot smaller, but black women did not let that stop them from forming strong and effective clubs. For example, the African American community in Albuquerque, New Mexico, represented only 1.6 percent of the state's population in the 1920s and 1930s. Yet middle-class black women in Albuquerque organized a handful of powerful clubs. Lula Black, a schoolteacher from Kentucky, started the Home Circle Club in 1914 to provide an outlet for the young, black, married middle-class women who did not work outside the home. The club focused on education and social responsibility, buying books about African Americans for the public library, for example, and creating a scholarship fund for college students.

Zenobia McMurry and several of her friends organized the Eureka Matrons Club in Albuquerque in 1934. McMurry had been born in Texas in 1909 but moved to Albuquerque in 1931. Unlike the Home Circle Club, which never expanded beyond Albuquerque, the Eureka Matrons had chapters in several other New Mexico cities. In its first year the club became a member of the state's Federation of Colored Women's Clubs, and in 1936 it joined the national organization. The Eureka Matrons Club focused on helping its members and other young African Americans in the city to improve their education. As McMurray wrote, "We were urged to go in and take courses in schools where we wouldn't have to be cooks and such in homes. And when our children came on—they didn't want to do those jobs anyway."

The Winona Art and Study Club in Albuquerque also put a high value on encouraging African American women's education and creativity. Florence Napoleon was one of twelve founding members in 1936. Born in Oklahoma in 1908, she had moved to Albuquerque with her husband and three children in 1935. She had taught elementary school in Oklahoma but was not able to get a teaching job in Albuquerque, so she turned to volunteer work, which she thought might unify white and black women. She believed that white and black women shared many of the same desires: "We can all relate to some things in our lives, if nothing [else], as mothers—we can all relate to that." The club's motto was "Let love and goodwill prevail; together we stand, divided we fail."

Hispanic and Native American women did not organize as many formal clubs as white and black women because their concerns and activities were usually more integrated into family, community, and religious structures. Hispanic women tended to focus on their families and their local Roman Catholic parish. For example, Anita Gonzalez Thomas, who descended from the earliest Spanish settlers in Santa Fe, New Mexico, noted that most Hispanics "are so involved with our own family and cousins and aunts and uncles and grandparents, etc." that they did not have as much time as Anglo women to participate in the club movement. She also thought that in Santa Fe the Anglo-American women's club membership stemmed from the fact that they were newcomers: "these Anglo women, they come, fall in love with Santa Fe, move here and one way to get to

know people is to volunteer to do all these things." Hispanic women
instead joined lay groups organized by the Catholic Church. Just
as Anglo-American clubwomen learned parliamentary procedures
and organizational techniques in their clubs, Hispanic women developed similar skills in church organizations such as the Young Ladies'
Sodality and the Altar Society. For example, Thomas was president
of the former group in 1936, where she learned parliamentary skills
and attended national conventions. These organizations also carried
out charity work, providing clothing to the needy and milk to school
children and establishing a health clinic in Santa Fe.

Women's clubs were the bedrock on which women's political
activism across the West was built. In small towns and big cities
alike, women organized to address a range of social and political
issues. The club movement was as divided by race, ethnicity, and
religion as the rest of the country, yet each club gave its members the
opportunity to learn basic organizational and political skills and the
chance to affect the world around them. As club members, women
learned how much they could accomplish if they worked together
but also the constraints that they faced because they were women.

Health Care

Western clubwomen also turned their energies to providing health
care in their communities. Large areas of the West had few doctors
and nurses, and many women believed that they had a special duty
to help care for their neighbors. The initiatives that health care activists promoted in the early twentieth century ranged from providing
better care for mothers and children in towns and cities to improving hygiene and medical practices on Native American reservations.
Their achievements often formed the basis for later government policies and organizations.

New Mexico offers good examples of both types of initiatives.
Public and private groups were concerned about health care because
the state was one of the poorest in the nation in the early twentieth

century. As a result, it had the highest rate of infant mortality in the nation in the late 1920s and 1930s, to give one example. In 1929, the first year for which the state compiled statistics, 140 babies died in their first year of life for every 1,000 born. This figure was more than twice the national rate of 61 per 1,000, and it continued to rise in the 1930s before dropping to 96 per 1,000 in 1940.

Local groups, including women's clubs, and state agencies like the Bureau of Public Health, made a concerted effort to address New Mexico's health problems in the 1920s and 1930s. The clubwomen's first major success was the state's establishment of the Child Welfare Service in 1919. Two years later they achieved a second major success, the creation of the Department of Public Welfare. These two arms of the state government provided some basic infrastructure to address the state's health-care woes.

The most important early funding for this infrastructure came from the Federal Maternity and Infancy Act, better known as the Sheppard-Towner Act (1921). Representative Jeannette Rankin of Montana (the first woman ever elected to the House of Representatives) had introduced the proposal in 1918, but there was little support for it until after the nineteenth amendment, granting women suffrage, was ratified, spurring Congress to address some of women's concerns. The Sheppard-Towner Act provided funding to set up public health centers, prenatal clinics, and hygiene and child welfare divisions in all the states, until Congress allowed the act to lapse in 1929. New Mexico received about $16,000, which it used to create programs to improve child and maternal health.

To administer the Sheppard-Towner funds, New Mexico merged its Child Welfare Service and Child Welfare Board into a new state Department of Public Welfare. The state required the new department's board to have at least two but no more than three women members, which reflected how rapidly the state's organized clubwomen had begun to flex their political muscles. Two of the first appointees were Bertha Nordhaus, a prominent Albuquerque clubwoman and former chair of the Child Welfare Service Board, and Adelina "Nina" Otero-Warren. The latter came from a leading Hispanic family in Santa Fe, was a longtime suffrage activist, school superintendent, future Republican candidate for the House of Representatives, and had served on the Board of Public Health since its founding 1919. The Department of Public Welfare created a new Bureau of Child Welfare and continued the Bureau of Public Health. By law, the director of Child Welfare was to be a woman with experience and training in child welfare work, a stipulation that recognized women's expertise in health and welfare.

New Mexico's health-care initiatives were not just taking place at the state level; some were as local and as important as a single clinic in a poor neighborhood. In October 1937, five women, Faith Meem, Peach Mayer, Mary Schmidt, Florence Davenport, and Mary Goodwin, established the free Maternal Health Center in Santa Fe, which had the fifth highest infant mortality rate in the nation at the time. The clinic was controversial because the founders used funds from national birth control activist Margaret Sanger's foundation to open the clinic in a mostly Catholic neighborhood. The Santa Fe women wanted to provide general health services for women and children, not simply or even primarily contraception, but that did not stop the Catholic Church from waging a heated campaign against the clinic. The campaign did not succeed, and the clinic soon became an indispensable part of the network of social services available in Santa Fe. It expanded to include prenatal, postnatal, and infant care classes, a unique home visit service, temporary and emergency medical care, and nursing consultation. In October 1938 the clinic had 577 patients enrolled as prenatal cases.

The clinic was run entirely by volunteers, the sole exception being the bilingual nursing director, Marjorie Stoll, RN. Board members, as well as local nurses and doctors, all donated their time and services. The first doctor to volunteer her time was Evelyn Fisher Frisbie, who came to the tiny clinic on Sundays, her one day off. A midwesterner who had moved to New Mexico in 1908, by 1911 she was a horse and buggy doctor, taking care of ranching communities within a 25-mile radius southwest of Las Vegas. She moved to Albu-querque in 1911 and became the first female president of the New Mexico Medical Society in 1915.

Six months after the clinic opened, the Sanger foundation with-drew its funding on the grounds that not enough birth control work was being done. A nine-woman finance committee raised enough money to keep the clinic open for another year and held regular fundraisers thereafter. The clinic's annual rummage sale became so popular that it evolved into a permanent thrift shop in 1947. Found-ing member Peach Mayer recalled, "We never asked for nor received any public funds—federal, state or county—but paid our bills from generous contributions and the rummage sales!"

Another New Mexico group focused its attention on improving health care for the state's Native American communities. In 1922 a group of female and male middle- and upper-class Anglo-Ameri-cans, most of whom were new arrivals in the state, founded the New Mexico Association on Indian Affairs (NMAIA) in Santa Fe, and its female members focused particularly on public health issues. Legally, the Bureau of Indian Affairs (BIA) was responsible for the health and welfare of Native Americans, but the BIA's efforts were sporadic, underfunded, often ineffective, and more focused on taking care of sick people than preventing disease. BIA field matrons who hap-pened to have some nursing skills provided the only care available on most reservations. As a result, many did not have enough health care personnel, a lack that compounded other problems, such as extreme poverty and poor sanitation. In New Mexico in the 1920s, malnutrition, tuberculosis, and a highly infectious eye disease called trachoma were all widespread among the Pueblo peoples.

By the 1920s the BIA began to recognize the value of having trained medical professionals working in the field. The NMAIA seized this opportunity in 1924 and, with the tacit approval of the BIA, began an experimental field nursing program among several northern New Mexican pueblos. In the spring of 1925 the NMAIA sent Elizabeth Duggan, a former Santa Fe County nurse, to Zuni

Pueblo, where conditions were unusually bad and the BIA-appointed doctor and agent unusually indifferent. Backed by Duggan's reports, the NMAIA appealed to the BIA to replace the underperforming employees. Duggan spent three years at Zuni and made significant headway in improving local people's health. The BIA then hired her to be the nursing supervisor for the whole Southwest. Augustine Stoll, a Red Cross nurse, started working at San Juan Pueblo in the spring in 1926. Her program to train Native girls to be nursing assistants was so successful that it expanded to other pueblos. At San Ildefonso Pueblo, Stoll established a laundry and bath house that became models for other pueblos.

In 1930 the NMAIA sent two more nurses to the Navajo reservation, Elizabeth Forster to the settlement at Red Rock and Molly Reebel to Nava. Both women lived a nomadic lifestyle, following the Navajo in their traditional seasonal round, because they recognized that they could only introduce better health-care practices and treat the sick effectively by keeping up with the temporary camps. Forster had been head of the Visiting Nurse Association in Colorado Springs, Colorado, for seventeen years and was ready for a new challenge. She and her partner, photographer Laura Gilpin, had taken a camping tour through the Navajo reservation, and the people had made a deep impression on both women. When Forster heard that the NMAIA was looking for a nurse to work in Red Rock, she applied eagerly and started the job in October 1930. In December she reported that she had already held four health-care clinics, treated 138 patients with everything from appendicitis and frostbite to tuberculosis and trachoma, and delivered one baby. She also coached a basketball team, assisted with funerals, dispensed legal advice, and organized Christmas parties. Her annual report for 1932 stated that although the government had sent extra food for Christmas, most of it was spoiled "and the poor Navajos who traveled thru the cold and snow were sadly disappointed." Forster invited ten residents for dinner and twenty more to socialize around her Christmas tree, "but found myself receiving some forty-odd" guests.

Forster was happy that the Navajos seemed eventually to accept her:

> When I came here…I soon realized that the Navajos hereabouts expected to find me antagonistic to their religious customs and were slow to consult me about illness until the medicine man had failed to help, but gradually they are showing more confidence in my good will and often notify me that they are having a sing [a healing ceremony] and invite me to attend. Sometimes I am invited to practice medicine with the medicine man, sometimes I am asked to wait until the conclusion of the sing so as to be on hand to take the patient to the hospital. I am surprised and gratified to find my medicine men friendly and often cooperative.

Determined to fit in without being presumptuous or condescending, she was able to laugh at herself and some of her "civilized" ways that were clearly inappropriate in the Navajo world. Unfortunately, her willingness to work with the traditional healers instead of challenging them led the BIA to fire her in 1933. The NMAIA hoped to keep her and her skills in New Mexico, just at another location, but BIA officials refused to provide any support for her work so Forster returned to Colorado Springs.

After July 1934, Navajo nurse's aides were available to assist the field nurses. Commissioner of Indian Affairs John Collier hired Elinor Gregg, the BIA supervisor of nurses, to organize a four-week nurse training institute in Santa Fe for young Navajo women. Ninety-six Navajo women attended, ranging in age from fifteen to thirty-five. The main purpose was learning how to treat trachoma by washing affected eyes daily, but the institute also included instruction in infant care and family hygiene. Unfortunately, this effort to train nurse's aides was not repeated, as the 1935 clinic focused instead on teaching "future wives, mothers, and neighbors" how to "prevent sickness, and promote health."

In 1935 the BIA took over the field nursing program completely and incorporated some of the changes and innovations that New

Mexico's female health care reformers had developed. By the mid-1930s, some of the nurses who had worked for private agencies like the NMAIA or public agencies like the Red Cross held influential positions with the BIA nursing administration and implemented some of the New Mexico nurses' more successful field experiments. The BIA maintained programs like the mobile dispensaries that Reebel and Forster had established among the Navajo sheep camps; Duggan's sanatorium for tubercular children at Zuni and new wells that provided better drinking water; and Stoll's laundry and bathing facilities and her program for training young Indian women as nurse assistants.

These examples from New Mexico are a microcosm of the kinds of health-care initiatives that women across the West launched in their communities. Although they were more successful than many other politically active women in terms of getting their reforms recognized and even enshrined in government policy, even then they had to recognize that those political successes depended on the goodwill of male politicians.

The Grange, the Farmers' Alliance, and Populism

The organizations discussed above had tens of thousands of women members in the West, but the women were not always able to achieve everything they wanted because they did not have the right to vote. Without this right, they had no formal voice in government, where men determined policies and budgets. As a result, some women realized that they had to step into the world of male-dominated political action. For rural women, taking that step often led to the National Grange of the Patrons of Husbandry (commonly called the Grange) or the Farmers' Alliance. Farmers on the Great Plains founded the Grange in the 1860s, and Southern white farmers founded the Alliance in the 1870s. Both groups had three clear goals. First, they wanted to improve the social and economic conditions of farm families by changing the financial system, which made it hard for farmers to prosper but easy for banks to foreclose on them. Second, they wanted to change the transportation system, which made it cheaper for eastern manufacturers to ship their goods to the West than for western farmers to send their goods to the East. Finally, they wanted to make rural life more appealing so that fewer daughters and sons left the farm for the city. From the outset the Grange and the Alliance welcomed women members, recognized women's contributions to farming, and were at least theoretically committed to sexual equality.

Women were far more involved at all levels of the Grange and the Alliance than Democratic or Republican women were in their parties during this period. Their contributions included the stereotypical feminine work of organizing and supplying the social functions that kept the farmers' organizations active, but many of the women members also began to find their own strong political voices. These activists worked with men on issues important to rural communities as a whole, not just rural women. Men certainly dominated the leadership, but women were active participants and officers. For example, in March 1895 the Lewis County, Washington, Alliance newsletter *The People's Advocate* reported that at one recent meeting "the ladies were even more enthusiastic than the gents." The main speaker at the county Alliance picnic in Toledo, Washington, in August 1895 was Mary Hobart. An *Advocate* reporter labeled her "one of America's brainiest women" because of her discussion of finances. Hattie Antrim and her husband joined the Hope Grange in Lewis County in 1904, when she was fifty-six. She made or seconded many motions over the years and served on many committees. In 1910 the county Grange elected her to office.

The Grange and the Alliance were not able to change the banking and transportation systems because of the power of these industries, so they knew that they had to move away from informal persuasive efforts and into formal electoral politics. Some of the locals worked with the Democratic and Republican parties at the state level, but in 1891 the Grange and the Alliance took the important step of working with urban working-class activists to create the People's Party (commonly known as the Populists). Women played a role in every stage of this transformation of regional farmers' organizations into a national political party, and some gained a new regional and national prominence with the Populists. For example, Luna Kellie of Nebraska had joined the first Farmers' Alliance in her area in the 1870s while raising her eleven children. She was an editor, secretary, bookkeeper, and speaker for the Alliance, and then threw her considerable energy behind the Populists. She wrote several Populist songs and edited the party's newspaper, *Prairie Home.*

Similarly, Mary Elizabeth Lease of Kansas, a former homesteader, became a charismatic speaker for the Alliance and then the Populists, giving more than a hundred and sixty speeches in 1890 alone. In a speech to the WCTU that year, she reportedly said that the "gray old world" was beginning "to dimly comprehend that there is no difference between the brain of an intelligent woman and the brain of an intelligent man" and that a golden age of justice for all was approaching thanks to movements like temperance and the Farmers' Alliance. Her most famous statement was that Kansas farmers should "raise less corn and more hell." In 1893 Kansas elected a Populist legislature and governor, who appointed Lease director of the state board of charities. In 1896, when the Populists merged with the Democratic Party to try to improve their chances in the upcoming national election, Lease opposed the merger and became a Progressive Republican to continue her work on behalf of women's suffrage.

Some women even ran as Populist candidates for public office. Ella Knowles of Montana had already successfully lobbied for a woman's right to practice law in the state and was the state's first female lawyer before she ran for state attorney general in 1892. She lost to a Republican, Henri Haskell, but he appointed her the first female assistant state attorney general in the United States. They married in 1895 but divorced a few years later. Knowles went on to be a prominent lawyer for the state's mining interests.

While the Populists gave some women a taste of the power of a formal political organization, women's participation in the party also highlighted the limits of their influence. Women could run as Populist candidates in some states, but they still did not have the right to vote in national elections. By the late nineteenth century, a small number of western women were no longer willing to accept this constraint.

Electoral Politics and the Suffrage Movement

Like the Populists, many politically active women turned to electoral politics when they realized that their inability to vote or be elected to office severely limited their ability to enact the changes they wanted. Most of these women did not want to overhaul the political system radically; they just wanted the right to speak publically and be heard on issues that affected their homes and families. Nebraska's Luna Kellie started thinking about involving herself in politics when men who did not have school-age children tried to shorten the local school year to reduce taxes. Kellie realized that she and other mothers of small children were hampered by the fact that they could not vote on the issue. "Right then I saw for the first time that a woman might be interested in politics and want a vote. I had been taught it was unwomanly to concern oneself with politics and that only the worst class of women would ever vote if they had a chance etc etc but now I saw where a decent mother might wish very much to vote on local affairs at least." Her husband and her father supported her and helped promote the legislation that eventually allowed Nebraska women to vote in local school board elections. Her husband also encouraged her to pursue further political action.

The fact that most western women could vote long before the nineteenth amendment enfranchised most women nationwide distinguished the westerners' formal political behavior from that of most women in other regions. Thirteen of the fifteen states that had enacted women's suffrage laws before World War I were west of the Mississippi River. Wyoming and Utah were the first to do so, in 1869 and 1870. Colorado was next (1893), then Idaho (1896), Washington (1910), and California (1911). Arizona, Kansas, and Oregon gave women the vote in 1912, and Montana and Nevada did so in 1914.

Women usually achieved suffrage in the West because of a combination of two things: women demanded it and male politicians granted it for reasons that usually had little to do with women's rights. In Wyoming, for instance, New York–born Esther Hobart Morris told William H. Bright in 1869 that she would support his campaign for the territorial legislature if he would support a women's suffrage bill once elected. Bright's wife was also a suffragist, and he kept his promise after he won his seat. In December 1869 Wyoming passed a bill allowing women twenty-one years of age and older to vote and hold political office. Territorial Governor John Wesley Hoyt later recalled, "Of course the women were astounded! If a whole troop of angels had come down with flaming swords for their vindication, they would not have been much more astonished than they were when that bill became a law and the women of Wyoming were thus clothed with the habiliments of citizenship." Given that there were barely a thousand non-Native American women over the age of ten in the territory, Wyoming's action was a way to advertise the state and attract more white women. A writer for the national magazine *Harper's Weekly* took this more cynical view when he quipped, "Wyoming gave women the right to vote in much the same spirit that New York or Pennsylvania might vote to enfranchise angels or Martians."

In March 1870 the first female jurors sat in a Laramie courtroom; the first Wyoming election in which women could vote occurred in September. Fifty-seven-year-old Esther Hobart Morris became the first female justice of the peace. Not until 1910, however, would Mary Godot Bellamy become the first woman to be elected to the Wyoming legislature. In 1924 Wyoming set another record when it elected the first female governor of the nation, Nellie Tayloe Ross (discussed below).

No women demanded the right to vote in Utah in 1870, but the Mormon-dominated legislature and Mormon leaders had strong reasons to give it to them. With the completion of a transcontinental railroad near their territory in 1869 and the enactment of new antipolygamy legislation in Congress, Utah gave women the right to vote to protect Mormon society and plural marriage and counter the public impression that Mormon women were slaves. Public criticism of Mormonism escalated sharply in the 1860s. Utah's territorial government wanted to do something to show that Mormon women had more rights than the rest of the nation believed and increase the number of pro-Mormon voters. The federal government abolished women's suffrage in Utah in 1887 as part of a legislative attack on polygamy and Mormonism, and women in the state did not regain the vote until 1895.

More than twenty years after the enfranchisement of women in Wyoming and Utah, Colorado became the third state to grant women's suffrage in 1893. Other western states followed eventually. A new generation of skilled, articulate leaders who fought to overcome the objections of male legislators won these later victories. Abigail Scott Duniway of Oregon was one of the most influential suffragists of her generation. An agrarian reformer and an ardent Oregon booster before she committed herself to the cause of suffrage, she also called for equal economic and property rights for women, divorce reforms, shared responsibility for housework and child care, and better education for women. She started a women's rights newspaper, *The New Northwest,* in 1871 when she was thirty-six, after witnessing the vicious press coverage national suffrage leader Susan B. Anthony endured during her 1871 tour of the Pacific Northwest. Duniway decided that if suffrage was to stand a chance in Oregon, it needed a press of its own to defend against the personal attacks so often aimed at suffragists. She wanted to use *The New Northwest* to raise readers' consciousness and motivate them to act politically on their convictions, not just convert them to the cause. Activists proposed the first women's suffrage amendment in Oregon in 1884 but opponents defeated it, along with the next four attempts. *The New*

Northwest was published until 1887, but women did not get the vote in Oregon until 1912.

Another leading western suffragist and journalist was Clara Bewick Colby, who established the *Woman's Tribune* in Beatrice, Nebraska, in 1883. Born in England in 1846, she was eight years old when her family moved to Wisconsin. In 1869 she became one of the first women to graduate from a coeducational class at the University of Wisconsin. She wanted to be a journalist, but no major newspaper would hire a woman for the job. When she and her husband moved to Nebraska, she finally got her start by writing regularly for the *Western Women's Journal,* a prosuffrage paper published in Lincoln. In 1881 she became vice president of the newly formed Nebraska Woman Suffrage Association, and in 1883 she became the first editor and publisher of its official newspaper, the *Women's Tribune.* She published the paper for twenty-six years, making it into one of the leading papers for the suffrage movement. In May 1885, national suffrage activist Elizabeth Cady Stanton said the *Woman's Tribune* was the best suffrage paper ever published.

Colby insisted that suffrage and equality for women were moral rights in a democratic society. She wanted to connect with readers who were already suffragists, but she also wanted to reach out to other women. The newspaper did not focus primarily on suffrage at first but instead discussed all aspects of women's lives, publishing articles on law, literature, political science, household hints, and children, as well as dozens of original poems, many of them written by Nebraska women. She also ran news items, petitions, speeches, constitutions, and resolutions from suffrage organizations across the United States and around the world. She challenged the argument that women did not deserve to vote because they could not join the military by pointing out that "aged, infirm men" who had to be "carried to the polls to vote" could not fight either. She never argued that women should get the right to vote because they would civilize society, the common suffragist argument at the time, instead insisting that women should have the right because they were human beings living in a democracy. Colby was determined that "women should have something to say about…the laws they live under." She accepted only educational advertising and never raised the subscription price from a dollar a year. She died in 1916.

In most states suffrage leaders worked with other women's groups to convince male legislators to support women's right to vote. They formed alliances with middle-class women's clubs, women in labor unions, and the WCTU, although alliances with the latter could be dangerous. Duniway, for example, cautioned against working too closely with temperance advocates because she knew that suffrage would lose every time if male voters believed that a vote for women's rights was a vote against the right to drink.

Success came slowly and unevenly. Women in Colorado formed the first territorial suffrage organization in Denver in 1876 to try to convince the territorial constitutional convention to guarantee women's suffrage in the new state. The convention voted against the amendment twenty-four to eight, but women gained some concessions. The state constitution granted them the right to vote in school elections and be elected to school district offices, and scheduled a referendum on the suffrage question in 1877. The Denver prosuffrage community shifted into high gear to prepare for the October 1877 referendum. Its members spent months organizing rallies and petitions and finding prominent guest speakers, but they still lost, 14,053 to 6,612. The mainstream press accused the women of unladylike behavior, and the suffragists realized that most of the women in the state were not yet ready for such a big change.

Colorado suffragists spent the next sixteen years changing people's minds gradually and working with other political organizations, including the WCTU and literary clubs. In 1879, Denverite Caroline Nichols Churchill started publishing a monthly suffrage paper called the *Colorado Antelope,* dedicating it to the "interests of humanity, woman's political equality and individuality." The state's WCTU elected as its president the prominent suffrage leader Mary Shields in 1880. In the late 1880s, working-class women in Denver also began pushing for suffrage through the organized labor movement. In 1887, Albina Washington began editing a "Woman's Column" for the *Labor Enquirer.* By the early 1890s, all these groups of organized women, including the middle-class WCTU and clubwomen and working-class women, came together in a renewed statewide suffrage movement. Part of their new motivation came from the creation of the People's Party in 1891 and its support for women's rights. Colorado held another suffrage referendum in 1893, and on November 7 Colorado women finally won the right to vote.

In Montana the suffrage campaign began relatively late, in 1895, at the instigation of the Helena Suffrage Club. In 1896 Montana Populist attorney Ella Knowles succeeded in putting a women's suffrage plank into the Populist state platform, and in 1897 she carried a petition bearing 3,000 names supporting women's suffrage to the Montana legislature. Not until 1914, however, did Montana give women the right to vote. Just three years later that state elected Jeanette Rankin as the first woman to the House of Representatives.

Few black women participated in western suffrage campaigns, because the racial oppression they shared with black men was a bigger problem than the gendered oppression they shared with white women. The African American women who did get involved with suffrage included activists like Naomi Anderson of Kansas, an official representative of the National American Woman's Suffrage Association in the West who played an active role in campaigns in Kansas in 1894 and California in 1896. In California she was able to garner the support of the Afro-American Women's League. Another black suffragist was Sarah M. Overton, a leader in suffrage organizations in San Jose, California, for many years who toured the state in 1911 to organize black support for a suffrage amendment. Unlike white women, who often focused exclusively on the right to vote, black suffragists always connected women's rights with the broader campaign for racial equality. Their work is a reminder that the West, a region often equated with freedom in the national mythology, was also for a long time a place of inequality for anyone who was not white and male.

Women in Public Office

Long before women got the state or federal franchise, western women actively participated in local electoral politics and served in a variety of local, county, and state positions. For example, Olive Pickering Rankin, Jeannette Rankin's mother, was the only woman on the school board in Missoula, Montana, for many years, and in 1908 Grace Reed Porter of South Dakota was elected county superintendent by a significant margin. Kansas and Arizona were particularly favorable to female politicians.

Kansas' unusual support for local women politicians in the 1880s may have grown out of the work of antislavery and women's rights activists in the 1850s. In January 1887, the town of Argonia elected the first female mayor in the United States, Susanna Madora Salter. A few months later, Syracuse, Kansas, elected an all-female town council. The five women were Caroline E. Barber, Sarah M. Coe, Mary E. Riggles, Hanna D. Nott, and Lizzie M. Swartwood. A year later, the local newspaper had to admit that the council had turned Syracuse into a city "renowned" for its "good government, good morals, [and] fine streets." None of the women ran for re-election in 1888, apparently having decided that they had made their point about women's abilities. In November 1887, Hamilton County (for which Syracuse became the center) elected its first female county school superintendent, Elizabeth Culver. She was single when she was first elected, and she refused to step down when she got married or when she was pregnant with her first child. Public opposition grew so intense, however, that she resigned in 1890. The next female candidate in the county was Sarah Catharine Warthen, an unmarried homesteader and teacher. She won the race for school superintendent by a bigger majority than any of the male officials elected that year. She served two terms, from 1891 to 1894, and kept her campaign promise to be a full-time administrator while also working as a journalist and notary public. In March 1894, she became the first woman admitted to the county bar and married a few months later. No women occupied public offices in the state for several years after that, and women did not get the state franchise until 1912.

As the example of Kansas demonstrates, a high level of local political activity among women did not necessarily translate into political gains for them, and in most western states women's enfranchisement did not quickly translate into female politicians' being elected at a state or national level. One of the exceptions was Arizona, where women won the vote in 1912 and turned a unique combination of circumstances into electoral success. Frances Willard Munds and Pauline O'Neill had led the campaign for suffrage in the summer of 1912. They built a remarkable coalition that included organized labor, the state Progressive Party, and Mormon voters. The women's campaign was so successful that 68 percent of the male voters supported the constitutional amendment enfranchising women, the largest margin of victory for suffrage in the nation at the time.

Munds and O'Neill lost little time launching their own political careers, and in 1914 Munds became the first woman to serve in the Arizona Senate. She and other women elected to the Arizona legislature proved very effective. They introduced more bills on average than men in the House and had higher success rates. From 1914 to 1928, 38 percent of all female-sponsored bills passed both houses, compared to an overall average of 30 percent. The list of legislation that women sponsored included a range of education and schooling initiatives; health and welfare issues; creating institutions for disabled children and delinquent girls; establishing a minimum wage for women; and legal reforms like prohibition and raising the age at which a person could legally marry.

There were four main reasons why Arizona women were more successful than other western women at getting elected and then being effective in the legislature. First, many Arizonans thought that women in public office would correct the state's wild and lawless image. In the early twentieth century most Americans believed white women had an innate ability to "civilize" their communities, and Arizonans thought that a more "civilized" state might be able to attract more newcomers and investment. Second, a significantly higher proportion of Arizona's female legislators before 1940 were born or raised in the West (63 percent compared to only 25 percent of male legislators and 17 percent of the state's population as a whole). Unlike their male competitors, then, female candidates were more likely to be able to campaign as "real" westerners who truly understood the state's needs. Third, a high proportion of the women politicians already worked outside the home for wages and were comfortable in the male-dominated world. Seventy-five percent of the women in the legislature also worked as teachers, clerical workers, attorneys, or business owners, a figure well above the average for female legislators in other states. The fourth reason why Arizona women had electoral and legislative success is that, with nearly twice the national average of widows in the state, mothers who had to work outside the home were more common and socially acceptable than in many other western states. Nearly 25 percent of the women in the legislature had young children when they first ran for office, but Arizona's unique circumstances meant that they were not judged as harshly (that is, as "unwomanly" or as "unfit mothers"), as they would have been in many other places.

In addition to these early suffrage and legislative successes, the first woman in Congress and the first woman governor were westerners. Jeannette Rankin of Montana was elected to the House of Representatives in 1917 and served until 1919; she was elected again in 1941 and served until 1943. A pacifist, she was the only member of Congress to vote against U.S. participation in both world wars. Nellie Tayloe Ross became governor of Wyoming in 1924 when her husband, William Bradford Ross, the Democratic governor of the state, died one month before the mid-term elections. Because he died so close to the elections, Wyoming law required that an election be held for someone to complete the last two years of his term. Supporters encouraged Nellie to run. She stayed home and let her friends and supporters campaign for her, yet she won by more than 8,000 votes, largely because of sympathy from Wyoming voters.

Ross carried on her husband's policies, then lost the 1926 election by just over 1,300 votes. In 1933 President Roosevelt appointed her director of the Bureau of the Mint, a job that she held for the next twenty years.

Nina Otero-Warren's 1922 campaign as a Republican candidate for the House of Representatives was not successful, but it set an important precedent. Not only was she the first woman from New Mexico to run for a federal office, but also she was the first Hispanic woman to do so anywhere in the United States. A key Hispanic leader in New Mexico's campaign for female suffrage, she was appointed Santa Fe's school superintendent in 1917, and in the 1920s she was active in the state's health-care movement. Otero-Warren's campaign suffered when it turned out that she was divorced, not a widow, as she had claimed. Although she won in four out of five Hispanic counties, she lost in counties with Anglo-American majorities. Another Hispanic woman, an Albuquerque Democrat named Soledad Chávez de Chacón, was successful in the 1922 election, becoming the first female secretary of state for New Mexico. Whereas Otero-Warren ran as an independent woman with a strong record as a political activist and officeholder, de Chacón emphasized her family ties and was listed on the ballot as "Mrs. Ed Chacón."

Native American women started to get involved in formal politics in the 1930s, thanks to the 1934 Indian Reorganization Act (IRA), and like white women, they earned their earliest electoral successes at the local level. The IRA (discussed in more detail in chapter ten) allowed Native American tribes to organize their own governments after the BIA approved a tribal constitution. Commissioner of Indian Affairs John Collier insisted that the new constitutions include provisions for female suffrage and office-holding, whether or not a tribe had traditionally included women in the formal political process. After the IRA passed, delegations to Washington, D.C., to discuss tribal organization began to include women. In 1935, for example, Irene Meade and two men comprised a Shoshone delegation, and in 1938, the six-person delegation from the Standing Rock

Reservation in South Dakota included three women: Josephine Kelly, Mary Long Chase, and Mary M. Wounds. Between 1935 and 1940, Native Americans elected women to at least fifteen tribal councils. Irene Meade and Josephine Kelly both became members of their respective tribal councils, and Kelly chaired hers in the 1940s. The fourteen-member council of the Colville Reservation in Washington State included two women, Florence Quill and Grace Coil, as did the Ute Mountain Council, on which Aileen Hatch and Emma South served.

Although women's participation in these councils and electoral processes may have been new, they were usually chosen for a traditional reason: they were already well known in their communities for their longstanding service to their people. Sarah Snipe, the first woman on the Fort Hall, Idaho, Business Council, is a good example. Born in 1895, she was a member of the Bannock tribe, and by the 1930s she was a grandmother. She had attended the Fort Hall boarding school and the Sherman Institute (discussed in chapter four), and throughout her life combined traditional and new activities and skills. She and her husband were well acquainted with modern business practices, as they operated a 240-acre farm with seventy-five cattle in addition to horses and poultry. She was quoted in 1940 in the BIA's magazine *Indians at Work* as saying, "It is our children's future that we should be interested in and not our own selfish interests. If we expect our children to make a living for themselves, we must help them."

With these words, Sarah Snipe summed up the reason why so many women became (and are today) politically active: to make the world a better place for future generations. Whereas most of the accomplishments discussed in this chapter resulted from women working together toward that better future, other women learned that sometimes all it took was a single voice. For example, in 1885 the San Francisco Board of Education barred eight-year-old Mamie Tape from attending her local elementary school because she was Chinese. Her mother, Mary Tape, attacked their decision, asking whether it was "a disgrace to be born Chinese? Didn't God made us all!!!" She continued, "I suppose, you all goes to churches on Sunday! Do you call that a Christian act to compel my little children to go so far to a school that is made in purpose for them." Mary stressed that her children were assimilated; they didn't "dress like the other Chinese," and "if I had any wish to send them to a Chinese school I could have sent them two years ago without going to all this trouble. You have expended a lot of the Public money foolishly, all because of a one poor little Child." Mary emphasized that her daughter's playmates were all "Caucasians" and had been "ever since she could toddle around," so why was Mamie "good enough to play with them" but not "good enough to be in the same room and studie" with them? Mary suggested that the board members visit her home to see that the Tape family was the "same as other Caucasians, except in features." She observed: "It seems no matter how a Chinese may live and dress so long as you know they Chinese. Then they are hated as one. There is not any right or justice for them." Mary closed her letter by noting that her daughter was already "more of an American" than the prejudiced board members.

Then Mary and her husband Joseph sued the San Francisco Board of Education and won. In his ruling the judge said that "to deny a child, born of Chinese parents in this state, entrance to the public schools would be a violation of the law of the state and the Constitution of the United States." The city evaded the ruling by setting up a separate school for Chinese children in Chinatown, to contain them there and prevent them from trying to get into "white" schools. Mary Tape's victory was partial, as so many of women's political victories were across the West, but the ruling was still a dramatic early victory for the rights of Chinese Americans in California, and it demonstrates how much one angry woman could accomplish when she had the courage to speak up.

Very few western women got involved in politics with the goal of fundamentally transforming women's roles. Indeed, they tended to use the language of appropriate femininity and domesticity to express their ambitions, and most of them focused their attention on practical, relatively respectable goals. They wanted to end the injustice of slavery, protect themselves and their families from the dangers of alcoholism, and preserve the beauty around them for future generations. They wanted to improve the social and economic lives of their communities, in the shape of a library for their children, trees in a town park, a health clinic for mothers and babies, or a fair deal for farmers. Only a minority wanted to expand the parameters of what it meant to be a woman. Together, the majority and the minority wound up dramatically reshaping the political landscape of the West and the nation through their activities.

Suggested Readings

Anderson, Karen. *Changing Woman: A History of Racial-Ethnic Women in Modern America.* New York: Oxford University Press, 1996.

de Graaf, Lawrence B. "Race, Sex and Region: Black Women in the American West, 1850–1920." *Pacific Historical Review* 49, no. 2 (May 1980): 285–313.

Dickson, Lynda F. "Lifting as We Climb: African American Women's Clubs of Denver 1880–1925." In *Writing the Range: Race, Class, and Culture in the Women's West,* edited by Elizabeth Jameson and Susan Armitage, pp. 372–392. Norman: University of Oklahoma Press, 1997.

Etcheson, Nicole. "'Labouring for the Freedom of this Territory': Free-State Kansas Women in the 1850s." *Kansas History* 21, no. 2 (Summer 1998): 68–87.

Handy-Marchello, Barbara. "Land, Liquor and the Women of Hatton, North Dakota." *North Dakota History* 59, 4 (Fall 1992): 223–231.

Heider, Carmen. "Adversaries and Allies: Rival National Suffrage Groups and the 1882 Nebraska Woman Suffrage Campaign." *Great Plains Quarterly* 25 (Spring 2005): 87–103.

Irwin, Mary Ann. "'Going About and Doing Good': The Politics of Benevolence, Welfare, and Gender in San Francisco, 1850–1880." *Pacific Historical Review* 68, no. 3 (1999): 365–397.

Jensen, Joan. *One Foot on the Rockies: Women and Creativity in the Modern American West.* Albuquerque: University of New Mexico Press, 1995.

Lomicky, Carol. "Frontier Feminism and the Woman's Tribune: The Journalism of Clara Bewick Colby." *Journalism History* 28, no. 3 (Fall 2002): 102–111.

Mackey, Mike. "Nellie Tayloe Ross and Wyoming Politics." *Journal of the West* 42, no. 3 (Summer 2003): 3–25.

Moss, Rosalind Urbach. "The 'Girls' from Syracuse: Sex Role Negotiations of Kansas Women in Politics, 1887–1890." In *The Women's West,* edited by Susan Armitage and Elizabeth Jameson, pp. 253–264. Norman: University of Oklahoma Press, 1987.

Osselaer, Heidi. *Winning Their Place: Arizona Women in Politics 1883–1950.* Tucson: University of Arizona Press, 2009.

Pascoe, Peggy. *Relations of Rescue: The Search for Female Moral Authority in the American West, 1874–1939.* New York: Oxford University Press, 1991.

Riley, Glenda. "'Wimmin Is Everywhere': Conserving and Feminizing Western Landscapes, 1870 to 1940." *Western Historical Quarterly* 29, no. 1 (Spring 1998): 4–23.

———. "Victorian Ladies Outdoors: Women in the Early Western Conservation Movement, 1870–1920." *Southern California Quarterly* 83, no. 1 (2001): 59–80.

Salas, Elizabeth. "Ethnicity, Gender, and Divorce: Issues in the 1922 Campaign by Adelina Otero-Warren for the U.S. House of Representatives." *New Mexico Historical Review* 70, no. 4 (October 1995): 367–382.

Schackel, Sandra. *Social Housekeepers: Women Shaping Public Policy in New Mexico, 1920–1940.* Albuquerque: University of New Mexico Press, 1992.

Stefanco, Carolyn. "Networking on the Frontier: The Colorado Women's Suffrage Movement, 1876–1893." In *The Women's West,* edited by Susan Armitage and Elizabeth Jameson, pp. 265–276. Norman: University of Oklahoma Press, 1987.

Vigil, Maurilio E. "The Political Development of New Mexico's Hispanas." *Latino Studies Journal* 7, no. 2 (Spring 1996): 3–28.

Watkins, Marilyn P. "Political Activism and Community-Building among Alliance and Grange Women in Western Washington, 1892–1925." *Agricultural History* 67, no. 2 (Spring 1993): 197–213.

Winchester, Juti. "'So Glad God Let Me Be an Outdoor Woman': The Conservationist Writing of Sharlot Mabridth Hall." *Journal of the West* 44, no. 4 (Fall 2005): 18–25.

CHAPTER NINE

Women and the Urban West

The stereotypical image of the West tends to be one of farms, ranches, small towns, wide-open spaces, a thinly spread population, and not much else. But in fact, by the end of the nineteenth century most westerners lived in cities and California was the most urbanized part of the United States except for New England. Western cities grew much faster than cities in the rest of the country. Denver, Colorado, grew from 35,000 people in 1880 to 256,000 in 1920. Los Angeles had the most spectacular growth, increasing from only 50,000 residents in 1890 to 1.2 million by 1930. In 1880, San Francisco, with a population of 234,000, was already the ninth largest city in the United States. It was also the first industrial city in the trans-Mississippi West: in 1880 its 30,000 workers produced more than the combined total of all the other western cities put together. Forty percent of all Californians lived in either San Francisco or Los Angeles by 1900.

This urban West was also the women's West: once the initial settlement phase ended, these booming western cities often had more women than men because of the economic opportunities available there. For every twenty young men who moved to the city, twenty-five or thirty young women did. Rural areas offered women fewer long-term opportunities, so many chose to take their chances in the big cities. Women moved to these cities from Europe and Asia, from eastern states, and from other parts of the West. Some had never lived in cities before, whereas others were already experienced urbanites.

Not all women could access urban economic opportunities equally, however; race, class, skill level, and even location significantly constrained many women's choices. Just as the influx of young women shaped western cities, the expectations and remarkable racial diversity of these new urban residents also shaped the cities. Asian, Native American, black, and Hispanic women moved to the cities looking for a better life, but once there they had fewer choices than white women. Women in bigger cities with more diversified economies had more choices than women in smaller centers. Nevertheless, all women worked within their individual situations to make the most of the new urban landscapes. A new job was not all that a woman found in a city; many women reshaped other aspects of their lives, too, and the urban environments around them.

Urban Newcomers

Chinese women were one of the smallest groups of women living in western cities in the latter half of nineteenth century; in 1852 only seven Chinese women lived in California. Most of the young Chinese men who were working in the United States at that time were unmarried "sojourners," which means that they intended to work temporarily as miners in the United States and then return home with enough money to marry and settle down. This option was not open to Chinese women, who normally only migrated to the United States as the wives of businessmen, students, and diplomats who had been granted permission to enter, or, more rarely, as slaves purchased by criminal organizations to work in the sex trade in western cities and towns. In 1882 the United States passed its first ever racially specific immigration legislation, the Chinese Exclusion Act, which dramatically reduced the number of Chinese men and women who could enter the country legally. From 1870 to 1900 fewer than 5,300 Chinese women were admitted to the United States, and most of them entered before 1882. The inaccurate belief that all Chinese women in the United States were sex trade workers fueled much of the anti-Chinese sentiment that led to the 1882 act and continued to hurt Chinese women's admission cases after the law went into effect. The categories of Chinese who could enter under the Exclusion Act (merchant, student, teacher, diplomat, and traveler) were positions that in most cases only men could take advantage of in nineteenth- and early twentieth-century China, making it even more difficult for Chinese women to enter the country. From 1910 to 1924, only 27 percent (2,107) of the Chinese women who entered the country did so as independent immigrants, and the remaining 73 percent (5,702) entered as dependents.

In the United States, most Chinese women and their daughters had to work because of their families' precarious economic situations, and their work was usually integrated with family life. If their families did not own their own businesses, the women worked as cannery workers, shrimp cleaners, or garment workers. None of these jobs paid much, but they could be combined with childcare and other family responsibilities, and the latter two could even be done at home.

As was the case with the Chinese migrants, males also dominated Japanese immigration until the early twentieth century. Most of the men lived and worked in the San Francisco Bay Area, which had a population of just over 7,000 Japanese men by 1910. Like Chinese men, most of the Japanese men had only come to the United States intending to work for a limited time before returning to Japan. In addition, in the late nineteenth century the Japanese government limited emigration by imposing strict controls over issuing passports for male and female emigrants. After American rumors about Japanese prostitutes on the west coast reached Japan, the Japanese government restricted the number of passports issued for female laborers but made it easier for the wives, children, and parents of men already living in the United States to get passports. In 1907 Japan and the United States signed the so-called Gentleman's Agreement to limit the immigration of Japanese men, but the accord contained a loophole that allowed men who could prove that they had enough money to summon wives and other relatives. The men began returning to Japan to marry or sending for "picture brides" (wives selected by matchmakers using photographs). More than half of the adult women who arrived in the United States from Japan between 1910 and 1920 were picture brides. Between 1909 and 1923 more than 33,000 Japanese-born wives (the Issei generation) immigrated to the U.S. mainland, and the population began to include American-born children (the Nisei generation). In December 1919 the Japanese government stopped issuing passports to picture brides; starting the following spring, it would only issue passports to wives who accompanied their spouses to the United States.

The Issei women came to the United States with the same high hopes that people from other immigrant groups had. They wanted to further their education, help their families economically, and experience new things. When they arrived, many of the picture brides were shocked to discover that their new husbands were much older and less attractive than the pictures they had sent. The second shock was having to change out of their comfortable kimonos and slippers into uncomfortable and confining American dresses and shoes. In Seattle a Japanese-run store located near the port helped many of the women change into American clothes. Mrs. Nomura recalled, "The lady there would show us how to use a corset—since we had never used one in Japan. And how to wear stockings and shoes."

The women had little time to adjust to their new surroundings, because their husbands expected them to start working almost immediately. Most of the women went into rural areas, whereas the rest stayed in urban areas and worked at their husbands' small businesses: laundries, bath houses, bars, markets, restaurants, boardinghouses, and pool halls. Others found work as domestic servants, seamstresses, or cannery workers. By 1920 approximately 20 percent of all Issei women over the age of fifteen worked for pay outside the home, more than half of them as domestic servants. The rest did clerical or service work in Japanese-owned businesses or worked in food processing and garment making, and a few taught in schools where Japanese was the dominant language.

Native American women, who were also new to western cities, went through substantial culture shock even though their journeys were much shorter than the one from Japan. In the early twentieth century, a huge gulf divided the life experiences of most Native Americans from those of other Americans because of the poverty on most reservations and the poor education offered by most government schools. Many of the Native American women who moved to western cities to work in this period had been students at government schools (see chapter four). Others were looking for better opportunities than they could find on their often poverty-stricken reservations. For example, in November 1934, a twenty-two-year-old Pomo woman named Frances Jack left her home at the Hopland Ranchería, a hamlet of fifteen cabins with no indoor plumbing or running water, twenty-five miles south east of Ukiah, California, to work in Oakland. She had never been so far away from home in her life. Hopland was one of six rancherías on the periphery of the greater Ukiah area, each community either purchased by Native Americans in the late 1880s or set up by the government beginning in 1906. Ukiah was the center of local government, employment, and social life, but in the 1930s it was also strictly segregated and whites there did not welcome the Pomo. Until 1927 Pomo children were barred from most of the schools in the county. Frances Jack left Hopland for Oakland because her mother wanted her to have better chances in life than she was ever going to get in Ukiah.

Jack's experiences were similar to those of many other Native American women from Lake and Mendocino counties in the 1930s. By 1941, more than a third of Ukiah Valley Indian women between the ages of fifteen and thirty had worked for some time in the San Francisco Bay Area to escape the racism and lack of jobs at home. Most young Pomo women sent as much money home as they could. Oakland Young Women's Christian Association (YWCA) official Mildred Van Every, who helped place many of the young women in Oakland jobs, commented, "I know of no group that sends home as much money as these Pomo do. They may not have money for anything else but they send it home and don't spend it on themselves." The women rarely stayed in the cities year-round, preferring to work there during the winter and return home in the summer to harvest hops, an ingredient in beer. And almost all the young women went home to their reservations when it was time to marry and settle down. Frances Jack returned to Ukiah in 1949, after training as a nurse and building airplane engines in Sacramento during World War II. She married and became the first tribal chairperson of Hopland's new government.

Black women were concentrated in western urban communities to a much greater degree than white women and had even fewer employment options, but like white women they had better chances and choices in the cities, where they often outnumbered black men. By 1940, 25 percent of all African Americans west of the Great Plains lived in Los Angeles. More black women than black men lived in Los Angeles from 1900 to 1920, and the same was true in Denver from 1900 to 1910. East of the Rocky Mountains, women made up more than half of the black population in several Kansas cities. Until the 1930s, a greater percentage of African American women worked for wages than any other group of American women. In the West, black women were less than 1 percent of the female population, but 2 percent of the women wage workers. Married black women were twice as likely to be employed as Native American or Asian women and five times as likely as white women. Most worked in domestic service. A minority opened their own businesses, such as boardinghouses and laundries, and some invested in real estate.

In 1900 about 100,000 Mexican-born people lived in the United States; by 1930 that number had risen to about 1.5 million. These newcomers tended to migrate to the cities and not the countryside, the way earlier Mexican migrants had done. Most of these new Mexican migrants lived in Los Angeles, California, and El Paso, Texas, because the industrial economy in those cities was growing rapidly and creating a huge demand for unskilled workers who would accept very low wages. El Paso's Mexican community grew from 8,748 in 1900 to 68,476 in 1930. The Mexican population of Los Angeles tripled in the 1920s, giving the city the largest population of Mexicans outside of Mexico City. By 1930 most urban Mexican communities averaged 116 men for every 100 women. Only Los Angeles had a fairly balanced sex ratio, because it tended to be the final destination where families reunited. Very few Hispanic women worked outside the home until the 1930s. Unlike many other women who moved to the cities, then, the move had less to do with finding better opportunities for themselves and more to do with helping the family as a unit.

Whether an individual or a family choice, one made freely or as a result of hard circumstances, moving to the cities changed many women's lives permanently. New opportunities pulled women to urban areas, but in many ways the cities also mirrored the larger patterns of racism and sexism that had helped push women there.

The Sex Trade in Urban Areas

Women from many different backgrounds moved to western cities in the hope of finding or creating better economic opportunities for themselves, but race, class, education, and gender often restricted their choices more than they realized. The most marginalized women, who had the fewest resources or lacked support systems, often wound up in the sex trade. As noted in chapter six, prostitution was an intrinsic facet of the economy in the West's rapidly growing cities because it was usually the first occupation available to women in a brand-new, resource-based town or city, and it would continue to be the only option available to the most economically marginalized women. In the nineteenth century there may have been as many as 50,000 women who sometimes or regularly had sex for money. Working conditions for prostitutes varied considerably according to the city and setting in which a woman worked and her race.

Women of all races worked in the sex trade, with white women usually forming the majority and the percentage of other racial groups varying depending on the location. More Hispanic women worked in the Southwest, and more Chinese women worked in California, for instance. Sacramento, California, in 1860 was unusual in that white women were in the minority among its sex trade workers; more than 75 percent were women of color and more than half were Chinese women. Hispanics made up another 15 percent, and a small number of black women made up the next largest group. In Denver in the 1880s, more than half of the identified prostitutes were white, almost 15 percent were black, fewer than 1 percent were Asian or Mexican, and nearly 25 percent were of mixed-race or unidentified backgrounds.

In bigger cities the sex trade was usually concentrated in working-class and multiethnic neighborhoods, and it exploited the real and perceived social and economic differences between groups of women. For example, white women could usually charge more than women from other racial groups because cultural norms placed a higher value on white women's sexual services. All women knew that they could charge white men more than others because the former probably made more money than nonwhite men.

Prostitutes usually worked in one of four kinds of spaces in the urban West. Brothel workers had the highest status and most protection; saloon and dance hall workers were second; below them on the ladder were women who worked in the cribs (small shacks or rooms clustered along an alley or a road, usually only big enough for a cot and a chair). At the very bottom were the women who had no other options but to work on the streets and in back alleys. The working conditions and level of police surveillance also varied according to the city a woman lived in. For example, sex trade workers in San Antonio and Austin, Texas, operated in very different contexts because of the different economies and social structures in the two cities. San Antonio's large military establishment produced a high demand for and tolerance of the sex trade. Before 1845 most of the sex trade workers were Spanish-speaking women who lived in slums. White women became the other main group of prostitutes as Anglo-Americans poured into the region after 1845. After the

Civil War, black women formed another, much smaller group. Only Mexican women had a lower status. San Antonio did not police the prostitutes too closely because people regarded them as providing a necessary service for the military.

By contrast, as the state capitol Austin did not have a big military population but it did have politicians who had to be careful with their reputations. As a result, an elite group of discreet white prostitutes worked for and were protected by influential clients. Politicians could not be seen to condone prostitution, however, so Austin's police conducted regular sweeps of the streetwalkers, arresting the small number of black prostitutes at a much higher rate than the larger number of white prostitutes.

Chinese women were one of the smallest groups of women in urban areas, yet they often comprised a disproportionate number of a city's sex trade workers. The number of Chinese women in the sex trade in California grew rapidly in the mid-1850s because Chinese criminal organizations called tongs had begun importing them as slaves. By 1860 there were fewer than seven hundred Chinese women in San Francisco, but more than 85 percent were trapped in multiyear contracts with the men who had brought them from China or men who purchased their contracts in California. Most did not live long enough to complete their contracts, and few leveraged their skills into the kind of independence that a onetime prostitute named Ah Toy achieved. She arrived in California in late 1848 or early 1849 and began working as one of the few independent Chinese sex trade workers. She invested her earnings carefully, married a white man, and became the madam of a Chinese brothel.

In spite of very real differences in the lives and experiences of sex trade workers, they had a lot in common no matter where they lived or what their background was. Violence, whether from customers, pimps, or other prostitutes, was a fact of life, as was extreme poverty for most. Most prostitutes were in their late teens or early twenties, and their earnings declined as they aged. Minors (those under age eighteen) comprised more than 60 percent of Sacramento's prostitutes in 1860, some as young as fourteen.

Another similarity in their lives was that women who worked in the sex trade were also wives, lovers, and mothers. Getting married did not necessarily mean that a woman left the sex trade, because she often wed her former pimp or the man who owned the bar where she worked. In these instances the husbands lived off of their wives' income and so expected them to keep working. Other husbands of prostitutes had seasonal jobs that took them away for months at a time. As a result, few prostitutes had stable, long-term marriages.

Raising children was difficult for women in the sex trade because they were poor, highly mobile, and were often raising their children as single parents. Many towns and cities took children away from their mothers if the family lived in a red light district. Other women left their children with relatives or paid another family to take them in. Many of the daughters of prostitutes ended up in the sex trade too, because there were few other options for them.

A sex trade worker's social circle was typically pretty small; her only friends might be the other women she worked with. Some women traveled in pairs and sought work together, and many of those pairs were also lovers. However, prostitutes also competed with each other for clients, and court records across the West show that nearly as many of these women ended up in court for assaulting each other or disturbing the peace as they did for prostitution-related charges. Yet even though their jobs could bring them into conflict, sex trade workers also had to rely on each other for help, protection, or comfort. When a woman died, for example, her coworkers often raised the money to pay for her burial.

The urban sex trade illustrates that moving to one of the West's rapidly growing cities could involve a lot of continuities as well as changes. The most obvious continuity is that prostitution remained the only paid work available to the poorest and most marginalized women. The most striking change was that so many other factors were now shaping the sex trade, including each city's economy and locally specific racial and class hierarchies.

Domestic Service

Whereas the most marginalized women in a town or city found work providing sexual services to men, slightly less marginalized women often found that the only other job they could get was providing domestic services for middle-class and wealthy families. The rapidly growing middle and upper classes in the West's booming cities wanted to hire domestic servants, but few were available in the late nineteenth and early twentieth centuries. This combination of high demand and limited supply meant that domestic work became a gateway into the urban labor force for women of many different backgrounds. It was the single most important form of wage labor for women, especially young, single women, from the nineteenth to the early twentieth century. Jobs were always available, but the occupation's low status and poor working conditions made it unattractive to women who could get other jobs. Few women chose to stay in a job that required them to clean for six and a half days a week for low pay and live under an employer's roof with little protection from potential sexual harassment or physical abuse, if they had any other options. Thus the field was left to the newcomer and minority women who had the fewest options.

Immigrant women were twice as likely to work as domestics than native-born women, and some ethnic groups were more likely than others. As with prostitution, the availability of domestic service jobs varied a lot according to a woman's location and her race or ethnicity. For example, in San Francisco in 1880 more than one-third of all single women worked in domestic service, but the percentage ranged from a high of 72 percent of Scandinavian-born and Irish-born women to a low of 16 percent for native-born daughters of native-born parents. In the same year in Portland, Oregon, on average 54 percent of single women worked in domestic service, but 92 percent of Irish-born unmarried women did so, compared with 37 percent of native-born daughters of native-born parents. In Los Angeles the overall percentage of young women was the same as in Portland that year, but 67 percent of German- and English-born women worked as servants, whereas only 40 percent of native-born daughters of native-born parents did so.

These numbers hint at the fact that each city had a distinctive economy, which helped determine the opportunities available to women, but the numbers also highlight the ways that ethnicity affected a young woman's employment. The high percentage of Irish-born women working as domestics indicates how central they were to the domestic servant supply across the West. As discussed in chapter six, Irish women left Ireland in huge numbers in the nineteenth century because there were more jobs for them abroad than at home. Without a doubt, their main prospect was domestic service. For example, in 1880 twenty-two-year-old Maggie McGouglan, an Irish immigrant, worked as a live-in domestic for a German clerk and his family in one of the newer middle-class suburbs west of downtown San Francisco. The ready supply of Irish women did not mean that they were the most popular group of domestics, however. In fact, Anglo-Protestant employers often viewed them as stupid, unclean, annoyingly independent, and stubbornly Catholic. Irish women generally refused to do more work than their wages warranted, refused to leave the city to work at a country home, and quit as soon as they could get a better job in manufacturing or if they thought they were being treated poorly.

Location mattered even more than race or ethnicity for domestic servants, however, because each city's economy contained a distinctive mix of job opportunities and constraints. For example, in 1880 San Francisco was a metropolitan city of nearly a quarter of a million people, with an economy based on commerce, manufacturing, and shipping. Portland and Los Angeles were tiny by comparison (18,000 and 12,000 residents, respectively) and had almost no local manufacturing. Residents of those towns could not buy a locally made hat, dress, or pair of shoes; instead, they ordered items directly from the San Francisco producers or from a hometown merchant whose stock came from San Francisco. As a result, San Francisco had a lot of jobs for women in the needle trades, light manufacturing, clerical work, and sales. A smaller percentage of young single women worked as domestics in San Francisco because there were many more jobs available in these other occupations. Manufacturing or clerical jobs were few and far between in Portland and Los Angeles, however, so a much higher percentage of women in all ethnic groups had to work as domestics. For example, twenty-year-old Minnie Dickson had been born in California to German parents but moved north to Portland. In 1880 she was working as a domestic for a lawyer, his family, and a boarder. In Los Angeles, a much smaller proportion of immigrant women worked in domestic service because it was just about the only paid occupation open to the large group of native-born Hispanic women in the city. Only 3 percent of Hispanic women in Los Angeles had white collar jobs, while more than 80 percent were domestic servants.

As it was for many other women, domestic service was often the first job a young Native American woman could get in the city, and the government-run schools often placed them in urban households as servants. The women who had graduated from or simply left the schools often turned to domestic service because they could not get other jobs. Like Frances Jack, many Native women combined wage work in the cities with seasonal agricultural labor at home and struggled to contribute to their families' economies. Jack's first job in California's Bay Area in November 1934 was as a housekeeper, cooking and cleaning for a man and his daughter while his wife recuperated from an operation. When she started, her employer had to show her how to use all of the appliances and teach her how to cook. She was scared of the electric iron and the gas stove, and it took her a week to learn how to light the oven. She had her own room, though, and the family dog kept her company. After the man's wife recovered, Frances left the household.

Another young Pomo woman named Opal also worked in the Bay Area in 1934 and was particularly frustrated that her employer would not pay her. In exasperation, Opal wrote to the BIA matron who had placed her with Mrs. L. N. David of Berkeley, saying that the woman owed her "ten dollars and she won't pay me for it. She accuses me of taking things which I didn't do..., and besides she accused the girl before me...of the same thing. I think it's just a stunt to get out of paying me....She didn't give me a moment's rest, so I think it's terrible that she doesn't want to pay me. Will you please try and make her give me the $10."

Native American women were also frustrated when they tried to get out of domestic service into other kinds of employment. In 1933 a woman named Margaret wrote directly to newly appointed commissioner of the BIA, John Collier. She said "I am an Indian a girl and a graduate from Sherman Institute.... I was sent out to that school to get an education. When I graduated I found I could not get any other job but as a housekeeper. Any girl knows how to do that sort of work I'm sure. My four years wasted. I found I could have accomplished more if I had attended a regular public high school." Margaret told Collier that her family had lost their land and become destitute: "The reason why we Indians in the middle part of California are backward is because we have nothing to get started with. The little we have doesn't amount to anything. We have no money to go to college to be somebody. Why doesn't somebody give us a break?" She was currently working as a housekeeper in Hollywood but wanted to go to nursing school. Not until 1942 was Margaret able to complete a training course at a hospital and get a temporary position as a nurse.

Whereas the daughters of European immigrants could often escape domestic service and find clerical and sales jobs and Native American women had the option of going home, institutionalized prejudice barred the Japanese and other visible minorities from most industrial and office settings. They remained heavily concentrated in domestic work until World War II. Only after the war did systemic racism diminish enough to allow them to move into other occupations.

As it did for other women, Japanese women's concentration in domestic service varied according to where they lived. It was the main occupation for Issei women in the Bay Area (more than one quarter of all employed Issei women in Oakland and more than one half in San Francisco), but only 6.4 percent of these women in Los Angeles and 3.3 percent in Seattle worked as servants. In Seattle, nearly two-thirds of the Issei women were employed in the service sector, as sales clerks or waitresses for example, because the city's high proportion of transient male laborers in lumbering and canning created many opportunities for small businesses catering to the men's needs. In San Francisco, by contrast, far more Japanese women had to work in domestic service because the city offered better job opportunities to almost every other group of young women.

A family-owned small business did not always guarantee that a woman could avoid domestic service, however. For example, when Mrs. Yoshida arrived in the United States in 1909, her husband had been there long enough to open his own laundry in Alameda, California. By 1912 they had the first two of what would be ten children, and she thought that they needed additional income, particularly since the cleaning business slowed down in the summer. "I started to work," she recalled,

> because everyone went on vacation and the summer was very hard for us.... I bought a second-hand bicycle from a friend who had used it for five years. I paid $3 for it. So, at night I went to the beach and practiced on that bicycle. At night nobody was at the beach, so even if I fell down, I didn't feel embarrassed. And then I went to work [as a domestic servant]. I worked half a day and was paid $1.... We didn't know the first thing about housework, but the ladies of the house didn't mind. They taught us how at the beginning; 'This is a broom; this is a dustpan.' And we worked hard for them. We always thought America was a wonderful country.

Mrs. Yoshida and her husband had planned on moving back to Japan once they had earned enough money, but they abandoned that plan after having ten children.

Women of all racial and ethnic backgrounds left domestic service as soon as they could because of the low wages, long hours, isolation, and vulnerability. One young Pomo woman wrote, "It's awful lonesome not knowing anyone down here. This morning when I woke I felt like packing my bags and going back home to Ukiah." Many young women working as urban domestic servants did not have this choice, however, so instead of moving back home they did their best to get out of domestic service and into a better job.

Factory and Clerical Work and Teaching

Factory and clerical work represented a huge step up for most women, but opportunities for such jobs again varied enormously. Young women preferred the regular hours and independence of a factory job, but there weren't a lot of these positions in the West compared to the east in the late nineteenth century. For example, San Francisco's thriving manufacturing sector only employed 6 percent of young female workers in 1880, compared to a national average of 20 percent. West coast factories employed an average of twenty-three women, whereas those in New York had forty-seven and in Boston seventy-two. One of the small number of women factory workers in San Francisco in 1880 was twenty-five-year-old Mary McAurey, who worked in a shoe factory and lived with her parents and four brothers in a working-class neighborhood.

A western woman was also less than half as likely as a woman in New York, Boston, or Philadelphia to have a clerical or sales job (often called "white-collar" to distinguish them from "blue-collar" manual positions). Los Angeles had a lower percentage of women working in manufacturing than San Francisco, but it had a much higher percentage of women working in white-collar jobs than that city or Portland. The large number of white-collar men who had chosen to move to Los Angeles for the weather needed to hire staff for their businesses, giving certain women more opportunities for this kind of job. The prevailing racism toward Hispanics meant that young, single, white, foreign-born women in Los Angeles were more than twice as likely to have a clerical or sales job than a similar woman in the other two cities.

Teaching was one of the first white-collar jobs that white and black women could find in a town or city, because of the widely shared belief that teaching was a natural outlet for women's supposedly nurturing temperaments. Los Angeles needed more teachers than other western cities because it had a much higher proportion of families with school-age children. Women teachers still represented only 9 percent of the working women in the city, however. Teaching was also the most accessible profession for black women, because most black students were not allowed to attend white schools and the segregated schools needed black teachers. For example, Elizabeth Thorn Scott opened the first black schools in Sacramento and Oakland, California. The number of black teachers dropped significantly when schools across the West began to desegregate in the late nineteenth century. By 1900 there were only fifteen black female teachers recorded in the West, and most of them were in states like Kansas that still had segregated schools.

Factory, clerical, and teaching jobs were harder to get than work as a domestic servant because so many more women wanted to have those jobs and there were fewer positions available. White-collar work was more respectable, paid better, had better hours, and freed women from having to live isolated lives in their employers' homes.

Working Together, Working for Each Other

Unlike women in rural areas, small towns, or mining camps who rarely worked alongside other women, working-class women in the cities had a completely new experience: factory jobs where dozens or hundreds of women working together. This shared workplace experience often led to collective action, such as striking to protest poor conditions or even forming unions.

White working-class women played a big role in San Francisco's labor unrest during the late 1870s and early 1880s, for example. They carved out a political middle ground between white working-class men and white middle-class women by refusing to be treated

as victims by either side and by forging their own distinct opposition to the Chinese men with whom they competed for work.
They attended labor rallies, gave speeches, and organized grievance
committees to demand better working conditions and higher pay
from employers.

In the late 1870s, working-class white women competed against
Chinese men for low-skilled and low-paying jobs in domestic service
and light manufacturing. A national economic depression occurred
in that decade, and thousands of Chinese men were unemployed
after completing the construction of the first transcontinental railroad in the late 1860s. This glut of workers meant that wages dropped
wherever white women and Chinese men sought the same jobs. For
example, between 1876 and 1880, the daily wage of white women
and Chinese men in the shirt industry in San Francisco fell from
$1.25 to a dollar. As a result, white working-class women actively
participated in three days of anti-Chinese rioting in San Francisco in
July 1877. They also criticized the middle-class white women who
hired Chinese men instead of white women as domestic servants.

White working-class anger against the Chinese continued to
build in San Francisco in 1880. Unemployed white men and women
gathered every week on the sand lot in front of the site where the
new city hall was being built to protest continued white unemploy-
ment and the presence of Chinese workers. Anna Smith became a
regular speaker at these weekly meetings. Born in New York City,
she migrated westward by taking a series of low-paying jobs, including domestic servant, janitor, nurse, and laundress. She arrived in
San Francisco in 1875, a widow with a son, and found work as a
nurse and domestic servant. On February 8, 1880, she stood on the
makeshift speaker's platform at the sand lot and stated that poverty was the real cause of working women's suffering: "There are
sewing women in this city who can only earn $3 a week for their
tedious toil. How, then, can they be expected to live comfortably
and respectably on so small a sum. It is impossible. They cannot
do it." When the city's employers responded that women were just

temporary workers looking for spending money and therefore did not need better wages, Smith insisted, "Women had the same right as men to earn an honest living. They did not wish to be compelled to go on certain streets to eke out an existence. They did not want to sell themselves, souls and bodies." The sand lot women formed a Committee on Corporations Looking into Laundries and spent two weeks confronting laundry owners, who soon promised that they would hire more white women and fewer Chinese men.

The white women who worked in San Francisco's commercial laundries pursued other strategies too, including alliances with middle-class women to establish institutions like the Women's and Girl's Protective Laundry and the Women's Protective League of California. The former occupied a three-story building and included living spaces above the laundry operations. It employed between twenty and thirty white women and girls, and its officers were all wives of prominent San Francisco businessmen. The middle-class members of the protective league promised not to hire any Chinese men as domestics or buy any household supplies from Chinese manufacturers. The league also functioned as an employment agency and temporary home for working women while they looked for work.

As a result of white working women's activism in the 1880s, the male-dominated Workingmen's Party of California (WPC) and unions like the Knights of Labor gradually addressed women's concerns over the next few years. The WPC began to support equal pay for women, helped unemployed women and men find jobs, raised money for impoverished women, and provided seed money for new businesses. For example, the WPC gave one woman sixty-five dollars to open her own business. Unions also began to accept women as members. Typographical Union Local 21 started to accept female members in 1883, and the Knights of Labor Ladies' Assembly 5855 met for the first time in 1888.

Whereas organized male workers tended to strike to gain something new, women workers tended to strike to get back something specific that an employer had taken away, such as a higher wage or a shorter work day. In 1887, for example, striking San Francisco glove makers said that they were not on strike to get "an increase of wages" but to protest the fact that they were getting paid less for each pair they made. In 1895, the hundreds of Hispanic women who worked at the Galveston Cotton and Woolen Mill walked out to protest a one-hour extension of their twelve-hour workday. Strike leaders cited the workers' family responsibilities to justify their opposition to the longer hours. An extra hour of work would cut into what little time they had to take care of their houses and families and to sleep. The company locked the women out for six weeks and refused to give most of them their jobs back when the strike ended.

A decade later in Seattle, white wage-earning women and the wives of unionized men began to create a new kind of working-class women's movement, one grounded in their awareness of their common oppression as working-class women. It began with the Seattle Women's Label League, founded in 1905. Organized labor started using "union labels" in the late nineteenth century to mark union-made goods and encourage people to buy them. The strategy's success depended on convincing women, who did most of the shopping for their households, to choose union-made goods over those not made by unionized workers. Most of the Label League's members were the wives of union men, but for the first five years they received little support or respect from the trade union movement. Washington state's suffrage victory in 1910 gave them a new political voice to express their concerns, and they began to get more support from the progressive labor movement in Seattle. The labor newspaper, the *Seattle Union Record,* had included a women's page for a few months in 1909 but it got little attention. The *Record* started a new page in 1910, edited by Phillipina McNamara, the wife of George McNamara, the newspaper's editor and manager from 1908 to 1913. In addition to cooking, cleaning, and fashion, the new page included columns on local and national women's political issues, the struggles faced by wage-earning women, and women's achievements outside the home. Phillipina also became one of the organizers of the new

Women's Union Card and Label League, founded in 1911, and its first president. In February 1912, the *Record* wrote, "The Women's Card and Label League is doing much good over the nation, but its field of usefulness is much greater in those states having woman suffrage than elsewhere. The last twenty-five years have shown a vast change in the ability and qualifications of women to take an active part in public affairs."

For the first couple of years of its existence, the league spent most of its time supporting the local union movement rather than women's issues specifically. League activists avoided working too closely with middle-class women because they saw the middle-class reformers as busybodies with too much time on their hands. However, by 1914 the league's membership had declined, and the organizers believed it was because the group had spent too much time on social events and not enough time on politics. To combat the decline, the new secretary, Mary Walker, wrote in the *Record* that the League was going to reinvent itself as a "training school for women." The members put aside their aversion to working with middle-class women and joined the King County Legislative Federation, a coalition of local women's organizations ranging from the WTCU to Parent-Teacher Associations and the women's auxiliaries of craft unions. The league now wanted to put itself "in the vanguard of the advanced Woman Movement" and the labor movement. League leaders urged women to quit the women's auxiliaries to their husbands' trade unions and join the league's "one big organization" for women.

This 1914 transformation succeeded and membership sky-rocketed. The Label League got its own section in the *Record*, and the members discussed everything from sex hygiene and the Russian Revolution to firetrap sweatshops. The league also continued to publicize union-made goods. League women never forgot their working-class loyalties, even when they worked with middle-class women. For example, in 1915 the League joined with women's clubs to found a municipal lodging house for girls. The league women pointed out that the new house was necessary because the YWCA had failed to provide a place for working-class girls. The League criticized the YWCA building as "a magnificent palace for the use of business and professional women, and for the giving of social functions by the lesser lights of society"—clearly not a place that was of any practical use to working-class women.

In 1915 the *Record's* stenographer, Sophia Kramer, became the new editor of the women's page and brought a new feminist edge to it. For example, under her leadership the page published a column by Edith Levi on the connections between women's suffrage and trade unionism and a spirited debate over the worth of its fashion section. One critic said that instead of "this silly fashion space," the *Record* should print articles demanding that the state bear the cost of babies. Another writer said that she liked the fashion pages but that some of the styles were not very "appropriate for the majority of working people." At the end of 1916, Kramer announced that the fashion column was going to be replaced by a column on labor law.

Seattle's working-class women's movement hit its peak between 1916 and 1918. The Label League and other working-class women helped create the Federation of Trade Unionist Women and Auxiliaries (FTUW&A) with the goal of uniting and organizing all women workers and advancing unionized women's causes through legislative channels. The FTUW&A brought the women of the Label League together with members of women's auxiliaries of the Carpenters' and Typographers' unions, female unionists of the United Garment Workers, the Waitresses' Union, and the Federal Labor Union. The new organization did not get much help from the state's male union hierarchy, so its leaders focused on the Seattle Central Labor Council instead. This strategy paid off: the council appointed a woman organizer, long-time Label League member Ida Levi, in the fall of 1917. She soon had female elevator operators, theater ushers, film inspectors, retail clerks, electrical workers, and machinists meeting to discuss the benefits of unionization. Within a year Levi moved on to state-level work and Blanche Johnson took her place. The women's gains did not survive the economic downturn and anti-union backlash after World War I, however, because the male-dominated union movement concentrated on protecting the rights of its male members.

In cities across the West, as women began to work in bigger workplaces with a lot of other women, they realized that they had many things in common. They recognized that some employers paid them less just because they were women and that their concerns over workplace conditions were often dismissed for the same reason. By working together in new urban workplaces, they recognized that they could also start to work together to change those workplaces.

Women Reshape Their Cities

As significant and visible as urban working-class women's efforts to improve their working conditions were, those efforts were only a small part of a much larger and more widespread pattern of women's responses to their new urban environments. Cities also gave women the chance to redefine themselves, their communities, and their cultural norms at a more personal level. Most urban women, for example, had fewer children than most rural women, reflecting the fact that urban families did not need children for additional labor the way rural families did. White middle-class women's efforts to address the social problems created by rapidly growing cities were another key part of the response. Just like the politically active women discussed in chapter eight, these women used their socially acceptable role as respectable, Christian women to try to improve urban life for themselves and others. They focused on issues that were of particular important to them as white, middle-class women, including children's welfare and the living and working experiences of working-class and minority women.

San Francisco's social problems grew as quickly as the city itself did, and from 1850 to 1880 in particular the city relied heavily on middle-class, Anglo-American women's charities for social services. These women genuinely worried about the struggles of working-class women and children and used their charities to pressure community members and state and local policy makers to do something for the more vulnerable residents of their city. In 1850 the women of the San Francisco Protestant Orphan Asylum (SFPOA) founded an orphanage that was the first social welfare institution in California. The SFPOA convinced city officials to allocate $125 per month to the orphanage and donate land for a building in 1855. Women reformers founded the San Francisco Ladies' Protection and Relief Society in 1853 and opened a home for working-class women in 1857. In 1866, activists created a Ladies' Depository to provide an income for both working-class women and any other woman who might find herself in need of work in the city's volatile economy. Managers took donations from private contributors and used the money to buy sewing materials, which they gave to seamstresses in need of work. The completed articles were sold in the depository's store. The managers gave 90 percent of the sale price of each item to the woman who had made it.

Although some middle-class white women wanted to improve the living and working conditions of white working-class women, another group focused on trying to get Chinese women out of the sex trade and convert them to Christianity. A group of Presbyterian women in San Francisco founded the Chinese Mission Home in 1874 to meet these two goals. By the late 1880s the home had an average of fifty residents per year, a number that rose to an average of eighty in the 1890s. The home put residents to work sewing items to be sold at fundraisers and local shops. In the summer time, the home sent residents to work for California's fruit growers. Home officials saved the women's earnings for them to help them get started when they left the home, ideally as the wife of a Christianized Chinese man.

The goals of the home's directors were not always the same as those of the Chinese women who used their services, however. Some of the residents were trying to escape the sex trade and find a husband, whereas others used it to escape unhappy marriages.

Fifteen-year-old Amy Chan moved into the home to avoid going back to China with her father because she feared he would arrange a marriage for her there. She used the home to get an education and avoid marriage altogether. Most of the residents eagerly sought new skills and an education but were less interested in the mandatory twice-daily Christian prayer sessions.

Middle-class white women in many other smaller cities in the West also actively worked to make their cities better places to live. In 1886 the Colorado branch of the WCTU opened the Colorado Cottage Home for unmarried mothers. In Tacoma, Washington, the Women's Study Club started in 1899 as a literary society, but within a year its members were working with other groups on city beautification and child labor problems. Soon they decided to add suffrage to their list of activities. In 1910 the club investigated Tacoma's water supply, passed resolutions to raise the salaries of local teachers, and petitioned the city council for a home for girls. In 1881 the Oakland, California, YWCA became the first branch in the United States to extend its work to girls who were still in school. From 1896 to 1909, the Oakland YWCA operated the Girls' Mutual Benefit Club, which managed a downtown lunchroom where working women could eat and relax in comfort. In 1896, the YWCA opened the Girls' Sewing School near the California Cotton Mills, a kindergarten, and the East Oakland Social Settlement (a neighborhood social welfare agency) for the female mill workers. It also provided an employment placement service. The goals of the Oakland YWCA were "not only to furnish a reliable and steady employment office for employers and employees, but also to bring the girls who are seeking employment in touch with the protective, educational, and social opportunities of the Association; that the girls will realize this is their Association and place for friends, clubs, and self-development."

The sheer number of women in western cities and the range of new opportunities they found also meant that women were often the catalysts of cultural change in their ethnic and religious communities. For example, American-born Jewish women in Portland had far more options than their European-born mothers for employment outside the home before they got married. They also had more power to make independent decisions about marriage partners, family structure, and civic participation. Jewish women in Portland assumed most of the responsibility for charity and welfare work among the city's Jews and provided critical leadership for Seattle's working-class women's movement (as discussed above).

Scandinavian women in Seattle also discarded many of the roles and responsibilities of women in their homelands. Most young Scandinavian women came to Seattle without any family and supported themselves as domestic servants. In doing so, they conformed to existing Scandinavian migration and labor patterns for women. They also married in their late twenties, which was normal in Scandinavia. After marriage, though, they broke two norms. First, nearly 40 percent of Norwegian and Swedish women married outside their ethnic group. Second, although women in Scandinavia usually kept working outside the home after marriage, women in Seattle generally did not, following middle-class American cultural norms rather than their own.

Western cities created new personal and cultural opportunities for African American women. A higher percentage of black women in the West than in other regions married, but they had fewer than half the children that black women in the South did. Western African American women also lived longer than their counterparts in the South. The longer life expectancies, smaller families, and urban concentration of western black women gave them a unique demographic profile, especially on the coast. Black women in the West also had a higher rate of literacy than those in other regions, and in the 1920s black girls in the West had a higher rate of school attendance than those in any other region of the United States. The West was the only part of the nation where more than half of black girls of high-school age were enrolled in school, even though many western states and territories tried to limit or eliminate educational opportunities for blacks. For example, though Sarah Lester's high grades and very light skin color enabled her to enroll in San Francisco's only high school in 1858, the school expelled her when it found out that she was African American. By 1880 courts and legislators forced western states and cities to integrate their schools and admit black students. A few states, such as Kansas, allowed some local school segregation, whereas others, such as Arizona, maintained completely segregated systems. But the African American students stuck it out, and as early as 1890 a higher percentage of black girls than white attended schools for six months or more of the year.

Urban African American women's efforts to reshape urban landscapes often began with demands to use basic services like public transit. Black women in San Francisco, for example, played a bigger role than men in the struggle for access to public transit. The ability to travel safely and in peace mattered more to them in a city in which men still outnumbered women by at least three to one, and in an era when being outside one's own home made a respectable urban woman a potential target of male harassment. The fight began in April 1863 when the Omnibus Railroad Company, one of two streetcar companies in the city, forced Charlotte Brown to get off one of its streetcars. Over the next few months, streetcar drivers kicked her off twice more. She sued. During the court proceedings, the company insisted that it had to bar all blacks from its cars to protect white women and children. The court ruled against the company and forced it to change its policy.

In 1866, Emma Jane Turner and a well-known San Francisco businesswoman, Mary Ellen Pleasant, brought lawsuits against the other streetcar company, the North Beach and Mission Railroad Company. Pleasant had moved to the city during the Gold Rush, and worked as a domestic and then as a boardinghouse owner. With her earnings she also financed various mining and real estate ventures over the years, made connections with the city's mining elite, and became very wealthy. Both lawsuits succeeded at the local level, but the California Supreme Court threw them out in 1868. The higher court agreed that the streetcar companies did not have the right to stop African Americans from using their services, but it stated that Turner and Pleasant had not proved that the company had discriminated against them or that the conductors' behavior was racially motivated. The suits had accomplished one thing, however: neither company ever tried again to deny access to a black person.

Two prominent members of the small African American middle class in the Northwest, Susie Revels Cayton of Seattle, Washington, and Beatrice Morrow Cannady of Portland, Oregon, devoted much of their lives to making their cities better places to live for African Americans. Cayton was born in Mississippi in 1870, the daughter of the first black senator in the United States, Hiram Revels. She married her husband Horace in Seattle in 1896. She was a college-educated journalist, and her husband founded the *Seattle Republican,* which was the second black newspaper in Seattle. The Caytons intended the *Republican* for black and white audiences. Susie became associate editor in 1900, and in the early 1900s the paper did very well. She and Horace could afford to live with their children in a wealthy white neighborhood and had a Japanese servant and a Swedish maid. In 1906 she founded the Dorcas Charity Club and later the Sunday Forum, an all-black discussion group.

Racism toward African Americans was on the rise in Seattle in the 1910s, however. The *Seattle Republican* folded in 1913, Cayton's husband was refused service in a restaurant and lost the subsequent court battle, and their white neighbors accused them of lowering property values. They moved several times in the 1910s and started a new paper, *Cayton's Weekly,* in 1916, this time aiming at a black audience. Susie was a contributing editor and the weekly ran until 1920. In the 1930s she joined the Communist Party and became more active politically than she had ever been. At the age of sixty-six, her typical week could include attending meetings of the American Federation of Labor, the Negro Workers Council, the Harriet Tubman Club, the Workers' Forum, and the Legislative Council. As she said in a letter to her daughter, "I'm having the time of my life and at the same time making some contribution to the working class, I hope."

Whereas Cayton eventually turned to communism to make the world a better place, Beatrice Morrow Cannady dedicated herself to the National Association for the Advancement of Colored People (NAACP). Born in Texas in 1890, she moved to Portland in 1910 and married Edward Daniel Cannady in 1912. He founded the city's main African American newspaper, the *Advocate*, and she became an assistant editor there in 1912. They had two children when she entered law school in 1919. When she was admitted to the bar in 1922, she was the first African American woman to practice law in the state. In 1914 she helped found the Portland chapter of the NAACP, and in 1928 she was one of the few women to speak at the NAACP's national convention in Los Angeles. She helped organize the successful 1925 campaign to repeal a range of Oregon's discriminatory laws but was not able to gain full and equal access to public facilities such as movie theaters and segregated YWCA buildings.

As the example of the Chinese Mission Home in San Francisco demonstrated, cultural change was not always initiated or even directed by the members of a specific racial or ethnic group. For example, the large numbers of Mexican-born women who immigrated to the United States in the early twentieth century found that their new life in the city included Americanization programs. These programs looked a lot like the education that the federal government imposed on Native American women in the nineteenth century, including classes on cleaning and household duties as well as the English language and the American system of government. As they had with Native Americans, reformers believed that if Mexican mothers assimilated Anglo-American norms, then they could assimilate the rest of their families, especially their children. Reformers also considered Mexican women good candidates for jobs as domestic servants, seamstresses, laundresses, and service workers throughout the Southwest, because there were not enough black and immigrant European women to fill these positions. Teaching Mexican women how to sew or clean the "American" way would prepare them for the jobs that employers needed to fill. At the Rose Gregory Houchen Settlement House, founded in El Paso, Texas, in 1912, the Americanization courses included citizenship, cooking, carpentry, English, Bible study, music, and hygiene, as well as working girls' clubs, Camp Fire Girls, and Boy Scouts. In 1920, the house assigned a nurse to try to counter the high infant mortality rate in the neighborhood. A few months later it opened a clinic offering prenatal and postnatal care, pediatric services, and later a maternity ward. Mexican-born women were happy to use the free medical care but had little interest in Bible study classes taught from a Protestant perspective.

The Americanization programs did not have a big impact on Mexican-born women, but they did affect their American-born daughters considerably. A 1928 survey of Mexican women in the paid workforce in Los Angeles concluded that most were under the age of twenty-three, two-thirds had been born in the United States, and 90 percent were unmarried. And they were Americanized, but perhaps not in the way that reformers intended. One Mexican mother complained that

> it is because they can run around so much and be so free, that our Mexican girls do not know how to act. So many girls run away and get married. This terrible freedom in this United States. The Mexican girls seeing American girls with freedom, they want it too, so they go where they like. They do not mind their parents; this terrible freedom. But what can the Mexican mothers do? It is the custom, and we cannot change it, but it is bad.

Many Japanese mothers might have shared the sentiments of this Mexican woman. In Los Angeles in the 1930s, young Japanese American women had one foot in the community of their immigrant parents and the other foot in the larger American community and its contemporary youth culture. About 35,000 Japanese Americans lived in Los Angeles in this decade, half of whom were American-born and most of whom were under twenty-one. Their labor was essential to their families and communities. Girls helped clean and operate small, family-run restaurants and grocery stores in the Japanese American neighborhood. Their families expected the girls, but not their brothers, to help with the housework and care for their younger siblings. However, these traditional family expectations did not stop some young Nisei women from adopting shorter, more fashionable hair cuts or demanding a greater say in choosing their marriage partners, an autonomy in keeping with the trend for American-born white women.

As adults, many Nisei women faced limited job prospects. They were educated and spoke English, but these skills could not overcome the entrenched racism of the time. A small number found work as secretaries and clerks for Japanese American professionals and merchants. As Monica Sone recalled of her youth in Seattle, "I knew that the Nisei girls competed fiercely among themselves for white-collar jobs in the Mitsui and Mitsubishi branch firms downtown, local newspaper establishments, Japanese banks, shipping offices, and small export and import firms." Others worked as teachers, nurses, seamstresses, and beauticians within their own community. Two of every five young working women were in domestic service.

Nisei girls and single women found much needed camaraderie in a wide array of urban Japanese American organizations. There were more than four hundred Nisei organizations in Los Angeles by 1938, including a number of young women's clubs, ranging from Buddhist and Christian groups to YWCA affiliates. These young women also formed Girl Scout troops and baseball teams; they sent their poems to ethnic newspapers and danced at Nisei clubs. In Portland, Oregon, the YWCA reached out to Nisei girls and young women, either recruiting them into the YWCA's existing girls' groups or supporting them when they formed their own groups. In 1936, for example, the Girls' Cultural Guild, one of several girls' clubs at the YWCA open to both white and Japanese girls, reported that it had recruited thirty Nisei girls. The Portland YWCA also had a Japanese Girls' Cultural Guild, Japanese Girl Reserves, Japanese Girls' Reserves Alumnae, and Japanese Young Women's Guild. Participating in these youth groups exposed urban Nisei girls and single women to mainstream culture at the same time as it gave them the chance to explain their norms and beliefs to the white girls.

New job opportunities were clearly only the tip of the iceberg when it came to the effect that western cities had on women, and women had on the cities. The population density and racial, ethnic, and economic diversity in a city meant that on a daily basis women could see that there were other ways to live their lives, and many of them seized the chance to make large and small changes.

As much as the West was an incubator of change and provided opportunities for women with diverse economic and ethnic backgrounds, those changes were even more rapid and concentrated in the cities. Urban life was a new experience for most western women in the late nineteenth and early twentieth centuries, and many took advantage of everything that cities had to offer. Some of their roles and experiences were familiar, continuing aspects of the lives they had lived before moving to a western city, but there were also many dramatic changes: new kinds of paid work, new forms of solidarity with other women, and new social choices to make. There were new problems, specific to urban settings, and women of all classes and racial groups responded to those problems with their own solutions. Perhaps even more than men, women sought new roles, experiences, and rights that challenged traditions and made western cities modern. Women had the opportunity to make their cities better places to live, within the social and legal constraints of the time, and many seized the chance to improve their own lives and often made them very different from their mothers' lives.

Suggested Readings

Butler, Anne. *Daughters of Joy, Sisters of Misery: Prostitutes in the American West 1865–90.* Chicago and Urbana: University of Illinois Press 1985.

DeVault, Ileen. "'Too Hard on the Women, Especially': Striking Together for Women's Workers' Issues." *International Review of Social History* 51 (2006): 441–462.

Gardner, Martha M. "Working on White Womanhood: White Working Women in the San Francisco Anti-Chinese Movement, 1877–1890." *Journal of Social History 33*, no. 1 (Fall 1999): 73–95.

Gayne, Mary K. "Japanese Americans at the Portland YWCA." *Journal of Women's History* 15, no. 3 (Autumn 2003): 197–203.

Glenn, Evelyn Nakano. "The Dialectics of Wage Work: Japanese-American Women and Domestic Service, 1905–1940." *Feminist Studies* 6, no. 3 (Autumn 1980): 432–471.

Ichioka, Yuji. "Amerika Nadeshiko: Japanese Immigrant Women in the United States, 1900–1924." *The Pacific Historical Review* 49, no. 2 (May 1980): 339–357.

Jacobs, Margaret D. "Working on the Domestic Frontier: American Indian Domestic Servants in White Women's Households in the San Francisco Bay Area, 1920–1940." *Frontiers* 28, nos. 1–2 (2007): 165–199.

Laslett, John H. M. "Gender, Class, or Ethno-Cultural Struggle? The Problematic Relationship between Rose Pesotta and the Los Angeles ILGWU." *California History* 72, no. 1 (Spring 1993): 20–39.

Lee, Erika. *At America's Gates: Chinese Immigration During the Exclusion Era, 1882–1943.* Chapel Hill: University of North Carolina Press, 2003.

Locke, Mary Lou. "Out of the Shadows and Into the Western Sun: Working Women of the Late Nineteenth-Century Urban Far West." *Journal of Urban History* 16, no. 2 (February 1990): 175–204.

Matsumoto, Valerie J. "Japanese American Women and the Creation of Urban Nisei Culture in the 1930s." In *Over the Edge: Re-Mapping the American West,* edited by Valerie J. Matsumoto and Blake Allmendinger, pp. 291–306. Berkeley and Los Angeles: University of California Press, 1999.

Oberdeck, Kathryn. "'Not Pink Teas': The Seattle Working-Class Women's Movement, 1905–1918." Labor History 32, no. 2 (1991): 193–230.

Pascoe, Peggy. *Relations of Rescue: The Search for Female Moral Authority in the American West, 1874–1939.* New York: Oxford University Press, 1990.

Patterson, Victoria D. "Indian Life in the City: A Glimpse of the Urban Experience of Pomo Women in the 1930s." *California History* 71, no. 3 (Fall 1992): 402–411.

Sánchez, George J. "'Go After the Women': Americanization and the Mexican Immigrant Woman, 1915–1929." *Unequal Sisters: A Multicultural Reader in U.S. Women's History,* 2nd ed., edited by Vicki L. Ruiz and Ellen Carol Dubois, pp. 284–297. New York: Routledge, 1994.

Taylor, Quintard. "Susie Revels Cayton, Beatrice Morrow Cannady, and the Campaign for Social Justice in the Pacific Northwest." In *African American Women Confront the West 1600–2000,* edited by Quintard Taylor and Shirley Ann Wilson Moore, pp. 189–206. Norman: University of Oklahoma Press, 2003.

Welke, Barbara Y. "Rights of Passage: Gendered-Rights Consciousness and the Quest for Freedom, San Francisco, California, 1850–1870." In *African American Women Confront the West 1600–2000,* edited by Quintard Taylor and Shirley Ann Wilson Moore, pp. 73–93. Norman: University of Oklahoma Press, 2003.

Wild, Mark. "Red Light Kaleidoscope: Prostitution and Ethnoracial Relations in Los Angeles, 1880–1940." *Journal of Urban History* 28, no. 6 (September 2002): 720–742.

A Navajo woman shearing a sheep, 1937. *National Archives (ARC 298582); Navajo Annual Extension Report, 1937 (#13 in the series)*

This 1934 photo shows a white woman teaching domestic skills to African American and Hispanic students as part of a Works Progress Administration project in Phoenix, Arizona. *Arizona State Library, Archives and Public Records, History and Archives Division, Phoenix, WPA Collection, #98-3380.jpg*

Dorothea Lange's famous 1936 photo, 'Migrant Mother'. *Library of Congress (LC-USF34-9058-C)*

A group of women at the Cheyenne River Agency standing next to a stack of mattresses they made, ca. 1940. *National Archives (ARC 285221)*

World War Two poster intended to recruit women into the armed forces. *National Archives (44-PA-820)*

31-year old Willa Beatrice Brown, the first African American woman to receive a commission as a lieutenant in the U.S. Civil Air Patrol during World War II, trained other pilots as well. *National Archives (208-FS-793-1) (ARC 535717)*

World War II poster intended to recruit more nurses into the Army Nurse Corps. ca. 1941–45. *National Archives (44-PA-205) (ARC 513648)*

A group of African American U.S. Army Nurses wait to disembark at Breenock, Scotland, 1944. *National Archives (111-SC-192605-S) (ARC 531204)*

Eleven young women who completed the nurses' aide course at the internment camp in Poston, Arizona, 1943. *National Archives (210-G-B493) (ARC 537101)*

Left to right are shipfitters Betty Pierce, Lola Thomas, Margaret Houston, Thelma Mort and Katie Stanfill, at the United States Navy Yard, Mare Island, California. ca 1943. *National Archives (ARC 296892)*

This photo shows the safety clothes that companies thought women workers needed during World War II, complete with a plastic bra. Los Angeles, California. ca. 1943. *National Archives (86-WWT-33-41) (ARC 522882)*

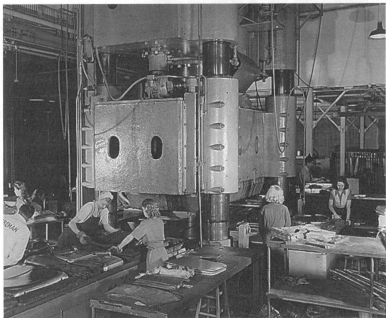

Women working at a hydraulic press making sheet metal parts at the Inglewood, California, plant of North American Aviation, Inc. 1942. *National Archives (6658(2) (ARC 195490)*

Welder-trainee Josie Lucille Owens working at the Kaiser Shipyards in Richmond, California. *National Archives (208-NP-1KKK(6)) (ARC 535803)*

This 1942 photo shows young Hispanic women bunching broccoli in Maricopa County, Arizona, for which they earned about $2.50 a day. *National Archives (16-G-159(2)AAA8172W) (ARC 512797); Creator Department of Agriculture, Office of the Secretary, Office of Information*

Pitch in and Help!

JOIN THE WOMEN'S LAND ARMY
OF THE U.S. CROP CORPS

Recruiting poster for the Women's Land Army. *National Archives (44-PA-1511) (ARC 515177)*

A young Japanese American girl waiting with her family's baggage before leaving by bus for an assembly center in the spring of 1942. *National Archives (210-G-2A-6) (ARC 539959)*

Japanese American women walk to their barracks at the Heart Mountain, Wyoming, internment camp in 1942. *Buffalo Bill Historical Center, Cody, Wyoming; Jack Richard Collection, PN.89.111.21238.3*

Ramona Fonseca in zoot suit, 1944. *Shades of L.A. Archives / Los Angeles Public Library, #00003660*

CHAPTER TEN

Women and the Great Depression

In many ways the 1930s were harder on women in the West than on men. Many men felt humiliated by not being able to provide for their families, but government responses to the economic crisis focused almost entirely on men's needs. For example, most local and federal relief efforts helped male breadwinners and did little for women workers. The Depression affected all women in one way or another, however. Even the women who were able to stay on their land or whose husbands kept their jobs witnessed the suffering around them. Two key factors determined how the economic collapse affected women: location and race. Rural women could potentially produce enough food so that they and their families would not starve, and these women could trade any surplus for other necessary items. But if grasshoppers or drought destroyed their crops and gardens or they could not pay bank loans or taxes, they might lose their land. Tens of thousands of farm families had to leave their land during the 1930s. Urban women, in contrast, could not produce their own food, but they had more access to paid work, however low the wage.

Even more than location, though, a woman's race determined her experiences during the Depression. White women, whether rural or urban, usually had more opportunities and resources than others. African American and Hispanic women had fewer options and resources even before the Great Depression, and state and local governments were less inclined to help them. Native American women experienced the first dramatic change in their relationship with the federal government since the Dawes Act of 1887 (see chapter four). The Depression affected all western women but not in the same way, and their choices and chances were shaped by factors over which they had little control.

Rural Women

The best-known images of the Depression come from the Dust Bowl of the Great Plains. Much of the West experienced periods of severe drought during the 1930s, but the Great Plains suffered the most because of too many years of over-plowing and cultivating marginal land. The soil was already so dry and loose that the wind just carried it away. Huge dust storms began sweeping across the plains in the spring of 1932 and many areas were drought-stricken throughout the decade. In South Dakota, for example, dust storms in 1933 and 1934 carried away the dry topsoil, and the state had grasshopper infestations every year from 1930 to 1935. In western Kansas, the drought began with a month of dust storms in 1933 and lasted until 1939, when enough rain finally fell to keep the dust down. In May 1934, a dust storm that began in Montana and Wyoming blew dirt all the way to the east coast; within a week it was falling on ships on the Atlantic Ocean. In 1935, the dust storms began in February and peaked on April 14, "Black Sunday," when a huge cloud of dust enveloped nearly the whole state of Kansas. For farm families, these environmental disasters were compounded by low prices for their products and foreclosures. Some of these financial and production problems had been plaguing farmers for decades and had helped fuel nineteenth-century groups like the Grange, Farmers' Alliance, and Populist movement (see chapter eight). The environmental catastrophes of the 1930s brought them to a head.

These challenges meant that western farm women had to use traditional strategies and develop new ones to keep their families fed and clothed. Farm women were critical to a family's ability to stay on its land when prices for crops dropped but taxes and mortgage payments did not. The traditional work of growing and canning as much fruit and vegetables as possible took on a new urgency, because women had to be able to supply a greater proportion of their family's food and produce a surplus that could be sold. One South Dakota woman planted an extra large garden in 1932, canned 50 quarts each of most vegetables, and stored 1,400 pounds of potatoes. Her efforts meant that her family had enough food to make it through the winter. In 1933, a poll taken by the *Dakota Farmer* newspaper showed that women canned an average of 228 quarts of food annually. In the early 1930s, a study in North Dakota showed that women saved their families $150–$300 a year by cultivating their own gardens. As the drought worsened, most women reported that they expanded their gardens every year.

In some parts of the West the drought was so severe that women could not harvest anything from their gardens, and they had to buy fruits and vegetables to can. For example, Martha Elizabeth Schmidt Friesen was in her late forties when the drought hit the 1,200-acre Kansas farm she shared with her husband George. In 1935 their farm was right in the middle of the Dust Bowl, and Friesen's garden was destroyed. She had to buy all of her fruits and vegetables for canning. From August to November 1937 she preserved nearly 20 gallons of peaches and nearly 18 gallons of tomatoes, and she put up twenty-eight jars of jams and jellies. She also raised poultry, a critical source of income for the farm. In 1935 she earned more than $220 from egg sales and $42 from chicken sales, while George sold only $134 worth of wheat.

Farm women were well aware of the value of their work. One woman summed it up in April 1935: "Our living expenses will come from our cream checks [the money she earned when she sold the cream from their dairy cattle's milk], garden and poultry." Women could trade chickens and eggs to local stores for the food and clothing that they could not make themselves, or they could sell poultry products for cash. In 1930, 90 percent of South Dakota farms had at least a small poultry operation, and most women expanded their efforts throughout the decade. Between 1932 and 1941, women sold 74 percent of the eggs that their chickens produced. They also raised turkeys, which would eat the grasshoppers plaguing the region and which were consistently in demand at Thanksgiving and Christmas. Turkey production in South Dakota doubled in the early 1930s. In the late 1930s, a study showed that nearly half of the income of an average South Dakota farm family was earned through "in-kind" trade (that is, bartered for other goods, not sold for cash). Most of this in-kind income probably came from trading the food that women grew and prepared.

Farm women contributed to the family's income in other ways, too. Whereas women usually had exclusive responsibility for the gardening and poultry, they shared the dairying with their husbands. Some helped feed and milk the cows, and most were in charge of separating the cream and making butter. Women also sold prepared food or took on small jobs to earn money, such as serving Sunday dinners for fifty cents a plate; doing another woman's washing, ironing, and mending; or working as cleaners and nurses. Farm women's work also meant indirect savings for their families. By sewing, mending, and altering clothes or making their own soap and other supplies, they saved the family's limited cash for other items. Some women had never stopped doing their own baking, and many more returned to the practice in the 1930s.

Not every western woman suffered dire straits during the Depression. Families that were not in debt before the decade began and did not experience the worst of the environmental disasters did not have to work so hard just to get by, and families sometimes could increase their landholdings if their neighbors had to sell land at a low price. One such woman was Kaia Cosgriff, whose family lived on an irrigated farm north of Big Timber, Montana, in the 1930s. Their land, milk cows, and machinery were all paid for. They kept a big garden; raised lambs, chickens, hogs, and cattle; and had easy access to a mill to grind their wheat. Cosgriff made most of her children's clothes, so all the family had to pay for was coffee, sugar, shoes, overalls, and underwear. When a neighbor lost everything and had to sell, she bought two cows and two calves, later selling the calves for more than she had paid for all four animals.

Farm women also responded to the crisis by reaching out to other women who were suffering and by trying to get someone in authority to listen. They wrote letters to the women's pages of rural newspapers, sharing practical suggestions and comfort with each other. Others wrote to politicians, asking for help and making suggestions for how governments could do more for struggling rural families. Mrs. H. Frederickson wrote to Montana Governor John Erickson in 1930 that she, her husband, and their six children had "worked very hard to try to make a home but it seems as if we can not raise means enough to do so any more." Her husband was disabled after an accident in 1926, so she and her children did all the heavy farm work. She worried that she would not be able to send her children to school past the eighth grade because the family had not been able to harvest a crop for three years and had lost their savings when the bank failed.

> So no money to pay taxes and intrests and we have never waisted a cent for shows and dances and so on…. I can not get a job and work for there is no work to be gotten here and I don't like to seperate my family. Can you advice me what do to do we have always payed our honest debts when we could rase the money to do so…. If only we could raise a crop again we could live.

In August 1931 Mrs. L. R. Lang, manager of the Women's Exchange in Wolf Point, Montana, wrote to the governor to suggest that merchants in every town in the state should put 5 percent of their daily receipts into a "helping" fund from which farmers could borrow.

There was nothing anyone could do about the drought and dust storms, so farm women focused on what they could do. Sometimes their production made the difference between a family's being able to stay on its farm and having to leave. But when all other strategies were exhausted, many farm families did have to leave their land altogether. Most farm families who made this decision headed to the west coast in search of work. At least 750,000 migrants moved to the far West during the Depression, most of them from the central plains states. For example, South Dakota experienced a net loss of more than 51,000 people during the decade. Seventeen counties lost 20 percent or more of their population, while one county lost almost half. The Depression was a painful reality check after some of the unbridled optimism farm women had experienced in previous decades (discussed in chapter seven).

Native American Women and the "Indian New Deal"

Native American women faced the same environmental catastrophes and personal challenges as other rural and small-town women during the Depression, but they did so from a socioeconomic position that the government had been weakening for decades. By 1930, Native American reservations were already some of the most poverty-stricken and under-served areas of the country. On South Dakota reservations in the 1930s, for example, 10 percent of all families had no permanent homes and nearly 5 percent lived in tents. The new challenges of the Depression made Native women's existing responsibilities harder, as they did for women in other poor communities. Bureau of Indian Affairs (BIA) staff on reservations across the West tried to help Native American women increase their gardening and canning activities, but the drought hampered these efforts. For example, women on the Cheyenne River Reservation in South Dakota planted nearly five hundred gardens in 1933 but lost them all to drought.

Native American women had few employment opportunities, particularly if they lived on reservations. Women were usually excluded from a reservation's cash-producing activities, such as farming, ranching, or forestry. They typically could only earn money by selling garden surpluses and by using their traditional skills with beadwork, quillwork, and basketry. These activities did not produce a lot of income, however, and women traded these items more often than they sold them for cash. The government-run schools (see chapter four) trained young women to do secretarial work, bookkeeping, domestic service, or nursing, but there were few job opportunities in these fields near or on the reservations. There were not even enough jobs in the BIA for all the young women and men graduating from the government's own schools.

In spite of these significant constraints, Native American women did everything they could to contribute to their families' survival during the 1930s. Some were able to get regular work through the BIA; irregular work through federal programs such as the Public Works Administration (PWA), National Youth Administration (NYA), and Federal Emergency Relief Administration (FERA); or emergency work with the Indian Emergency Conservation Work program (IECW, more commonly known as the Civilian Conservation Corps–Indian Division or CCC–ID). Most of the federally funded jobs provided by these programs, however, were in construction and intended for men. When women were employed in the same jobs as men, they were usually paid less.

The CCC–ID occasionally hired Native American women for jobs usually not considered women's work. Among the Apache in Arizona, for example, the BIA authorized the employment of women for gopher eradication. The white supervisors' stereotypes about women led them to assume that the Apache women would not want the job or would do it poorly, but more women enrolled in the program than there was equipment. By the end of the gopher project, the supervisors had nothing but praise for the women. The Western Shoshone agency in Nevada conducted a similar project, in which sixteen girls treated 1,500 acres with hand sprayers to eliminate the swarms of crop-eating insects nicknamed "Mormon crickets." The project foreman and the U.S. Biological Survey representative praised the "capable handling of their jobs by this crew of girls."

During the 1930s, female social workers began to take over the jobs previously performed by field matrons (see chapter four), and many of the new employees were graduates of the government-run Indian schools. For example, the Lakota and Nez Perce woman Mylie Lawyer was hired by the BIA in 1932 after graduating from Willamette University. She helped Blackfeet women at the Two Medicine Camp in Montana prepare food for the winter and reuse old garments, and she taught them new sewing, embroidery, and quilting techniques. She also encouraged the women to practice traditional crafts that they could sell for additional income. She was later transferred to the Flathead Reservation in Montana and then the Yakima Reservation in Washington state.

The BIA also recruited older women, like Naomi K. Sippi, a San Carlos Apache and social worker for her own community in Arizona. She worked five days a week visiting homes and the CCC–ID camps to instruct women on child care, sanitation, and home improvement. Like Lawyer, she encouraged women to make clothing, quilts, and baskets and to do beadwork. She cared for many older people around San Carlos, and in her off hours she made clothes for the elderly and children whose families could not afford to buy them. She also advocated for improved facilities in the camps and on the reservation, although BIA officials rarely took her advice. Several times she approached officials about the need for a community bath house—a place to which water could be piped—to relieve women of the necessity of carrying buckets of water to their tents. Her request fell on deaf ears because the BIA did not want to invest in the project.

Federal paternalism changed but did not end completely when Congress passed the Indian Reorganization Act (IRA) in 1934. More commonly known as the "Indian New Deal," this legislation was part of the sweeping "New Deal" program President Franklin Delano Roosevelt launched shortly after taking office in 1933 to end the nation's suffering and get it out of the Depression. Thanks to the efforts of reformers in the 1920s and early 1930s, Roosevelt included Native Americans in that New Deal. In 1933 he appointed John Collier, one of the most outspoken critics of federal Indian policy in the 1920s, to head the BIA. The Reorganization Act represented Collier's effort to correct all the errors that he believed the BIA had made. For example, the legislation ended the allotment policy of the 1887 Dawes Act (see chapter four) and tried to give Native Americans more autonomy in tribal government, economic development, and culture.

The Indian New Deal ended the allotment program, but the BIA did not stop trying to make Native Americans conform to Anglo-American gender norms. In keeping with other New Deal programs, the BIA's economic development and relief efforts focused on creating jobs for Native American men and training Native American women to be responsible housewives. Like all New Deal officials, BIA policymakers did not see Native women as independent economic agents. The one small exception was that, as noted above, the BIA itself started hiring more Native Americans, which gave a handful of women on the reservations clerical, teaching, nursing, and social work jobs. Also, as discussed in chapter eight, Native American women finally got the right to vote and hold office because the BIA insisted that the new tribal constitutions drawn up under the IRA grant Native women these rights. A more substantial improvement came in 1935, when the BIA finally agreed to recognize tribally sanctioned marriages and divorces and stop trying to force white marriage and divorce practices on Native Americans.

These sweeping changes in the BIA's policies and attitudes garnered mixed reactions from Native Americans and produced mixed results. At one end of the spectrum, the BIA's new support for Native American culture created some new jobs for women and opportunities for women artists and educators. On the other end of the spectrum was the herd reduction campaign among the Navajos. The Navajos objected to the government's efforts to limit the number of sheep they could have, refused to create a new constitution as ordered by the IRA, refused to send their children to government schools, and refused to cooperate with white officials trying to implement the new policies.

Navajo women were at the heart of many of these protests. For example, local newspapers in Winslow, Arizona, and Gallup, New Mexico, reported in 1936 that the women on the Navajo Reservation were inciting a revolt against Collier's herd reduction policies. During a community meeting at which a group of men had gathered to talk to the superintendent of the Navajo Service (a branch of the BIA formed in 1935 to consolidate the local Navajo agencies), an elderly woman named Denehotso Hattie scolded them all. She criticized the government's herd reduction policy and the Navajo men who were going along with it. She spoke so rapidly and heatedly that the government translator could not (or did not want to) keep up.

Collier hoped that his conservation program, which included herd reduction, would halt the environmental and human calamity taking place on reservations across the West. Not since the seventeenth century had the Southwest suffered through such an extreme drought. By the 1930s nearly one million sheep, goats, horses, and cattle ranged across the Navajo Reservation, and the damage caused by overgrazing and drought could no longer be ignored. Collier believed that if the situation was allowed to continue, the animals would starve and so would the Navajos. What he failed to recognize was that the ownership of herds of sheep and goats reflected powerful gender and cultural norms and that, like most of the earlier white reformers discussed in chapter four, he was trying to tell Native peoples how to live their lives.

The Navajos lived in a female-centered culture. They were a matrilineal and matrilocal people (terms discussed in chapter one), Navajo women owned most of the sheep and goats, and acquired the right through their mothers' lineages to use certain lands for pasturing their animals. The flocks provided both food and the wool that women used to make blankets, which were highly valued trade goods. In a society that measured wealth and prestige by livestock, the women who owned the biggest flocks had more autonomy and authority. They did not accept the demand to reduce those flocks without a fight.

Navajo women's rebellion against the stock reduction program did not start immediately. The program began in the winter of 1933–34, when the BIA bought more than 86,000 sheep from willing owners. That was fewer than the goal of 100,000, but the partial success led Collier to believe that the Navajos understood and accepted the program. The turning point came with the 1934 announcement that nearly all the goats on the reservation were to be eliminated. Conservationists targeted the goats because they had little market value and could eat their way through both rangelands and forests, but for Navajo women the goats often meant the difference between survival and starvation. Goats were a more dependable source of food because they survived the winters better than sheep. Families could drink goat's milk and eat goat cheese and meat while keeping their sheep to breed or barter. The loss of the goats would be devastating.

Collier convinced the men who served on the Navajo Tribal Council to go along with the plan by promising programs to save smaller herds or help poorer families trade their goats for sheep. All of the men, from the white government agents to the Navajos on the council, underestimated how hard the women who owned goats were going to fight for them. They were angry that the men had agreed to the plan and even angrier that they could not do anything to stop it. Some women chose to reduce their flocks their own way by butchering the animals for home consumption. Some of the male council members tried to convince the BIA to allow the tribe to reduce the herd through home consumption and sale to the reservation schools, but the BIA representative refused on the grounds that it would take too long to reduce the herds that way.

Collier first felt the women's wrath at the ballot box. The IRA was the cornerstone of his Indian New Deal, and the Navajos rejected it by a narrow margin in 1935, seeing the vote as a referendum on the stock reduction program and Collier himself. The BIA commissioner recognized that women voters may have tipped the balance, noting that the belief that the act meant continuing the herd reduction program "undoubtedly controlled the votes of a great many of the older Indians, particularly the women."

Despite this opposition, the herd reduction program continued. By 1936, range managers estimated that the reservation could carry roughly 560,000 sheep and goats or their equivalent in cattle or horses. (Each sheep or goat counted as one "sheep unit," whereas cattle counted as four sheep units and horses as five because they needed more forage.) But after nearly three years of reductions, the reservation still had more than 918,000 sheep units. The BIA wanted to reduce that number by 40 percent, so administrators set a maximum number of livestock that each family could own. In some regions the limit was as low as sixty-one sheep units. A family that had fewer than the maximum did not have to get rid of any animals, but it was not allowed to acquire new ones, either. In an additional assault on women's traditional power, the BIA assigned the permits for livestock to male heads of household, thus stripping Navajo women of their herds and their grazing rights.

Navajos' resistance grew when the new grazing program got underway. In early 1938 the grazing district supervisors began issuing the official grazing permits that specified how many "sheep units" each family could have grazing on their land. Some Navajos refused to accept their permits and others burned them. Although there were some violent confrontations, petition drives became the most common form of protest. At trading posts, schools, and dances, the Navajos signed petitions denouncing stock reduction, John Collier, and the entire New Deal. As early as 1937, when the official livestock counts began, thousands of women and men gathered to register their objections. Most could not write, so they marked the petitions with their thumbprints. More than 40 percent of the people who came to convey their displeasure were women. Women also raised money to send a delegation to Washington, D.C., to meet with First Lady Eleanor Roosevelt and beg her to intervene. One of the delegates, 'Asdzáá Nez, explained through an interpreter, "Our sheep are our children, our life, and our food." In 1940 one woman wept in anger as she told her story to a sociologist. Ever since Collier came to the reservation, she said, "We have seen nothing but trouble," and she emphasized that she could barely feed her family of six.

> This may sound awful for me to say, but I really hate John Collier....When I think of what he has done to us, I realize that I could even kill him myself just like I could kill a mad dog. I don't like to feel about anyone the way I feel about John Collier, but he has ruined our home, our lives, and our children, and I will hate him until the day I die.

In 1943 the Navajo Tribal Council finally passed a series of resolutions that attempted to cancel the herd reduction program. The council had been very weak politically in the mid-1930s, but by the early 1940s it was much stronger and willing to unite against the program. Collier vetoed the resolutions, but they signified the beginning of the end for the program, which the BIA finally cancelled in 1947.

At the other end of the spectrum of Native American women's experiences during the Depression was the Blackfeet Indian Craft Shop in northern Montana, one of the most successful Native businesses of the decade. The 1930s was certainly not the first time that Native women had tried to ease reservation poverty by selling their work to tourists, but their efforts took on a new urgency and scale during the Depression. Women were also frustrated by the so-called "Indian" craftwork, such as the reproduction baskets and blankets sold in the Southwest, that were increasingly being mass-produced cheaply by white companies. Forming marketing cooperatives to promote their own goods seemed like the only way to protect the value of their traditional skills and make money from traditionally made goods. Native American women used community workers, social workers, home economic teachers, home extension agents, and the BIA's new Arts and Crafts Board (created in 1936) to learn how to market their work more effectively.

Blackfeet women had produced beadwork for sale in the early 1930s but had not been able to profit from it because of the lack of a clear marketing plan. BIA community worker Jessie Donaldson Schultz, who had been working on the reservation since 1934, became the catalyst for the Blackfeet Indian Craft Shop. A group of Blackfeet women decided to form a crafts cooperative in March 1936. That summer the Glacier Park Curio Shops in Glacier Park, Montana, refused to sell Blackfeet crafts unless the women made "something of buckskin with a few beads" that could be sold to tourists for a few cents. The shops would not sell traditionally made items, which took longer to make and were of much higher quality, because the store managers believed that white tourists would not pay more money for better goods. Eight women then decided to sell their traditional work directly to tourists. They opened the first Blackfeet Indian Crafts Shop in a tipi in the camp circle and made a $31.50 profit.

Jessie Schultz and the Blackfeet artisans appealed to the local BIA superintendent for a permanent building for the shop. The BIA remodeled an old building at the agency for their use. The shop refused to cater to non-Indian tastes and only sold superior quality items decorated with traditional Blackfeet designs and made with traditional materials and techniques. Only native dye colors were to be used, moccasins and beadwork had to be stitched with sinew, and each bead had to be tacked individually to the buckskin. Beaded bags and moccasins, along with miniature tipis and dolls with real hair dressed in traditionally beaded buckskin, were staple items at the shop. Some men even supplied the shop with toy replicas of warrior shields, drums, and bows and arrows.

The success of the craft shop led the Division of Education of the Works Progress Administration (WPA), another New Deal initiative, to hire two Blackfeet workers, Louise Berrychild and Mary Little Bull, to start craft projects elsewhere on the reservation. In the spring of 1937, ten local crafts groups with a combined membership of four hundred organized the Blackfeet Cooperative Society. In January 1938 the group used a $7,500 Indian Rehabilitation Grant Loan to pay advances to the artists, buy supplies and tools, add another staff member, and refurbish a shop at St. Mary's Lake, about 25 miles northwest of Browning, Montana. They also moved a cabin to a good location on a highway in Glacier National Park to use as a shop for the 1938 season. By this time the original craft shop had entered the national market, selling clothing to Abercrombie and Fitch and to individuals through mail order. In 1937 the society earned just under $3,500; in 1938 it made more than $16,500. Blackfeet women went on to organize a reservation-wide Arts and Crafts Council, and in 1943 the Blackfeet Agency became the headquarters of the Northern Plains Indian Arts and Crafts Association.

The Navajo women's petitions and Blackfeet women's shop are only two of the more dramatic examples of Native American women's agency during the Depression. Women also seized opportunities for new kinds of political activism. They sat on tribal councils, served as members of livestock associations and electoral officers, and made their voices heard. Women at the Cheyenne River Agency frequently criticized the poor management of their reservation during the Depression, writing letters to everyone from their agency superintendent and BIA Commissioner John Collier to First Lady Eleanor Roosevelt. For example, in 1936 Virginia LeCompte wrote to Collier to complain about her husband's dismissal as foreman on a Public Works Administration construction project, but she also demanded an investigation into the federal government's wage scales, claiming that white men received "first class wages," while Indian men got "second class wages for first class labor."

Another significant and positive change for Native American women in the 1930s was the emergence of a new generation of female leaders, including Ella Cara Deloria and Helen Peterson of the Sioux and Ruth Muskrat Bronson of the Cherokee. Peterson and Bronson both served as executive director of the National Congress of American Indians (NCAI), a pan-Indian organization. Raised in a traditional, Dakota-speaking home even though her father was also an Episcopal priest, Deloria graduated from Columbia Teachers' College in 1915 with a bachelor of science degree. For the next four years she taught at the All Saints boarding school in Sioux Falls,

South Dakota, where she herself had been a student. In 1919 the YWCA hired her to be the health education secretary for Indian schools and reservations, and she later taught at the Haskell Indian School in Lawrence, Kansas. In 1927 Franz Boas, the pre-eminent American anthropologist of the time, asked her to translate and edit some written texts in the Sioux language, marking the start of her academic career. She assisted Boas as a research specialist in American Indian ethnology and linguistics until his death in 1942. She published *Dakota Texts,* a bilingual collection of Sioux stories, in 1932; *Dakota Grammar* in 1941; and *Speaking of Indians* in 1944. She also started work on a novel, *Waterlily,* in the 1940s. When she died in 1971, she was the leading authority on the Sioux.

The experiences of the Navajo and Blackfeet women and the life of Ella Deloria illustrate that the 1930s were years of depressing continuities and striking changes for Native American women. The IRA continued old patterns by trying to set the terms of Native Americans' reform, change, and progress, but it also created new political and creative opportunities for some Native women. The desire for agency and an increasing insistence on Native rights and the value of Native voices and culture continued through the Depression, World War II, and the postwar era.

Hispanic Women

Unlike rural white and Native American women, for whom environmental problems and weak or unwanted government policies created the biggest problems of the decade, women in the cities faced an entirely different set of economic problems as employers cut jobs and wages. Racial and ethnic minority women were already barely hanging on at the edges of the economy, and the Depression made it even harder for them to find and keep jobs.

Mexican American women, for example, were among the most economically disadvantaged of women before the Depression started. Many Hispanic women worked for pay outside the home in spite of conservative gender norms in the Mexican American community that prescribed that women were supposed to stay home. The two biggest Hispanic communities in the United States were in Los Angeles, California, and San Antonio, Texas; in 1930 the two cities were home to about 90,000 and 83,000 Hispanics, respectively. Although similar in size, the two communities occupied very different positions in their cities. In San Antonio, Hispanics were the largest visible minority and far outnumbered the small black community. A much larger proportion of Hispanic women worked outside the home in Texas than in any other state, with California a distant second. Most of the domestic servants, seamstresses, and laundry workers in San Antonio were Hispanic women. They had also begun to work in textile and clothing factories, where they faced appalling conditions in unsafe, poorly ventilated buildings. In 1933 wages ranged from one to five dollars a week for a six-day workweek, and some employers broke state law by making the women work more than nine hours a day.

Low wages and poor working conditions were also the norm for Hispanic women in other cities. For example, in 1934 the El Paso (Texas) League of Women Voters conducted a survey of employers of Hispanic domestics. It found that some domestics earned as little as ten or fifteen cents per day, and the highest wage was seven dollars a week. Many employers bussed their domestics in from Mexico because they thought that Mexican-born women were more compliant (and thus easier to exploit) than Mexican American women. They were also cheaper, earning as little as one dollar a week for a full-time job and fifty cents a week for part-time work. In 1935 the Texas State Department of Vocational Education reported that "long hours of drudgery and starvation pay are the rule rather than the exception" for domestics working in El Paso's wealthiest homes. By comparison, in 1932 Anglo women earned as little as $4.15 per week in a pecan-shelling company or as much as $12.45 at a department store, whereas Hispanic wages ranged from $2.65 to $9.00 per week and African American wages from $2.65 to $7.25 per week. In 1932 women in Texas industries were the lowest paid women workers in the nation.

The incredibly low wages and poor conditions for domestics were the main reasons why the El Paso elite had such a hard time finding Mexican American women to work for them. To solve the problem, wealthy Anglo-Texans asked the city to disqualify Mexican American women from local relief programs (which were supposed to "relieve," at least a little, the economic hardships of the Depression). This move would force more of the Mexican American women to work as domestics for the wealthy Anglos. The city complied by announcing that any woman who refused to accept a job would automatically be cut from the relief rolls. This act left Mexican American women with two choices: work for extremely low wages as a domestic servant or have no income at all.

San Antonio's economy depended so much on cheap Mexican labor, especially women's, that the city leaders made few concerted efforts to repatriate them (that is, send them back to Mexico). In other western cities, repatriation was a common strategy for creating more jobs for whites and getting rid of Hispanics. Cities were not shy about deporting Mexican Americans who had been born in the United States but, like most whites at the time, had no paperwork to prove their citizenship. Over the course of the 1930s, poverty and repatriation programs forced more than 400,000 Mexicans and their children to leave the United States.

Hispanic women only worked outside the home, away from their husbands or fathers' supervision, as a last resort. Most wives did the kind of paid labor that could be done at home. In Los Angeles in the 1930s, a study of ninety Hispanic families found that wives worked for pay in only twenty-eight of the households, and ten of these women engaged in waged work at home. Half of the working wives contributed less than 20 percent of family incomes. In San Antonio, the Hispanic women who did industrial jobs in their homes typically worked for eight to twelve hours a day, six days a week, and made less than three dollars a week. They earned less than an Anglo-American woman even when the two did exactly the same job in the same location. Pecan shelling and sewing were the two main forms of industrial employment women did at home. In San Antonio in the mid-1930s at least 4,000 people were doing these kinds of jobs, and anywhere from 15,000 to 20,000 families relied on industrial homework to survive. By the late 1930s, wages for pecan shelling had fallen to four cents a pound, and an adult worker made an average of $2.50 a week.

Not all Hispanic women tolerated low wages and poor conditions in silence. Being the lowest paid workers anywhere in the country prompted some Hispanic women in Texas and California to become highly organized and vocal. They unionized and participated in several major strikes in the 1930s. In 1933, for example, El Paso's Hispanic laundry workers and domestics unionized in response to the National Industrial Recovery Act. The NIRA was passed in 1933 as a key part of the New Deal and was intended to inject federal money into the economy, regulate employers and industries, and give workers more rights to organize unions and bargain collectively. Laundries and domestic service were the two biggest employers of Hispanic women in El Paso, and within the first month after NIRA's enactment, the domestics' union had more than seven hundred members. The union's first act was to send letters to its members' employers demanding a minimum weekly wage of six dollars. Within a few weeks, only one employer had refused and 169 had agreed. The group also tried, this time unsuccessfully, to reduce the hours that the U.S.–Mexico border was open, hoping to make it harder for employers to bus women in from Mexico.

In San Antonio, the International Ladies Garment Workers' Union (ILGWU) organized the city's female garment workers, most of whom were Hispanic and earned such low wages that garment workers elsewhere in the country could not compete. The ILGWU had two key organizers in San Antonio: Rebecca Taylor and Myrle Zappone. Taylor was an educated, bilingual, Anglo-American resident of San Antonio. She was in her twenties and teaching night classes at a vocational school when the ILGWU approached her to become an organizer. She had no previous union experience but spent the next twenty-five years as a major figure in the San Antonio labor movement. Hispanic organizer Myrle Zappone joined the union after several years as a garment worker. By the end of the decade, the ILGWU had more than 1,000 members in the city and had conducted several strikes.

Their efforts had mixed results for workers, however. For example, Taylor and Zappone helped unionize the Halff and the A. B. Franks garment factories in 1934 and 1935. One of the plants closed as soon as the workers unionized, and the other plant switched to making men's shirts, which meant it could get rid of its unionized workers and hire new ones. An ILGWU strike in 1936 against the Dorothy Frocks factory led to fourteen union members being fined and/or jailed, before the company signed a contract with the union. The ILGWU made more progress in the late 1930s, gaining another, better contract for the workers at the Shirlee Frocks company after another strike.

The garment industry in San Antonio was not the only one affected by Hispanic women's militancy in the 1930s. The first major Depression-era strike in San Antonio occurred in August 1933 at the Finck Cigar Company, where about four hundred women, mostly Hispanic, walked off their jobs as cigar rollers and tobacco strippers. They were some of the lowest paid workers at the factory. Mrs. W. H. Ernst, a Mexican American woman whom Finck had fired for trying to organize her fellow workers, led the strike. The strike ended within a month when the company signed an agreement with the National Recovery Administration (another New Deal agency). The agreement promised a forty-hour workweek and lower penalties for improperly rolled cigars, in exchange for a low wage scale ranging from seventeen to twenty-two cents an hour. However, the company did not honor the agreement and refused to rehire the strike leaders. The 1933 strike was the first of several against the company. The Finck workers became more militant over time and the later strikes lasted longer, but the local police consistently intervened on the company's behalf, and the union workers made fewer gains with each strike.

Hispanic women also participated in strikes in San Antonio's pecan shelling industry in 1934, 1935, and 1938. The first two strikes achieved very little, but the 1938 strike, which was the longest and most bitter of any of San Antonio's Depression-era strikes, transformed the industry. The Texas Pecan Shelling Workers' Union went on strike on February 1, 1938. They had affiliated with the Congress of Industrial Organizations, a militant new national union. Most of the strikers went back to work in March when both sides agreed to arbitration. In April the arbitration board agreed to a seven-month contract with a tiny wage increase, but when the owners refused to comply with federal labor legislation, the workers walked out again in October. In December the U.S. Department of Labor Regional Labor Board ruled against the larger employers, who had asked for a six-month delay in implementing a minimum wage of twenty-five cents per hour. In response, most of the smaller companies closed their businesses and the larger operators converted to machine shelling, effectively eliminating all of the jobs that Hispanic women had in the industry.

Emma Tenayuca, a well-known local Hispanic labor sympathizer and proud Communist, played a key leadership role during the strike. She was very popular in the city's Hispanic community, but her ties to communism also made her a favorite target of the San Antonio police. She was arrested often in the 1930s and finally had to withdraw from the local labor movement in 1939.

Industrial workers in Texas were not the only Hispanic women in the 1930s who walked off the job to protest low wages and poor working conditions. In southern California most Hispanics worked as agricultural laborers, doing very hard work for low wages. For example, men and women who worked in the cotton fields picked an average of 200 pounds during a ten-hour day. One woman recalled,

> I'd have a twelve-foot sack....I'd tie the sack around my waist and the sack would go between my legs and I'd go on the cotton row, picking cotton and just putting it in there....So when we finally got it filled real good then we would pick up the [100-pound]

sack, toss it up on our shoulders, and then I would walk, put it up there on the scale and have it weighed, put it back on my shoulder, climb up on a wagon and empty that sack in.

When California growers cut their workers' wages in 1933, a wave of strikes occurred. Just as women in mining towns did during strikes, Hispanic women farmworkers ran kitchens and cared for children at strike camps, marched on picket lines, and distributed food and clothing to the poorest striking workers and their families. Some women attended and spoke at strike meetings, and it was usually women who confronted strikebreakers, because they knew that the strikebreakers were less likely to harm women physically. Bar owner Lourdes Castillo of Corcoran, California, stored food for strikers at her business and was responsible for distributing it fairly. She also kept a log of who came in and out of the strike camp and who spoke at meetings. After a long and bitter strike, the employers gave in and raised the farmworkers' wages.

Like other workers, Hispanic women did their best to support themselves and their families during the Depression, including unionizing and striking when they could. Though most New Deal programs favored men, working women took advantage of new labor laws that made it easier to unionize. But local police, courts, and employers often blocked their efforts, and the mainstream labor movement organized women and nonwhite workers last. Their struggles for better pay and working conditions continued until World War II, which provided some of them with new opportunities.

Relief Programs

As previous sections have noted, helping women was not a primary goal of early New Deal projects. All levels of government were more concerned about getting men back to work because officials assumed that heads of household were mainly men and that men, not women, were entitled to help in fulfilling their roles as breadwinners. During the Depression, however, women in government positions began insisting that the government had to do more to help women, particularly those who did head their own households. In 1933 Harry Hopkins, director of FERA, admitted that "women as a group have had less attention than any other unemployed group" and promised to fund more women's projects. He created a Women's Division within FERA, but the neglect of women workers continued. Of the 1.6 million Americans who received federal work relief in 1934, only 142,000 were women. The federal government itself fired 1,600 married women from federal jobs, on the grounds that married women supposedly had husbands to take care of them and thus were taking a job away from a man who needed it more. State and local governments quickly followed suit. Across the West, relief administrators typically saw women as temporary workers who were primarily homemakers. Officials tended to frown on any project that hired women to do tasks that they saw as nontraditional. For example, although women in Texas had worked as agricultural laborers and laundry workers for years, the Texas WPA refused to fund projects for women in those areas on the grounds that women could not handle the physical labor.

The projects for women generally focused on improving their domestic skills and were racially segregated. In San Antonio, for example, the Housekeeping Aid Projects employed Anglo and Hispanic women to help with housework and child care when parents were ill or unable to manage on their own. African American women could get relief under a completely separate program, the Household Workers Project, which was intended to teach them how to be "capable domestics." The racial separation continued even in larger-scale projects, such as the government-funded cannery that opened in San Antonio in 1934 and the sewing room that opened in 1936.

Relief officials often actively discriminated against African American women. Lula Gordon of San Antonio, for example, wrote to President Roosevelt to complain about the treatment she had received at the local relief office: "I have three children. I have no husband and no job. I have worked hard ever since I was old enough.

I am willing to do any kind of work because I have to support myself and my children. I was under the impression that the Government or the W.P.A. would give the Physical fit relief clients work. I have been praying for that time to come." At the local relief office, she had spoken with a Mrs. Beckmon, who had made it very clear what kind of work she thought African American women should do.

> Mrs. Beckmon told me to phone a Mrs. Coyle because she wanted some one to clean house and cook for five dollars a week. Mrs. Beckmon said if I did not take the job in the Private home I would be cut off from everything altogether. I told her I was afraid to accept the job in the private home because I have registered for a government job and when it opens up I want to take it. She said that she was talking people off of the relief and I have to take the job in the private home or non. I ask her if I take the job would I be transferred when the W.P.A. jobs open. She said there was no such thing as that. She was giving me a job and if I wanted work take the job and if I did not I wouldn't get that and nothing else. I have read in the paper that the Government is not going to put any one to work in private homes, that is why I was afraid to accept the job. I had to accept the job because I have to have work to live, but Mrs. Coyle was talking to someone looking for work when I phoned her. She told me if she need me she would let me know. If she does not need me what will I do? If she does need me is that the kind of work the government is giving the women. I need work and I will do anything the government gives me to do.

Many African American women left the paid workforce completely during the Depression, which was a very unusual trend because their participation in the paid workforce traditionally had been much higher than white women's. Relief programs often forced married black women to stop working because their husbands would only qualify for help if the wives were not employed. The increasing number of white women looking for paid work also squeezed black women out of their jobs. If nothing else, black families were accustomed to deprivation, as African American club woman Florence

Napoleon of Albuquerque, New Mexico, said: "We didn't have so much, so the Depression wasn't such a jolt as it would be to a person who was used to lots of things."

The discrimination against racial minorities in relief programs did not occur only on federally funded projects. In fact, local relief efforts were usually far more discriminatory. As in the case of El Paso's white elite using the local relief office to blackmail Mexican American women into working as domestics, relief officials often used their resources to discriminate against racial minorities. For example, in Cochise County, Arizona, an Anglo-American family of five received fifty-six hours of relief work a week, whereas a Mexican American family of five got only thirty-six hours.

Being white did not necessarily mean that a woman had a positive experience while on relief, however; Julia Trees of Montana recalled how embarrassed her mother and other women were about the "awful shapeless dresses" they had to wear as uniforms while working on a WPA sewing project. The dresses announced "to the whole town each day that [the women] were on the welfare projects," and they undermined her mother's self-esteem and sense of capability. "They were good sewers and made nice clothing and flannel sleep wear for distribution to needy people. They didn't mind the eight hours a day bent over a machine but never should they have been singled out in this way with uniforms." Julia got a National Youth Administration clerical job that let her finish school and start teaching.

Although the thousands of relief projects discriminated against women workers in general and racial minority women in particular, there is no doubt that they did also provide much-needed employment for thousands of women. Eva McLean of Montana was very suspicious of the work programs at first. She entered the relief office for the first time "outwardly defiant but with inward self-loathing." She changed her mind when she became the cook at a dormitory built and run by the WPA so that rural children could attend school. She later got a job in the WPA Recreational Division, and she was proud of being able "to release my husband from common labor, to educate my boys, …to dress them and us all well." Her husband resented her professional success, however, and she eventually chose to stop working rather than strain her marriage any further.

In an effort to create manufacturing jobs for women, the Women's Division of the FERA announced a mattress-making project in August 1934, the first national work project designed specifically for women. The program had three goals: to provide work relief for more than 60,000 women then on direct relief; to reduce a nation-wide cotton surplus; and to provide mattresses for needy families. The program paid workers the going local rate but no less than thirty cents an hour. New Mexico's state relief agencies promptly bought thirty bales of cotton and 3,000 yards of mattress ticking, and requested another two hundred bales and 17,100 yards from the Federal Surplus Relief Corporation. New Mexico soon had 152 women and twenty-six men employed in ten counties.

Employment in the mattress workshops increased when the WPA encouraged shops to begin to produce clothing and bedding as well as mattresses. By November 1934, twenty-four sewing rooms across New Mexico employed more than six hundred women working a six-hour day. The women were proud of their work and the income they received for it, and they were happy to be helping other people through their labor. It also lifted their spirits. Ena Walter Mitchell stated that the sewing project in Hidalgo County was a "wonderful thing" because "some of the women were alone [that is, unmarried] and that was the only income they had."

But the project's benefits did not go as far as they could have. In June 1936, Lena Robbins, a seamstress with the Clovis project in Curry County, New Mexico, wrote to Eleanor Roosevelt to complain. Work in the Clovis sewing room had been cut from full time to part time and the sewers' wages were cut from forty-four dollars per month to twenty-two dollars per month. Robbins was angry that the money seemed to be going to the white women who had the steady, well-paid administrative jobs at the public welfare head-quarters in Santa Fe instead of to "the women whom the plan was originally intended to help."

New Mexico had a much higher rate of women working on the sewing projects than the rest of the country: 84 percent of the women receiving relief in the state worked in WPA sewing rooms, far above the national average of 56 percent. Unique to New Mexico was the woman-directed task of plastering the exteriors of adobe buildings, particularly rural schools and churches. The local WPA office hired Hispanic women in three other counties at forty cents an hour to finish the adobe once the men had done the heavy labor. Other work for women included cataloguing and rebinding books in public libraries and translating Spanish documents in the Historical Society of New Mexico. In Albuquerque, a soap-making project employed five women to render scraps and spoiled meat from cattle slaughtered as part of a FERA drought relief program. In two weeks the women made 1,500 one-pound bars of laundry soap, which were then distributed to needy families.

Relief programs for Native American women, like those for non-Indian women, consisted mainly of textile and food preservation projects. On the Flathead Reservation in Montana in 1936, for example, the reservation received a railway carload of fabric rejected by the army and additional fabric from the WPA warehouse in Butte. Officials set up five sewing units, four of them in government buildings. Flathead women made hundreds of garments and household linens from the fabric and used the scraps to create rag rugs. The completed projects were distributed to local families on relief.

Yet another New Deal agency, the Resettlement Administration (RA), launched an ambitious project with the Arapahoes in Wyoming in 1936. It organized the Arapahoe Cooperative Canning Association, with 104 tribal members each contributing a fifty-dollar share. The RA loaned the Arapahoes $13,200 to get started, and WPA workers remodeled a school to house the cannery. One year later the cooperative opened for business. Most of the workers were women who cleaned and prepared the vegetables for canning on a piecework basis. The project hired men, paying them by the hour, to do the heavier work. It divided the profits made from selling the canned goods, with the producers receiving 40 percent and the factory keeping 60 percent. The association enlarged the cannery in 1937, by which time a total of 83 acres were under cultivation to supply the factory. In the fall of 1937 the cannery processed more than 38,000 cans, more than double the 1936 total.

Many of the reservations had far more women who wanted to work than they had jobs and equipment. At the Flathead Reservation's sewing centers, a shortage of sewing machines meant that only twelve to fifteen women could be employed at a time. They worked ten eight-hour days each month, for which each woman received forty dollars. Of the five sewing centers, three operated during the first half of the month and two opened during the second half. Agency officials on the Blackfeet reservation in Montana reported similar conditions. More women wanted to work than there were sewing machines, so each woman could only work for thirty hours a week.

In addition to the limited scope of relief efforts, sexism and racism continued to hinder women's relief programs in the West. In January 1936, all the women working in the sewing rooms in one New Mexico county had their hours cut in half, on the orders of the state WPA administrator Lee Rowland, who "did not believe women should earn as much as men." Margaret Reeves, the director of New Mexico's branch of the FERA, believed that New Mexico did not need as many work projects for women because such projects were better suited to Anglo-American communities in more industrialized areas. New Mexico's population was half Hispanic and had an average of five children per family; Reeve wanted to provide employment for the men so that the women could stay home and care for their large families. In Nevada, only 109 of 680 eligible non-reservation Shoshones in three counties received relief. Alida Bowler, the superintendent of the agency, complained that the Nevada Emergency Relief Administration was denying the Shoshones relief on the grounds that it would make them dependent and lazy.

For women in a position to provide services, as administrators, social workers, or office personnel, New Deal programs offered opportunities for better jobs and a great deal of authority. A few women even got the rare chance to develop and apply executive skills as project and agency administrators. They managed vast sums of money, supervised thousands of employees, and helped promote programs and policies. In New Mexico, for example, Margaret Reeves had served as director of the state's Bureau of Child Welfare since 1924 and became director of New Mexico's FERA branch in 1933. Nearly six million dollars in FERA money crossed her desk in her first year. In January 1936, however, the new governor fired her because he wanted his own people managing the money.

Government relief for women during the Depression ranged from nonexistent to blatantly racist, but in between those two extremes it did eventually aid many thousands of women across the West by giving them jobs and an income, however small. For some women, relief jobs were the only help they got during the 1930s, but for most women they were only one part of their survival strategies.

Witnessing the Crisis

The Depression affected every woman across the West in one way or another, but not every woman faced the hardest choices. Most women kept their jobs or stayed on their farms, and as a result they became the witnesses to the crises around them. For some, witnessing the traumas suffered during the Depression was part of their jobs. For example, Charlotte Edwards worked as a secretary in the Agricultural Adjustment Act (AAA) office in Broadus, Montana. Congress created the AAA to fix production quotas and buy surplus crops and stock in an effort to raise farm commodity prices. Edwards later wrote that she had not realized before what an "enormous tragedy that this was for the individual ranchers because they were losing everything....I had never seen grown men cry and many of them did when they came in to sign their forms....I realized that life was not a carefree fun time....Many people left Powder River County during that period and sought jobs or lost their places and never came back."

In 1936, Linda Cameron Burgess was the wife of a geologist working for the Anaconda Mining Company in Butte, Montana. The Depression had hit Butte hard, but Burgess wrote that the locals believed the worst was behind them "now that the mine is working at 2/3 capacity." She was very sympathetic to the unions and strikes in Butte in the late 1930s. She wrote that the labor activism stemmed from "terrible abuses such as having no ventilation in the mines at which time men would be carried out in a stupor." The women she hired as domestic servants provided her closest contact with Butte's working class. Even while subsisting on a budget of $175 a month and renting a two-bedroom apartment for $55, the Burgesses consistently hired domestic help. In April 1937 she wrote that there was a scarcity of available help because the Works Progress Administration had "many provisions for women…and naturally they prefer that with higher pay, better companionship and regular hours of work." By November, however, she believed that mine closures had driven more women into the workforce. "It isn't so hard to get help now because of the closing of the mines which means many wives and daughters are earning the family income," she explained.

The best-known observers of the Depression in the West were the women photographers who worked for the Farm Security Administration (FSA). Congress created the FSA in 1937, and one of its programs paid photographers to document rural conditions to foster public support for New Deal programs. Several women worked for the FSA, including Esther Bubley, Marjory Collins, Marion Post Wolcott, and Dorothea Lange. Marion Post Wolcott was born in New Jersey in 1910, the daughter of an activist who had worked with birth control advocate Margaret Sanger in New York. The FSA sent Wolcott to Montana from early August to late September 1941. She later recalled that

> people were curious that I was out there doing that kind of job.…
> They would ask more questions, watch where I went, what I did. I
> was much more conspicuous. I was gossiped about. They noticed

where I stayed—and I couldn't stay in certain tourist cabins oth-
erwise my reputation would suffer.... On a couple of occasions I
was "arrested," taken down to the police headquarters and questioned, or stopped by sheriffs and taken to their offices. They were
just curious and didn't have anything better to do.

She spent hours gaining the confidence of the people she wanted to
photograph. "I sometimes hang around and talk and help peel potatoes, wash and dress the children, help hang out the clothes or see
that the beans don't burn. I may give them a lift to town or perhaps
do five minutes shopping for them in the evening and bring it back
the next day."

The most famous FSA photographer was Dorothea Lange, who
produced hundreds of photographs of migrant workers, California
migrant labor camps, and destitute men in bread lines. Her job was
to document the plight of people who had fled from the Dust Bowl
disaster in Oklahoma and Texas to seek work in California. She
wrote to her boss at one point, "I saw conditions over which I am
still speechless." Her most famous image is the 1936 photo "Migrant
Mother, Nipomo, California." It is probably the best-known image
of the American West during the Depression. In a 1960 article Lange
described how she got the picture:

> I saw and approached the hungry and desperate mother, as if
> drawn by a magnet. I do not remember how I explained my pres-
> ence or my camera to her, but I do remember she asked me no
> questions. I made five exposures, working closer and closer from
> the same direction. I did not ask her name or her history. She told
> me her age, that she was thirty-two. She said that they had been
> living on frozen vegetables from the surrounding fields, and birds
> that the children killed. She had just sold the tires from her car to
> buy food.

By refusing to back away from what they saw, or in Lange's case
by insisting on getting as close as she could to the face of suffering,
the women who acted as witnesses to the Great Depression served
vital roles at the time by creating awareness and understanding of

the effects that the Depression was having on the people of the West. Images such as "Migrant Mother" continue to put a human face on the suffering so that modern viewers can also understand better how hard the decade was.

The Depression had a profound effect on the West and the women who lived there. It put unprecedented constraints on most women's economic and personal lives, while creating some new opportunities and choices for other women. Many girls had to leave school at an earlier age to help out, and women of all racial groups waited longer to get married. It forced a lot of women out of work and off their land, while bringing some women into the paid workforce for the first time. Women stood up for themselves in ways that they never had in the face of changes over which they had little control. The New Deal and other government programs sometimes helped and sometimes hindered them, because the Depression highlighted a broader societal tension between women's roles as domestic dependents and as independent adults who deserved practical help. The same conflicting impulses marked government programs and public responses during World War II, but that tension had far less of an impact on the huge increase in women's choices and opportunities during the war.

Suggested Readings

Anderson, Karen. *Changing Woman: A History of Racial-Ethnic Women in Modern America.* New York: Oxford University Press, 1996.

Blackwelder, Julia Kirk. *Women of the Depression: Caste and Culture in San Antonio, 1929–1939.* College Station, TX: Texas A&M University Press, 1984.

Chávez Layva, Yolanda. "'Faithful Hard-Working Hands': Mexicana Workers During the Great Depression." *Perspectives in Mexican American Studies* 5 (1995): 63–77.

Deutsch, Sarah. *No Separate Refuge: Culture, Class, and Gender on an Anglo-Hispanic Frontier in the American Southwest, 1880–1940.* New York: Oxford University Press, 1987.

Haywood, C. Robert. "The Great Depression: Two Kansas Diaries." *Great Plains Quarterly* 18 (Winter 1998): 23–37.

Laslett, John H. M. "Gender, Class, or Ethno-Cultural Struggle? The Problematic Relationship Between Rose Pesotta and the Los Angeles ILGWU." *California History* (Spring 1993): 20–39.

Murphy, Mary. *Hope in Hard Times: New Deal Photographs of Montana, 1936–1942.* Helena: Montana Historical Society Press, 2003.

Pentland, Brenda. "Letters from 'World's End': A Young Couple's Portrait of Butte, 1936–1941." *Montana: The Magazine of Western History* 53, no. 4 (Winter 2003): 36–49.

Riney-Kehrberg, Pamela. "Separation and Sorrow: A Farm Woman's Life, 1935–41." *Agricultural History* 67, no. 2 (Spring 1993): 185–196.

Schackel, Sandra. *Social Housekeepers: Women Shaping Public Policy in New Mexico, 1920 to 1940.* Albuquerque: University of New Mexico Press, 1992.

Schweider, Dorothy. "South Dakota Farm Women and the Great Depression." *Journal of the West* 24, no. 4 (1985): 6–18.

Sundstrom, William A. "Discouraging Times: The Labor Force Participation of Married Black Women, 1930–1940." *Explorations in Economic History* 38, no. 1 (January 2001): 123–146.

Weber, Devra Anne. "Raiz Fuerte: Oral History and Mexicana Farmworkers." In *Unequal Sisters: A Multicultural Reader in U.S. Women's History,* 2nd ed., edited by Vicki L. Ruiz and Ellen Carol Dubois, pp. 395–404. New York: Routledge, 1994.

Weisiger, Marsha. *Dreaming of Sheep in Navajo Country.* Seattle: University of Washington Press, 2009.

CHAPTER ELEVEN

Women and World War II

World War II was a definitive turning point for women in the West, as it was for the region as a whole. From significant new federal investment in infrastructure and wartime industries to internal migration patterns and Japanese internment, the war affected the West to a much greater extent than it did any other region of the country. In the midst of wartime upheaval, western women of all races and classes made unprecedented choices and took extraordinary chances. They forged remarkable new opportunities for themselves and lived through the unexpected consequences of war. Some joined the military, whereas others took new, temporary jobs in war-related industries, filling positions left empty when men went off to war. The war even affected women's traditional jobs and volunteer work, creating new constraints for women at the same time as the need for their work grew dramatically. Japanese women on the West Coast faced the worst constraints because the U.S. government interned them and their families after Japan attacked Pearl Harbor in December 1941, the act that finally drew the United States into a war that had started two years before. Yet despite this mass imprisonment, many of the young Japanese American women carved out new career opportunities when they got out. Women of all racial groups felt entitled to better treatment and more options, and the war provides some of the most dramatic examples of this new assertiveness of any period in the West's history.

Women in the Military

Western women from many different racial and ethnic backgrounds joined the military by the thousands during World War II. By the end of the war, a total of 350,000 women from across the country had served in the various branches: 140,000 in the Women's Auxiliary Army Corps (usually called the Women's Army Corps or WAC for short); 100,000 in the Navy's Women Accepted for Voluntary Emergency Service; 23,000 in the U.S. Marines; 13,000 in the U.S. Coast Guard; 60,000 in the Army Nurse Corps (ANC); and 14,000 as U.S. Navy nurses. The rationale for recruiting women was that they were "releasing men to fight"; that is, women could do most of the noncombat jobs to free the men for combat positions. Women also enlisted for personal and patriotic reasons. Many genuinely wanted to serve their country in a time of crisis, whereas others seized the chance to learn new skills and see new places and to be with other women. Most of the women employed by the military worked in clerical positions, but thousands also filled almost all noncombat occupational specialties. These included work as radio operators, chemists, cartographers, weather forecasters, control tower operators, gunnery specialists, pilots, carpenters, plumbers, electricians, and mechanics.

Most of the western women who served in the military were white, because the military made no effort to recruit women from any minority group except African Americans. The War Department and WAC director Oveta Hobby decided that black women should make up 10 percent of the corps' strength, but they never made up more than 4 percent and remained in segregated units. The only exception to this segregation was the training center at Fort Des Moines, Iowa, where Hobby had ordered that the officers' housing, mess halls, and service facilities be integrated. There were so many criticisms of the Fort Des Moines policy that the WAC made no other efforts to desegregate.

About eight hundred Native American women volunteered for the armed forces, and their white colleagues accepted them much more readily than they accepted black women. Three newspapers published for Native American readers even publicized the contributions of Native women who enlisted. *Indians at Work,* the magazine published by the Bureau of Indian Affairs (BIA), carried a story about two women from the Standing Rock Reservation, Roselyn Eagle and Myrtle Fool Bear, who joined the WAC after walking thirty-two miles in a sleet storm to Fort Yates, North Dakota. *The Indian Leader,* published by the Haskell Institute in Kansas, and the *Indian School Journal,* published by the Chilocco Institute in Oklahoma, ran special columns about former students who had enlisted in the armed forces. In a 1943 edition of the former, Margie Williams, a Lakota graduate of Haskell and a WAC, wrote that

> as in every progressive organization, our race is well represented in the Women's Army Auxiliary Corps. It is with much pride that the Indian woman dons the uniform of her country to aid in settling the turmoil. As in battles before, the Redman is proving to his white brother that he can make an outstanding contribution, both on the home front and behind the firing lines. With the same pride and devotion, the Indian woman is proving herself to be one of Uncle Sam's priceless daughters.

Barbara Fielder LeBeau served as a WAC from 1943 to 1945, and was assigned to the Office of the Port Inspector General as Assistant Chief Clerk at the Los Angeles Point of Embarkation. She often accompanied her white commander when his duties took him off the base, and she recalled that he usually told people she was "an Indian girl." She did not like the way he singled her out because she did not feel that being Native was a factor in her work. "I always felt like what I was doing was the best I could do, regardless of who I was or what I was. And I never once gave it a thought that my Indian blood had something to do with it."

The government did not allow Japanese American women to join the WAC until April 1943, although it did allow Japanese American men to enlist in the armed services before then. Between the spring of 1943, when the ban was lifted, and the end of the war in 1945, more than four hundred Nisei (second generation) women enlisted. The military initially planned on segregating the Nisei women as they had with black women, assuming that whites would not want to serve with people who looked like the enemy, but it abandoned the plan because so few Nisei women enlisted and African Americans were already challenging the segregation policy. The first Nisei woman to become a member of the WAC was Frances Iritani, inducted in November 1943 in Denver. Most Nisei WACs worked in clerical positions, like other women in the service, but some worked in intelligence, translating war documents, and the army assigned others to the Military Intelligence Service Language School at Fort Snelling, Minnesota.

Ruth Fujii of Hawaii had the distinction of being the only Japanese American woman to serve in the Pacific theater during the war. She did secretarial work in the Philippines. She and three other Hawaiian Nisei women had enlisted for patriotic reasons. Another young woman, Hisako Yamashita, said that she had become interested in joining the WAC during a conversation with her Nisei friends about how to prove their loyalty to the United States. "We said, 'You know, the war started, the men…volunteered…and why don't Japanese women join in because that would be something we'd be doing for the country. And although the enemy was Japanese and we're Japanese…[,] we're not the same people….We're Americans and they're from Japan, and there was a difference.'"

Another minority group that contributed to the war effort was not racial but sexual: many lesbians joined the armed forces to serve their country. The U.S. military needed as many people as it could get, so it tolerated lesbians (and gay men) temporarily. Officers tried to prevent any disruptive witch hunts that might discredit the WAC and its recruiting program during the war, but they also discouraged any overt same-sex behavior. Military officials instructed WAC officers to discharge only those women whom they could prove to be "addicted to the practice" and warned that "any officer bringing an unjust or unprovable charge against a woman in this regard will be severely reprimanded."

Life in the military and wartime tolerance gave many women opportunities to form lesbian relationships in this new all-female environment. That tolerance evaporated quickly as the war came to an end, however, because the armed forces no longer had to worry about attracting and keeping as many servicewomen as possible. The military now vigorously pursued witch hunts against lesbians and gay men and discharged as many as possible. If a lesbian or gay man was discharged specifically for homosexuality, his or her discharge papers were printed on blue paper, which marked the holder as an "undesirable." Some blue discharges even had "HS" stamped on them, for homosexual, a designation that disqualified the recipient from receiving any veteran's rights and benefits and often prevented her or him from getting civilian jobs.

Many of these returning veterans were dropped off at the first available port city and were often reluctant to go home. As a result, lesbian communities in such cities as San Francisco grew rapidly by war's end. Pat Bond, who was originally from Davenport, Iowa, and had served in the Women's Army Corps, stayed in the California city when she returned from the Pacific theater after demobilization. She kept in touch with many of her wartime friends and developed a new social life in the lesbian bars of postwar San Francisco.

Nurses also had a complicated relationship with the military, which could not decide whether they were soldiers or ladies. The Army Nurse Corps was founded in 1898 and became a permanent part of the U.S. Army's Medical Department in 1901, but nurses did not receive relative military rank (that is, the title, pay, and benefits of a commissioned army officer) until World War II. They did not receive actual commissions until 1947. Sixty thousand nurses served in the ANC, many of them overseas, during the war. Like most soldiers, the nurses went overseas on crowded ships that had been converted into troop carriers. Barbara Gier of Nebraska sailed from Boston with her unit, the 203rd General Hospital, on board a ship in which ten or twelve nurses had to share rooms designed for two to four people. The women bathed by filling helmets with water from taps that were only turned on twice a day. Another Nebraska woman, Catherine Flannery Prussa, remembered the nurses of the 167th unit carrying "life jackets like teddy bears" out of fear of a German attack.

Once the ships arrived in Europe, the army assigned many ANC nurses to field and evacuation hospitals, which followed the troops closely. Florence Fattig of Nebraska and the other nurses with the 104th Evacuation Hospital unit landed on Utah Beach, France, in July 1944, about a month after D-day, the June 6th invasion of mainland Europe by American, British, and Canadian forces. The chief nurse ordered the women to wear their dress uniforms because she wanted the members of her unit to arrive like "ladies." Giving this impression was not easy, however, because after crossing the English Channel in one ship the nurses had to jump into a smaller boat and then wade ashore.

Working conditions were often poor. Nebraska's Phyllis Vavra Johnson was assigned to a hospital train in France. The army gave her and the other nurses only two days to prepare the train for use as a hospital. They had "emergency things and not much more....We could give morphine, we could give sleeping tablets, we could give codeine. That's about it. We didn't have the boys on the train that long." It took the nurses nearly a full day to get each load of about three hundred wounded soldiers to Paris from the front line near Aachen, Germany. The nurses stacked litters three or four deep along the walls and restrained some of the battle fatigue casualties on the floor with straps because "they were just wild. You had to jump over those and hoped that they never got loose while you had them....But after all they were the boys. They were shell-shocked, poor fellows." What was then called "battle fatigue" or "shell shock" would now be called post-traumatic stress disorder, and all the nurses could do was keep the distraught men restrained until they could be delivered safely to the army hospital.

Although most of the ANC nurses were white, many minority women also joined. The 239th General Hospital unit was one of the first racially integrated hospital units in the U.S. Army. Some black nurses had been accepted into the ANC earlier, but they had always been placed in all-black units to care for African American soldiers or prisoners of war. Marcella Ryan LeBeau, a Lakota woman from South Dakota, worked in various army hospitals in North America and Europe, and at one point she was asked to help when a young Indian serviceman was brought in as a double amputee. The army initially barred Japanese American nurses from joining the ANC, but this ban did not deter some young women who wanted to serve. Mary Yamada, for example, wrote to the Office of the Surgeon General many times seeking permission to apply. In February 1943 the army finally told her that she was eligible to apply, but the ANC still did not accept her until the spring of 1945.

All women in the armed forces experienced a complex mix of opportunities and constraints. The military tolerated lesbians when it needed their service, but it hounded them out at war's end. It expected nurses wading ashore at Normandy to be "ladies," even when they about to take on some very unladylike wartime nursing. A Japanese American woman who wanted to be an army nurse did not get the chance to serve during the war because of her heritage. In short, the armed forces were willing to bend temporarily some of the normal rules about women's behavior and appearance during the war because they desperately needed women's labor, but they were not about to throw those rules out completely or permanently.

New Jobs in Wartime Industries

The same tension was evident, if considerably more muted, in women's experiences in wartime industries such as shipbuilding and aircraft manufacturing. Although western women of all races and ethnicities had been working for wages for decades, the government and public at the time and historians since have paid a disproportionate amount of attention to the women workers of World War II. It was not just that new groups of women, such as married middle-class white women with children, were working for pay for the first time, but that they were doing jobs that had previously only been done by men and that the federal government actively recruited women for the first time. More than half the women who worked during World War II had been working before the war. As the war continued, women already in the work force experienced increased occupational mobility. Although patriotism certainly motivated many women, most needed the higher wages paid by the defense industry and eagerly seized the chance to learn new skills.

War jobs paid much higher salaries than other work available to women. In 1940, for example, most white women who worked in restaurants in Salt Lake City made about $13.00 a week. They earned about $12.00 a week if they worked in a laundry, and about $10.50 a week if they worked in a department store. In comparison, a woman who worked at the Remington Small Arms Plant in Utah could make $22.56 a week, while in Clearfield, Utah, women who worked as supply handlers and lift operators earned $30.72 a week. The difference between men's and women's pay remained, however: in 1942 Utah's Ogden Arsenal paid female ammunition loaders $4.40 a day, but it paid male loaders $5.50 a day.

Recruiters encouraged women to fill wartime jobs by insisting that the work would not threaten their femininity, often by comparing war work to more traditional female activities. As with the nurses in the military, the public seemed to need reassurance that war workers could still be ladies. For example, a newspaper article quoted Mary Owens of Utah saying that her job washing ball bearings "is a great deal like doing dishes and the technique is much the same."

Recruiting strategies aside, most of the new jobs available in wartime industries were not particularly feminine or ladylike, and they required women to learn how to do jobs that men had done. Among the most dramatic new workplaces for women were the shipyards on the west coast, which was a magnet for hundreds of thousands of people from all over the United States during the war. Dozens of large and small shipyards were in operation from southern California to northern Washington, and there were so many in the San Francisco

Bay Area alone that it became one of the most crowded destinations for newcomers. Before the war shipbuilding had been an exclusively male preserve, but that changed rapidly during the war. Only 2 percent of the entire shipyard workforce was female in 1939, and those women were clerical workers. By January 1944, however, between 10 and 20 percent of all shipyard production workers were women. The Kaiser Corporation's yards in Portland, Oregon, and Vancouver, Washington, had the highest percentage of women workers. Kaiser's 40,000 women workers represented 27 percent of the company's production force in 1944. Women did nearly half of all the welding at Kaiser's many shipyards.

Women also did most of the heaviest, dirtiest cleaning jobs at most military industrial facilities. In May 1943, for instance, 65 percent of the cleaners at Kaiser's Swan Island shipyard in Portland, Oregon, were women, and all-women crews were usually assigned the most undesirable jobs in the yards. As one caption under a picture of twenty-nine women storage tank cleaners at Commercial Iron Works declared, the job was "too smelly and too dirty for men."

The hard realities of industrial work did not deter many women. Pat Koehler was eighteen when she and a friend started working in the shipyards. They wanted to do "something more exciting than typing," she remembered, so they applied to become electrician's helpers at the Kaiser Vancouver Shipyards. They started on the day shift, making 85¢ an hour, and took training classes at night. Being promoted to "electrician trainee" raised their pay to 95¢ an hour, then to $1.10 and $1.15. When they finished the training and became journeyman-electricians, their pay increased again to $1.20 per hour. They "celebrated by applying for jobs on the hookup crews, which worked aboard ships at the outfitting dock." Koehler's new supervisor had never had a female employee, and he doubted her abilities at first. So for the first few days she "followed his every move, anticipating what tool he needed next and handing it to him before he could ask. After a few days of this he relaxed and began teaching me the ropes—or, rather, the wires." Koehler liked working with her hands and "liked the feel of the tools." She and her friend were too busy and too tired to spend any of the money they made, and after a year and a half of working at the shipyards they had enough money to pay for two years at college, including tuition, books, and room and board. "Best of all," she observed years later, "we had acquired new confidence and maturity."

In 1943 Joanne Hudlicky, a divorced mother who was working as a sales clerk at a cigar store in Vancouver, Washington, got an office job at the new Kaiser Corporation shipyard. When she learned that the production people made a lot more money than the office staff, she quit and got a job as a helper in the yard. The job was boring, so she asked how she could become a crane operator. The man in charge of the crane operators asked whether she thought she could do the job, and she replied, "Well, I don't know why not; other people are doing it." As a single mother, she needed the higher wages, but she also really enjoyed the physical challenge of crane operating. She knew that she always had to be "a little bit better" than the male operators. "There might be a man relieving for a crane operator and maybe he wasn't as good an operator as the man he was relieving but they wouldn't have cared. I put everything into it I could 'cause I really wanted to do it and I think that it's that way with a lot of women. I think I was a real good operator."

Women workers' enthusiasm did not earn them a warm welcome at their new workplaces, however. The shipyard unions did not want them and channeled them into separate auxiliaries. White women got a much better reception than minority women did. Employers avoided hiring minority women until it was absolutely necessary, and the powerful unions did not want them as members at all. By the spring of 1943, however, severe labor shortages and vocal criticism from the African American community forced employers to hire and unions to accept black women. Shipyard work represented a significant step up for most black workers, and it allowed many black women to get out of domestic service for the first time. A woman who had migrated from Marshall, Texas, explained, "I am a colored woman and I am 42 years old. Now, you know that colored women don't have a chance for any kinds of job back there [in Texas] except in somebody's kitchen working for two or three dollars a week. I have an old mother and a crippled aunt to take care of....I went to work for Kaiser and saved enough money to bring my aunt and mother out here."

Finally getting hired at the shipyards did not mean an end to the racism, however. Employers usually paid black workers less and concentrated them in the dirtiest, lowest-status jobs, and the shipyard unions continued to discriminate against them. The exclusionary practices of the Boilermakers' Union were the most extreme. Union membership was a prerequisite for shipyard employment, but the union did not accept black members at first. Pressure from workers eventually forced the unions to form segregated "auxiliary unions" for black workers. For instance, in 1942 Frances Mary Albrier passed the welder's test "with flying colors," but Kaiser's Richmond Shipyard Number Two rejected her application because Kaiser "had not yet set up an auxiliary to take in Negroes." Albrier threatened to sue Kaiser if she was not allowed to join Local 513, the all-white union. The union decided to let her pay her dues in Richmond, California, but then sent the dues to the black auxiliary at Moore Dry Dock in Oakland, thus maintaining segregation technically until it established the black auxiliary Local A-36 in Richmond. Mrs. Etta Germany wrote to President Franklin Roosevelt to protest the way the unions treated her and other black shipyard workers:

> I wish to call your attention to a very disgraceful and UnAmerican situation that now exists in the Boilermakers and Welders Union Local 513 of Richmond California. I am a Negro girl. Three weeks ago I and lots of others enrolled in the National Defense Training Classes to become welders. I applied for a job at the yards several times. But each time myself and others of my race were give the run around....[B]ecause of being Negro I was not allowed to join the Union. Now Mr. President there are a great many Negroes in Defense Training as myself who upon completion of the course

will be subjected to the same treatment as myself....We are all doing what we can to assist in winning the war. I sincerely feel that this is no time for our very own fellow citizens to use discrimination of this type.

Some women used their new positions and skills to intervene directly in racist situations. At work one day, Lyn Childs, a black shipyard welder in San Francisco, saw a white man beating a Filipino man while the men standing around did nothing to stop it. She turned up the flame on her welding torch until it was "about six to seven feet out in front of me," walked over to the white man, and threatened to "cut [his] guts out" if he did not stop. The white man started crying, saying he had been trained in boot camp that anyone who was not white was inferior. Not knowing what else to do, Childs sat down with him while he cried. When her supervisor called her into his office, all the men came with her to show their support and because they were ashamed that they had not intervened as she did. The supervisor accused her of being a communist, which in the 1940s and 1950s was often used to denigrate anyone who was sympathetic to equal rights. Childs replied, "A communist! Forget you!" She said that if it was wrong to try and stop "the kind of treatment that man was putting on the Filipinos....then I am the biggest communist you ever seen in your life. That is great. I am a communist." She repeated the term so loudly that the officer quickly ushered her out of his office and told her to forget the whole incident.

Not all efforts to challenge entrenched racism were as successful, and many black women never achieved their goal of working in a wartime industry. Beatrice Marshall, an African American college student in Illinois who wanted to help the war effort, trained as a steel-lathe and drill press operator in a National Youth Administration (NYA) program, along with her sister and two friends. Marshall loved learning to use the machines. "I felt like I was a champion on the drill press, and I really did like it." The NYA paid the four women's train fare to Portland, Oregon, and paid for their first night's accommodation at the Young Women's Christian Association (YWCA). The four had papers certifying that they had passed their tests, and they were eager to start working as shipyard machinists. Whey they got to the shipyards, they were told that there were not any jobs available as lathe or drill-press operators, but that they could be painter's helpers or sweepers. The women complained that these were not they jobs that they trained for, and in the face of their persistence, the personnel office finally admitted that there were openings in the machine shop, but not for black workers. The four women worked for a while as painter's helpers before quitting the shipyards entirely. Marshall was very angry and confused about what had happened: "They was doing all this advertising and wanted us to do this, and here I am spending time and getting trained and qualified and couldn't get it.…I was real mad."

Black women were not the only minority women who wanted to take advantage of the new opportunities offered by defense industry work. The Kaiser Corporation made a point of trying to recruit Chinese American workers, and by 1943 about five to six hundred Chinese American women were working for or had worked for defense-related industries in the San Francisco Bay Area. Most were unmarried women, like Maryland Pong and Edna Wong, the first two Chinese American women to work at the Moore Dry Dock in Oakland, California. Betty Lum worked as a nurse before the war started, but she quit to learn welding at a Richmond, California, shipyard. Mannie Lee's husband Henry was a shipyard welder, and Mannie, her two daughters, and one daughter-in-law worked at the same yard in the electric shop. Jane Jeong started working as a welder at Richmond's Shipyard Number Two just four months after marrying her husband, a merchant seaman. She had accumulated two hundred flying hours toward her dream of being a pilot and fighting the Japanese in China, but after the war started, she realized that she could help China and the United States by building ships instead.

Not all of the new industrial workers were young women. Ah Yoke Gee was a widow and her two children were in high school when she started work as a welder in Kaiser's Shipyard Number Two. Every morning before leaving for work she cooked enough food for the family for the day, and on the weekends she did the shopping, washing, and cleaning. She only missed one day of work from July 1942 to April 1945, and she only took that one day off to spend time with her oldest son, a serviceman who was passing through San Francisco on his way to the Pacific theater. One of Gee's daughters, Maggie, worked as a drafter at the Mare Island shipyard while saving her money to go to aviation school. She later became one of only two Chinese Americans in the Women's Air Force Service Pilots (WASPs).

It is impossible to know exactly how many Native American women worked in defense industries because at least one government installation, Mare Island Navy Yard in California, classified Native workers as white. The experience of twenty-five-year-old Faith Feather Traversie, a Yankton Lakota, shows how it worked. She moved to California in 1943 with her first husband just before he shipped out to serve overseas. After he left, she stayed to take advantage of the better job opportunities on the west coast. When she applied for work at Mare Island, she was required to identify her nationality, but "American Indian" was not on the list of options so she left that part of the form blank. "Lady," the secretary asked when she handed in the form, "if you're not one of these nationalities, what in the world are you?" Traversie responded, "American Indian," and the secretary became agitated and talked to several other people to figure out what to do. Upon the secretary's return, she said, "Well, we'll have to classify you as White. Since you're a ward of the government, we'll have to put 'W' on your badge for White." Once Traversie's application was accepted, she "gladly took" the welding training because "welders were the highest paid in the yard," and she earned about $2.67 an hour. Out of a class of twenty-eight, she was one of only two women and six men to pass the practical exam.

Shipbuilding was not the only defense industry hiring large numbers of women; the nation's booming aircraft industry also had to do so. Aircraft manufacturing employed more women than any other defense industry, and 40 percent of its wartime workforce was female. The jobs often brought the harsh reality of the war home in ways that the shipyard workers never had to confront. Workers who repaired combat planes at Hill Field, Utah, cleaned blood, skin, and hair out of the cockpits. Pilots often left messages and drawings inside their planes. Retha Nielson, who worked on B-24s, wrote, "I got a lump in my throat as I read the names of the men who had piloted them. Some of them had given the planes a name....I would walk up to the big plane and touch it and wonder if all the men had come out alive, what had happened and why they had named it what they had." Macel Anderson received two letters from the federal government stating that parachutes that she had made had saved two soldiers' lives.

Just after the bombing of Pearl Harbor in December 1941, Wichita, Kansas, became a "twenty-four-hour city" when its three major aircraft manufacturers added a third shift to keep the factories working around the clock. The new shift meant that the factories needed to hire a lot of new workers. In early 1942 the federal government announced plans to offer aircraft manufacturing training programs in Wichita and specified that women who applied had to be high school graduates between the ages of twenty-one and thirty-five. Single women with dependents and married women whose husbands were in the service could sign up for the program. By the first week of February 1942, more than seven hundred women had put their names on a waiting list to attend the National Defense Training School. Roseva Babcock Lawrence moved to Wichita with her father in 1942 to attend the school. The school admitted her father immediately, but her name went on the waiting list because she was not yet twenty-one, the minimum age to work in the plants. She studied with her father in the evenings so that when she started taking the class, she was able to complete the course in four weeks rather than the usual six. But she was still only twenty when she graduated, so she needed to find another job while she waited for her birthday. Within a month Roseva was hired at the Beech Aircraft Company as an x-ray technician.

The Boeing Aircraft Company was not convinced that women could work as efficiently as men, despite a government report that indicated that only fifty-six out of 1,900 war occupations were unsuitable for women. The company claimed that many women could not withstand the rigors of a full day in the shops and that female employees had trouble understanding and complying with safety practices. The company even started a physical fitness program for its female workers in early 1943, because it believed that the women were all housewives who were not used to hard work. The fitness program did not last long because the women were doing their jobs well, and they considered it an unnecessary demand on their time. For example, forty-year-old Boeing employee Katherine Abraham certainly did not have any time in her schedule for fitness classes. She was married and had four children when she started working at Boeing in January 1943. She worked the 5 p.m. to 5 a.m. shift, making dinner for her family before she went to work. Her husband and oldest daughter worked the 5 a.m. to 5 p.m. shift, and cared for the younger children in the evening.

Of all the women employed in the aircraft industry during the war, only a few served in administrative positions. Whereas companies considered the production jobs temporary and thus an acceptable wartime aberration in normal hiring practices, administrative jobs were more permanent, so women were unwelcome in those positions and thought to be unqualified. Doris Massey Buchner was one of the few women to hold such a position in the aircraft industry during the war. While in high school before the war, she had convinced the principal to let her enroll in the male-dominated drafting and woodworking classes. When she went to work for Boeing in Wichita in June 1942, she started in an assembly section, where her drafting skills were immediately put to use. She was one of only two women in her office, and Boeing eventually promoted both of them to inspector positions. Doris inspected the wing tips and tunnels of the B-29 aircraft. Her colleague recommended that Doris wear her hair on top of her head to make her look taller and help project a more forceful, authoritative image. A small number of these women kept their jobs after the war. Grace M. McLean started her career as an ammunition inspector during the war and when she retired in 1978, she was the only female explosives safety specialist in the U.S. Air Force.

Far fewer black women worked in the aircraft industry than in shipbuilding. One of these women was Julia Scott Nelson, a riveter. Born and raised in rural Oklahoma, Julia heard about the job opportunities in Wichita in 1943. After training at a defense school, she got a job with Boeing, where her sister already worked. She recalled some initial hostility from a young white woman she worked with, but she was determined to retain her dignity and poise, and by the end of her first summer the two had developed a comfortable relationship. Margaret Wright was able to get a job on the assembly line at the Lockheed plant in 1943. She liked the fact that, unlike domestic service, she got paid for her overtime and did not have to work alone. "I was always with a bunch of other women," she remembered. Lockheed segregated blacks from whites at first, and it usually paid them less than a white worker earned for the same job.

The BIA also wanted to take advantage of wartime employment opportunities and quickly recognized that its graduates could earn more money—and attract positive attention to the bureau—if its boarding schools shifted their focus to industrial training. In 1942 the BIA designated several of its western boarding schools as defense training centers. Chilocco Indian School in Oklahoma was one of the first to adapt a sheet metal course to defense needs. In 1942, 175 male and female students completed the nine-week course, and 85 percent of them found employment. The courses were particularly attractive to women: in one class that year there were twenty-one women and only three men. By the following year, the school had trained almost three hundred students, and its female graduates found jobs paying an average of $40 a week. Although some companies, such as the Glenn L. Martin Aircraft Corporation, refused to hire black workers, male or female, there were no such restrictions on hiring Native women. The *Indian School Journal* announced that several aircraft companies specifically sought Indians trained at Chilocco and Haskell Institute, and the March 1942 issue of *Indians at Work* stated that the aircraft industry in southern California had already hired about two hundred Indians. Elizabeth Ortega, a California Mission Indian and a graduate of the Sherman Institute, worked as a welder at the Solar Aircraft Company. The military gave her the highly prized Army-Navy "E" pin for excellence in war production, and company officials invited her to accept the pin and speak at their awards banquet.

Wartime defense work provides the most dramatic examples of the new opportunities women seized during World War II. The shipyards and aircraft factories pulled in thousands of women who had never worked for wages before, and thousands of other women who jumped at the chance to make better wages than they ever had before. Women proved that they could do the jobs that men had done, even such stereotypically masculine ones as welding. These new jobs could not, however, change the fact that the most challenging work that women did during the war was only publicly acceptable because it was temporary. Nor did the new workplaces make any real strides toward dismantling the racism that structured women's wartime experiences.

Housing and Child Care Challenges

Although the military, business, government, and the general public praised women for their contributions to the war effort, they did little to help women with specific challenges such as finding adequate housing and child care. Despite the ways in which women's work lives were changing, most Americans still expected them to take care of their families. Those traditional responsibilities got a lot harder during the war, as everything from housing to consumer goods was in short supply and the new jobs rarely came with handy child care. For example, in Richmond, California, in 1943 there were so many shipyard workers and so little housing that some workers had to travel up to 150 miles a day to get to their jobs. In Los Angeles, the flood of African Americans looking for work was unwelcome in the segregated city, and black newcomers had a very difficult time finding places to live. One woman recalled that a realtor told them that the house they wanted had already been sold, refused to take their deposit, and said that no other houses were for sale in the area.

The government built some wartime housing in particularly heavily affected cities like San Diego, but these facilities did not meet the demand and were often inadequate. Kay Hill lived in a wartime housing project in San Diego called Linda Vista, which consisted of 3,500 houses built in early 1944. Water and sewer services were poor, and there were few places to shop. Every two weeks she walked three miles to the closest grocery store, and she recalled that "one of the constant features of life in Linda Vista was a kid at the back door saying, 'My mother wants to borrow a cup of sugar.'" Another San Diego resident, Mary Jane Babcock, had to live in a garage after her marriage in 1942, because she had no other options. "It was supposedly this two bedroom house and it had a tacked-on kitchen and a tacked-on bathroom." After her husband left for the war and termites forced her out of the garage, she was lucky to find a one-bedroom apartment in Ocean Beach, which she and her newborn son shared with another woman and her five-year-old daughter. The other woman had followed her husband to San Diego from South Carolina. Babcock and her son slept in the bedroom, and her roommate and her daughter slept on a Murphy bed in the living room. The cramped quarters at least made it easier for the women to take turns caring for each other's children while the other was out working or shopping. Babcock had to support herself and her newborn son because her husband was a low-paid cadet in the Army Air Corps, so she got a job working nights at the Southern California Telephone Company.

Although housing remained a problem throughout the war, employers, especially the big defense industries that employed so many women, assumed that day care would be their female employees' biggest difficulty. As Henry Kaiser explained in October 1943 to the House Naval Affairs Committee:

> Women need more care and attention than has ever been provided in plants, in order that they may want to work, in order that they should work, in order that she may have happiness in the work and that conditions may be right. It isn't properly provided now. This manpower situation could be tremendously improved, instantly, if we could have child care and proper shopping centers and some amusement. Women can't work ten hours a day under abominable conditions; you must do things for them, and they must have recreation. It is a new situation which we all have a great responsibility to achieve.

Even when women had access to day care facilities, however, they did not use them in the numbers that employers and the government expected. After the federal government passed the Lanham Act in 1943 to provide funding for nursery schools, day care centers, clinics, elementary and secondary schools, and recreation facilities, the day care facilities were usually the ones with the fewest users. The facilities often opened at times that conflicted with women's shifts or were located too far away from the residential quarters. Kaiser's paternalism led him to provide more services for his female workers, particularly child care and health care, than any other wartime employer. The Kaiser shipyards had day care centers on site, and at the U.S. Navy's dry docks the centers were open twenty-four hours a day and gave the children hot meals. In Wichita, Kansas, by the spring of 1943, the federal government was operating four day care centers near the large housing projects constructed close to the aircraft plants.

In hindsight, the amount of money and the statements of support that the federal government and employers gave to such services as day care during World War II seem remarkably progressive, and the day care centers that were established did help many women.

That support was only temporary, however, as was public support for mothers working outside the home. Women faced a much wider range of challenges during the war than simply accessing affordable day care. At the heart of these challenges was the fact that a public, temporary acceptance of them as workers did not change in any way the reality that, world war or not, the same public still held them responsible (and they themselves felt responsible) for all of their usual household duties.

The Women's Land Army

There was another kind of army at work in the United States during World War II: the Women's Land Army (WLA), modeled after similar programs already operating in Great Britain and Canada. The federal government created it in the spring of 1943 as part of the Emergency Farm Labor Program, which it set up to help the nation's farmers get the additional workers they desperately needed. The WLA recruited women over the age of eighteen and sent them wherever their labor was needed most. Economist Florence L. Hall, who had grown up on a farm in Michigan, headed the WLA. A long-time federal employee, she had been an advocate for farm women for years.

Tens of thousands of women, including university professors, students, and homemakers, joined the WLA. It became the largest single group of wartime agricultural workers, with more than three million women involved nationwide. In its first year alone it recruited and placed more than 600,000 women. Most of the women spent a minimum of one month on a farm as short-term emergency workers, usually during planting or harvesting. The WLA was not welcome in all western states, however. Whereas farmers on the west coast were happy to hire female labor, those in the Great Plains and Rocky Mountain states tended to be less supportive. Utah, Texas, New Mexico, Nevada, and Arizona did not organize WLA units; states like Utah had many non-WLA female farm workers, and the more southerly states avoided hiring female workers altogether.

Much of the support for the WLA in the west coast states stemmed from the fact that they already had effective labor recruitment programs before the war and were accustomed to hiring women when necessary. For example, California growers had employed women and high school students to pick the state's citrus crop for years before 1943. The state's farmers employed more than 169,000 women in their agricultural operations from 1943 to 1945. A walnut farmer in Contra Costa County reported that the "women are picking cleaner than any group that ever worked for us. The spirit of the women is excellent....We sincerely appreciate their help." Producers in the state's wine-producing region also praised the female crews, and some even paid them the same wage as male workers. "I hate to admit it," one foreman said, "but they do a better job than the men did."

Several thousand Oregon women joined the WLA and worked as part of the so-called "Housewife Special," which transported women daily from their homes to the fields and back again. One Oregon grower said of his of thirteen women employees that they "are the best crew I've ever had but they work too hard. They are paid by the hour (75 cents) and they just won't stop to rest." In Umatilla one all-female crew of university students harvested peas, and their boss reported that "Marilyn Glenn is the truck driver, Pat Mann, the tractor driver, and Mrs. Norma Mann, her sister-in-law, operates the loader."

West coast states were not the only ones to support the WLA, however. In 1943 North Dakota farmers expected bumper crops and a severe labor shortage, so the state eagerly recruited any available workers. Its early support for WLA workers allowed for successful harvests instead of production cutbacks and eliminated the need to recruit male labor from outside the state. Women assisted in all aspects of production, in some cases as members of all female harvest crews, as well as on livestock and truck-crop (fruit and vegetable crops delivered to local markets) operations. One crew of six women picked almost 775,000 pounds of potatoes in 1944.

The WLA enjoyed less support in the Rocky Mountain states because producers thought that inexperienced female workers could not handle livestock or crops such as wheat and sugar beets. In Wyoming, Ellen R. Lindstrom, a state labor supervisor, reported, "The main agricultural enterprises, sugar beets, hay, range cattle and sheep do not adapt themselves to inexperienced labor." Nevertheless, thousands of non-WLA women worked as farm laborers in the these states during the war. In 1943 8,000 women, only thirteen of whom were registered with the WLA, worked on Montana farms and proved that they could do the work that had to be done. They drove equipment; branded, herded, and cared for livestock; milked cows and delivered the milk to houses and creameries; thinned and topped beets; cultivated and harvested fruits and vegetables; hayed; and fixed fences. After seeing how successful women were in the 1943 season, the Montana state agricultural agents began to work with the WLA in 1944, placing more than five hundred WLA women in farm and ranch jobs. That summer in Flathead County, the agent reported that Mrs. Bob Seeve did "a man's work…including driving the tractor, hauling grain, cutting hay and general farm chores." In Carbon County, Wyoming, agent Nels Dalquist offered similar testimony: "In many instances in the county, women worked during the haying season in the hay field. Two ranchers in the Elk Mountain Community used a hay crew composed of women entirely and reported that this crew did an excellent job."

Western farmers needed additional help during the war just as much as wartime defense industries did, and many also turned to women to fill the gap, often finding them through the WLA. This program was most successful in mixed-farming regions (where farms raised livestock and grew crops) or states with pre-existing programs for recruiting seasonal labor, because farmers in those areas had an easier time imagining how they could use women workers. In spite of the praise that farmers who hired women heaped on them, growers in other areas refused to believe that women could do the necessary work.

Volunteerism

Although new kinds of paid work constituted some of the most dramatic changes in western women's lives during the war, a much larger number of women made their contributions by stepping up their traditional volunteer work. As noted above, most women tried and were expected to maintain their traditional responsibilities as wives, mothers, and homemakers even during the war. The *San Diego Union* noted that a woman's "main job right now is seeing to the needs of her husband and growing children, putting them first." The newspaper suggested that homemakers "keep up family morale by keeping up family and home standards."

Women kept up those standards in many ways, including turning their household responsibilities into patriotic service to their country. For instance, the highly successful salvage campaigns, which recycled common household items into usable war materials, depended completely on women's participation. In June 1942 federal Conservation and Salvage officials (employed by the War Production Board) stated, "Show the ladies the vital need of salvage, what they can do, when and how they can do it and you will create the irresistible drive so essential to the success of this great wartime effort." The Conservation and Salvage division's goal was to have one woman leader "on each block in every community in every state" to run the program and educate the public on the necessity of salvage. The leader was called a Minute Woman because she stood ready to disseminate information in her area and carry out a war job any time she was notified.

Utah was the first state to have a Minute Woman on every block. The Salt Lake Minute Women Committee formed in August 1942, and it drew on the knowledge and expertise of the presidents of local Parent-Teacher Associations, Latter-Day Saints' relief societies, and women's clubs. At their first mass meeting on September 12, 1942, the Minute Women produced a flyer with a checklist of ninety-three items that could be contributed to war effort, including everything from old irons and radiators to rubber garters and toys, old sheets and men's shirts, rope and burlap bags, "and anything else you can find made out of metal, rubber, cloth or hemp." They distributed charts showing exactly how salvaged items were used. One chart showed that one tank car full of fat (about 60,000 pounds) could be turned into 6,000 pounds of glycerin, which would be enough to make nitroglycerin for 240,000 anti-aircraft shells or 30,000 pounds of dynamite. Similarly, the Minute Women distributed a letter stating that "1. There is enough tin in 3 salvaged cans to make a *Hand Grenade*. 2. *One tin can* yields enough tin for a pair of *Binoculars*. 3. A family of four saving its tin cans for two weeks will save sufficient tin to supply this metal for a portable *flame thrower.* 4. A month's savings of cans will make the bushings for 3 *machine guns.* Save 'em, Wash 'em, Clean 'em, Squash 'em." By the end of the war the Utah Minute Women had collected more than 300 million pounds of salvage material.

Another organization that used women's traditional skills and networks to make life easier for servicemen and their families was the Spanish-American Mothers and Wives Association of Tucson, Arizona. A man named Rosalio Ronquillo founded the organization in the spring of 1944 to unite and glorify the Hispanic women of Tucson through their "ardent and patriotic longing." He believed that the association could help win the war and then help care for servicemen when they came home after the war. Although its upper management was all male, the organization had three hundred women members who did everything they could to reach out to Tucson's Hispanic soldiers fighting overseas. Its name singled out mothers and wives but sisters, daughters, fiancées, and neighbors joined, too. They produced 9,000 surgical dressings for the Red Cross in one thirty-six hour marathon. To raise money to buy war bonds (which the federal government sold to raise money for the war effort), they sold homemade enchiladas, tamales, tortillas, tostadas, tacos, and coffee. As a result, the women purchased thousands of dollars worth of bonds, exceeded their quotas, and received certificates of honor from the Treasury Department.

The women also supported the families of local servicemen. Club members commiserated with Carmen Ríos, the mother of five sons fighting in the war, when one was wounded and again when one was killed. They celebrated with members whose male relatives came home on leave. Starting in June 1944, the organization published a newsletter called *Chatter* that it sent to Tucson's soldiers overseas. Editor Rose Rodríguez worked as a secretary at city hall and typed the newsletter during her lunch hour and free time. At first the paper was called *Chismes* (Gossip) and was written in Spanish; it soon turned into *Chatter* at the request of its English-speaking readers. The four-page newsletter was full of information about fellow Mexican American servicemen and servicewomen, lists of the latest hit songs, horoscopes, and notices about local weddings, births, and deaths. Local Mexican-owned stores sold copies for five cents each, and people mailed it overseas by the thousands. Across the ocean, Abe Mendoza read about the piñata party held on July 6, 1944, to celebrate his twin children's second birthday. A solider named Carlos read the following note after the name of a new member of the Spanish-American Mothers and Wives Association: "(Carlos: She looks fine—and cute as ever.)"

In spite of all the attention historians have paid to women workers during the war, the vast majority of western women did their part for the war effort by increasing their traditional volunteer activities and turning those skills to new uses. Women made the national salvage programs possible, raised huge sums of money for the federal government by buying war bonds, took care of military families, and reminded soldiers that they had not been forgotten.

Internment

When Japan bombed the U.S. Navy base at Pearl Harbor, Hawaii, on December 7, 1941, it not only brought the United States into the war, but it also unleashed a wave of hostility against Japanese Americans. On December 8, the federal government froze the Japanese-born Issei's assets, and the FBI began rounding up community leaders. On February 19, 1942, President Franklin Delano Roosevelt signed Executive Order 9066, which authorized the removal of 110,000 immigrant Japanese and their American-born children from the west coast. Very few Japanese Americans were interned on Hawaii because they made up a much larger proportion of the population and were harder to persecute; also, the islands were already under martial law, and so the local Japanese Americans were seen as less threatening. Some families moved away from the coast voluntarily, but many stayed home until forced to leave. The War Relocation Authority (WRA), which was created by the federal government in 1942 to handle the internment process and manage the camps, began the involuntary evacuation in the spring of 1942. Families got only a week's notice to wind up their affairs, store or sell their belongings and homes, shut down their businesses and farms, and report to an assembly center. Individuals could only bring as much clothing and as many personal items as they could carry. By November 1942, the government sent the evacuees to ten permanent relocation camps: Topaz, Utah; Poston and Gila River, Arizona; Amache, Colorado; Manzanar and Tule Lake, California; Heart Mountain, Wyoming; Minidoka, Idaho; and Jerome and Rohwer, Arkansas.

The removal of the Japanese Americans changed the face of cities like San Francisco. Renowned African American writer Maya Angelou was thirteen when her family moved to the Bay Area during the war. In her memoir *I Know Why the Caged Bird Sings,* she recalled that in the city's Fillmore district,

> the Yakamoto Sea Food Market quietly became Sammy's Shoe Shine Parlor and Smoke Shop. Yashigira's Hardware metamorphosed into La Salon de Beaute….The Japanese shops which sold products to Nisei customers were taken over by enterprising Negro businessmen, and in less than a year became permanent homes away from home for the newly arrived Southern Blacks. Where the odors of tempura, raw fish and cha had dominated, the aroma of chitlings, greens and ham hocks now prevailed.

The American-born Nisei, most of whom were born between 1910 and 1940, were more shocked than their elders about the government's reaction to the bombing of Pearl Harbor and its decision to intern all the Japanese Americans on the west coast. Yuri Kochiyama was nineteen and living in San Francisco when the Japanese attacked Pearl Harbor. She recalled that she was "red, white, and blue when I was growing up. I taught Sunday school, and was very, very American." Her father, who owned a fish market, had just come home from the hospital after surgery when he was arrested. The FBI arrested all of the Japanese men, including community leaders, men who were "Japanese school teachers, or were teaching martial arts, or who were Buddhist priests." While her father was still in prison, her twin brother came home from university and volunteered for the military. "And it seemed strange that here they had my father in prison, and there the draft board okayed my brother. He went right into the army." The government released her father on December 20, but he died a few days later because of the rough treatment he had received so soon after surgery.

Kochiyama's family was lucky in that their white next-door neighbors were willing to help. They "offered to do our shopping for us, if we needed," she recalled, because the government had imposed strict curfew and travel limits on Japanese Americans. The neighbors even offered to take care of the Kochiyama family's house and find someone to rent it while the family was interned. In April 1942 the WRA sent her family to an assembly center at Arcadia, California. It was the biggest on the coast and held nearly 20,000 people. They lived there, in a horse stable, until October. Everyone

> slept on army cots, and for mattresses they gave us muslin bags, and told us to fill them with straw.... So it was just makeshift. But I was amazed how, in a few months, some of those units looked really nice. Japanese women fixed them up. Some people had the foresight to bring material and needles and thread. But they didn't let us bring anything that could be used as weapons. They let us have spoons, but no knives.

Kochiyama could not believe that her country could

do a thing like this to us. This is the greatest country in the world. So I thought this is only going to be for a short while, maybe a few weeks or something, and they will let us go back. At the beginning no one realized how long this would go on. I didn't feel the anger that much because I thought maybe this was the way we could show our love for our country, and we should not make too much fuss or noise, we should abide by what they asked of us.

Her disbelief and anger grew when officials told Japanese Americans that the assembly center was temporary and that they were being sent to permanent quarters elsewhere in the country.

The WRA sent Kochiyama's group to the center at Jerome, Arkansas, which required a five-day train trip. "We stopped in Nebraska, and everybody pulled the blinds to see what Nebraska looked like. The interesting thing was, there was a troop train stopped at the station too. These American soldiers looked out, and saw all these Asians, and they wondered what we were doing on the train." Both groups opened their windows, and the Japanese Americans were pleased that there "was none of that 'you Japs' kind of thing." The young women on her train were about the same age as the soldiers, so they quickly exchanged addresses and promised to write to each other. She recalled that she wrote to some of the soldiers for a long time.

Although the living conditions in the ten internment camps varied, all were harsh. For example, when Kochiyama's group reached the camp in Jerome, Arkansas, officials put them into barracks with two hundred to two hundred fifty people in each block. Barbed wire and armed soldiers surrounded them. Although some people were shot and killed for going too close to the fence, most were too scared to try to escape because of the swamps around the camp. The interned Japanese Americans had to cut trees for wood for heating in the winter and build their own drainage systems. They were not allowed to have radios and felt very cut off from the rest of the world, so they asked roofers working on the camp buildings to bring them newspapers. At the Heart Mountain camp in Wyoming, a married woman with a family wrote,

> Last weekend, we had an awful cold wave and it was about 20 to 30 degrees below zero. In such weather, it's terrible to try going even to the bath and latrine house…. It really aggravates me to hear some politicians say we Japanese are being coddled, for *it isn't so*!! We're on rations as much as outsiders are. I'd say welcome to anyone to try living behind barbed wire and be cooped in a 20 ft. by 20 ft. room….We do our sleeping, dressing, ironing, hanging up our clothes in this one room.

In spite of the extreme constraints and limited choices they faced in the camps, Issei and Nisei women were determined to take advantage of whatever opportunities they could find. For many Issei women, internment was the first time since they had come to the United States that they had significant leisure time. For Nisei women, life in the camps, as restrictive as it was, offered new kinds of employment and social opportunities.

Camp officials expected the internees to work in the camps for very low wages. Doctors, teachers, and other professionals earned the most money, $19 per month, but this was only $3 more than most of the other workers earned for doing every other job in camp. This new pay equity and the variety of jobs gave many women a chance to try different things. At the camp in Poston, Arizona, one young woman recalled that she "wanted to find art work, but I didn't last too long because it wasn't very interesting…so I worked in the mess hall, but that wasn't for me, so I went to the accounting department—time-keeping—and I enjoyed that so I stayed there." Her sister started out as a secretary and then "went to the optometry department. She was assistant optometrist; she fixed all the glasses and fitted them….That was $16 [per month]." Kochiyama said that although she had been made to feel like being Japanese was a bad thing, "I felt so proud of the Japanese, and proud to be Japanese" when she saw how much work everyone did in the camps.

Another new career path opened up for many of the young Nisei women as a result of the extreme shortage of health care personnel in the camps. There were not enough white doctors and nurses willing to work in the camps, and the WRA was reluctant to hire black nurses, so camp officials had to train internees to work as nurse's aides. The aides, who were mostly young women in their late teens and twenties, soon provided most of the actual nursing care under the supervision of better-trained white graduate nurses. Sachi Kajiwara, a nurse's aide at the Topaz camp, recalled that she only got three weeks of training, and she "didn't even know the names of the instruments. I felt terribly inadequate to take care of some very sick people." By 1944 in the Poston camp, fourteen graduate nurses (five white, five black, four Issei) were assisted by seventy-five Nisei nurse's aides.

This training, however limited, created an unexpected educational and employment opportunity for the Nisei women even in the midst of internment. To supplement the limited training inside the camps, the WRA helped Nisei women enroll in nursing programs outside the camps, and many chose nursing as a career. By July 1944 more than three hundred Nisei women were enrolled in over one hundred nursing programs in twenty-four states. One such student wrote from Minneapolis, "Work here isn't too hard and I enjoy it very much. The patients are very nice people and I haven't had any trouble as yet. They do give us a funny stare at the beginning but after a day or so we receive the best compliments."

These new jobs were not the only opportunities Nisei women pursued in the camps. Just as the Issei women took advantage of their new, involuntary leisure time by socializing and offering or taking classes at the makeshift community centers, the Nisei suddenly found themselves with an instant, all-Nisei peer group. The camp inmates started newspapers that often included a women's column. The *Mercedian* included Lily Shoji's "Fem-a-lites"; the *Daily Tulean Dispatch* had a "Strictly Feminine" column; and the *Poston Chronicle* had "Fashionotes." The columns gave their readers advice on skin care, romance, and the latest fashions, the same topics that could be found in mainstream American magazines and newspapers. The columns also provided advice for the young women who left the camps for jobs. The fashion news may have been particularly incongruous given that the internees had few choices in clothing, but the columns reflected the young women's desire to keep in touch with the world beyond the barbed wire fence and keep up their morale in a depressing environment.

By the end of 1942, only a few months after the internment camps opened, the WRA began to encourage the Japanese Americans to move east and resettle as soon as they could get jobs. They were not allowed to move back to the west coast, but many of the Nisei women seized the chance to get out. In December 1943, twenty-year-old Iris Watanabe became the first Nisei internee to join the WAC. Among the first women to venture out of the camps were college students. The National Japanese American Student Relocation Council was a nongovernmental agency that helped more than 4,000 Nisei, more than one-third of whom were women, to go to college between 1942 and 1946.

Issei parents were reluctant at first to let their daughters go, but they gradually began to allow their daughters to leave for education and employment. One Nisei daughter noted that her father "became more broadminded in the relocation center. He was more mellow in his ways…. At first he didn't want me to relocate, but he gave in….I said I wanted to go [to Chicago] with my friend, so he helped me pack. He didn't say I couldn't go…but he helped me pack, so I thought, 'Well, he didn't say no.'" Some women were not able to go because they had to care for their elderly or infirm parents in the camps.

Women who left the camps were often nervous that they might face anti-Japanese hostility, but those fears faded as reports of warm receptions at their new college and university campuses outnumbered stories of hostility. May Yoshina wrote to her family in the Topaz camp from her new place at the University of Utah, explaining that most local employers were perfectly willing to hire Japanese

American university students. Still, women in that first wave of freed inmates were very aware of the position they occupied and the level of scrutiny they had to endure. As Lillian Ota's "Campus Report" in the Topaz magazine *Trek* warned, "Those who have probably never seen a Nisei before will get their impression of the Nisei as a whole from the relocated students. It won't do you or your family and friends much good to dwell on what you consider injustices when you are questioned about evacuation. Rather, stress the contributions of [our] people to the nation's war effort." By the time the camps closed near the end of the war, two-thirds of the Nisei women sixteen years old or older had already relocated.

The government's internment of Japanese Americans provides the most dramatic example of the constraints that some women faced during the war. American-born women and their families lost their homes, livelihoods, and liberties and were shipped away to camps with a low standard of living. It is perhaps surprising, therefore, that the camps also provide some of the most dramatic examples of young women creating new opportunities for themselves and seizing the chance to make their postwar lives better.

Choices and Chances

All of these stories tell us something about the extraordinary challenges, choices, and chances that western women had during the war. What is even more striking, perhaps, is the deeper effect the war had on women's self-confidence and the unprecedented opportunities that they created for themselves. Quite simply, women who had faced some of the most difficult challenges and fewest opportunities before the war now decided that they deserved so much more.

A first example can be seen in Richmond, California, where a handful of black women who did not like either of their two main employment options (domestic service or the shipyards) became entrepreneurs instead. They established or ran some of the blues clubs that flourished in the area during the war. Willie Mae "Granny"

Johnson from Arkansas opened the popular Savoy Club and did all the hiring, firing, and bookkeeping. Billye Strickland and her husband Lawrence built the "B and L Club" with a motel next door, and Billye took over as sole manager when Lawrence was drafted. Margaret Starks managed the Tappers Inn and booked the talent for all the North Richmond clubs. She was also the bouncer at Tappers and was rarely seen without her .38 revolver. Minnie Lue Nichols, originally from Georgia, leased and operated her own club, Minnie Lue's. In one three-day period her jukebox brought in sixty dollars, which was more than the previous owner had made in a month.

These clubs catered to the tens of thousands of Southern blacks who had moved to the Richmond area, and they also provided a new degree of economic and personal autonomy for the women who owned and operated them. As Nichols explained, "It was just easier to take care of a club, give them music in a club, than it was to work all day and night in the yards, then turn around and work at home taking care of babies. Besides, if women were going to cook, they could make some real money off it." The women served southern food and played southern music, and as a result they became power brokers in their communities. Margaret Starks earned the nickname the "mayor of North Richmond" for all of her activities in and out of the club. She published Richmond's first black newspaper, *The Richmond Guide,* out of the back room of the Tappers Inn, and she became the secretary of the Richmond branch of the National Association for the Advancement of Colored People (NAACP) when she and other local black leaders formed it in 1944. Starks explained that "everyone knew where to find me if they needed something or had something to tell me. Everyone came through those clubs. We plotted many strategies there."

A more unusual example of women's new confidence and willingness to challenge established norms is the behavior of sex trade workers in wartime Honolulu. Prostitution was technically illegal, but in practice the local police had permitted and carefully managed it for years. The women had to follow a long list of rules, including having licenses, undergoing medical inspections, living and working only in the designated red light district, and only allowing themselves to be seen in public at certain times. In exchange for the annual license fee of one dollar, the approximately two hundred fifty women who registered with the Honolulu Police Department could earn on average between $30,000 and $40,000 dollars a year at a time when the average working woman was lucky to make $2,000. The brothels took in more than $10 million each during the war, and the madams earned between $150,000 to $450,000 a year. Wartime upheaval, and the new military government, in power because the islands were under martial law during the war, gave the women an opportunity to fight back against the rules, especially the ones that required them to live and work in the red light district and restricted their ability to move freely in public.

Women volunteered their time and housing after the bombing of Pearl Harbor, donated huge sums of money to the war effort, and believed they were doing vital war work for the troops. One madam received a special citation from the Secretary of the Treasury for selling $132,000 in war bonds, most of them no doubt to fellow sex trade workers. They were caught, however, in the power struggle between the local police, who wanted to force them to follow the prewar rules, particularly about where they could live and work, and the military governor, who was willing to ignore most of the rules to keep the troops happy. Although the military police were willing to let the women live and work outside the red light district, for example, they refused to let the women charge more for their services. When the women tried raising their prices, from three to five dollars per sexual transaction, Frank Steer, head of the military police, declared crudely that "the price of meat is still three dollars."

Frustrated with the local police force's efforts to make them follow the prewar rules, Honolulu's sex trade workers went on a three-week strike in June 1942. They walked a picket line outside police headquarters, which was just a few blocks from the red light district. The building also happened to house the military police, whom the women considered tentative allies. The women carried placards protesting their treatment and the rules that restricted their freedom. The strike was not about better pay but better treatment and full citizenship rights. As one of the women stated, "We pay some of the highest taxes in town. Where, I ask you, are the beneficial results of our taxes?" As a result of the strike, the women were able to force the military and local police to relax some of the rules about residency and mobility.

A third example of the unusual opportunities for women to change their lives during the war is that of the second-generation Mexican American women in Los Angeles, who adopted a new youth subculture that rejected both traditional Mexican and mainstream American definitions of respectable femininity. During the war some young Mexican American men adopted the "zoot suit," consisting of loose, tapered trousers and a fingertip-length jacket, as a defiant challenge to the mainstream society that excluded them. Some young Hispanic women took up the new fashion, too, sometimes substituting a short skirt for the tapered pants. They combined the suit with a pompadour hairstyle, plucked eyebrows, and heavy makeup to create a blatantly sexual look. Known as *pachucas* (a label the mainstream press created to suggest an affiliation with Hispanic "pachuco" gangs) or female "zoot suiters," the young women also embraced a politicized Mexican American identity that rejected their second-class status.

Most Mexican American women had not had been able to access the new jobs that had opened up for many other women during the war, and they were tired of discrimination against Hispanics and the resulting poverty. Most whites and many older Mexican Americans saw the pachucas as accomplices in whatever trouble the male zoot suiters caused, but their rebellion was all the more disturbing for the mainstream press and the Mexican American community because they were female. In the view of the Mexican immigrant generation, young women were not supposed to be seen in public in most circumstances, never mind wearing a controversial outfit and flaunting their sexuality. But that familial control eroded quickly during the war, as dance halls and movie theaters attracted young people from many racial and cultural backgrounds to what had been the predominantly white public spaces of Los Angeles. The small number of Mexican American women who did get jobs in the defense industry, such as seventeen-year-old Aida Loya, who was hired to make bombs in the summer of 1942, now had a new independence that resulted from earning wages outside the home. She went so far as to wear a zoot suit to her high school graduation to flaunt her independence and remembered that her mother never forgave her for it. Most pachucas were simply trying to express their independence and a sense of adventure, not engage in sexual or illegal behavior, but their appearance was enough to get them in trouble. A small minority went as far as Teresa Quiñones, who threw rocks at white girls at her junior high school because they were "down on the Mexicans."

To both the Anglo and Hispanic communities, these young women represented everything that was wrong with the growing public role of women during the war. Many observers feared that these young women and the millions of other women who took on new roles during the war would not want to return to the home when the war was over. In a way, those fears were justified, despite the seeming return to "normalcy" in the years after the war. When the men returned home, employers fired most women from the well-paid jobs that they had found during the war. Politicians, clergy, and social commentators worked frantically to retrench traditional gender norms during the postwar years. But it was too late to reverse the changes in women's experiences and attitudes. Their labor force participation rebounded quickly in the 1950s, and their wartime experiences led many women to the civil rights movements of the 1960s. They knew the value of what they had done during the war and were not going to just forget the opportunities they had seized and enjoyed.

Suggested Readings

Anderson, Karen. *Changing Woman: A History of Racial-Ethnic Women in Modern America.* New York: Oxford University Press, 1996.

Angelou, Maya. Excerpt from *I Know Why the Caged Bird Sings.* In *Eyewitness to the American West: 500 Years of Firsthand History,* edited by David Colbert, pp. 313–315. New York: Penguin, 1998.

Bailey, Beth, and David Farber. "Prostitutes on Strike: The Women of Hotel Street During World War II." In *Women's America: Refocusing the Past,* 5th ed., edited by Linda K. Kerber and Jane Sherron De Hart, pp. 426–435. New York: Oxford University Press, 2000.

Bérubé, Allan. "Marching to a Different Drummer: Lesbian and Gay GIs in World War II." In *Hidden from History: Reclaiming the Gay and Lesbian Past,* edited by Martin Duberman, Martha Vicinus, and George Chauncey, Jr., pp. 383–394. New York, Meridian, 1990.

Blakesley, Katie Clark. "'Save'em, Wash 'em, Clean 'em, Squash 'em': The Story of the Salt Lake City Minute Women." *Utah Historical Quarterly* 71, no. 1 (January 2003): 36–51.

Campbell, D'Ann. "Servicewomen of World War II." *Armed Forces and Society* 16, no. 2 (1990): 251–270.

Campbell, Julie A. "Madres y Esposas: Tucson's Spanish-American Mothers and Wives Association." *Journal of Arizona History* 31, no. 2 (Summer 1990): 161–182.

Conte, Christine. "Changing Woman Meets Madonna: Navajo Women's Networks and Sex-Gender Values in Transition." In *Writing the Range: Race, Class, and Culture in the Women's West,* edited by Elizabeth Jameson and Susan Armitage, pp. 533–552. Norman: University of Oklahoma Press, 1997.

D'Emilio, John, and Estelle B. Freedman. *Intimate Matters: A History of Sexuality in America,* 2nd ed. Chicago: University of Chicago Press, 1997.

Escobedo, Elizabeth R. "The Pachuca Panic: Sexual and Cultural Battlegrounds in World War II Los Angeles." *Western Historical Quarterly* 38 (Summer 2007): 133–156.

Fagan, Michelle L. "Overseas with the ANC: Experiences of Nebraska Nurses in World War II." *Nebraska History* 76, no. 2 (Summer/Fall 1995): 106–121.

Gouveia, Grace Mary. "'We also serve': American Indian Women's Role in World War II." *Michigan Historical Review* 20, no. 2 (March 1994): 153–182.

Hall, Kimberley A. "Women in Wartime: The San Diego Experience, 1941–1945." *Journal of San Diego History* 39, no. 4 (December 1993): 260–279.

Johnson, Judith R. "Uncle Sam Wanted Them Too! Women Aircraft Workers in Wichita During World War II." *Kansas History* 17, no. 1 (March 1994): 38–49.

Kesselman, Amy. *Fleeting Opportunities: Women Shipyard Workers in Portland and Vancouver During World War II and Reconversion.* Albany: State University of New York Press, 1990.

Kochiyama, Yuri. "Then Came the War." In *Race, Class, and Gender in the United States,* 7th ed., edited by Paula S. Rothenberg, pp. 407–414. New York: Worth Publishers, 2007.

Koehler, Pat. "Reminiscence: Pat Koehler on the Women Shipbuilders of World War II." *Oregon Historical Quarterly* 91, no. 3 (Fall 1990): 285–291.

Lemke-Santangelo Gretchen. "'Women Made the Community': African American Migrant Women and the Cultural Transformation of the San Francisco East Bay Area." In *African American Women Confront the West, 1600–2000,* edited by Quintard Taylor and Shirley Ann Wilson Moore, pp. 254–275. Norman: University of Oklahoma Press, 2003.

Manley, Kathleen E. B. "Women of Los Alamos During World War II: Some of Their Views." *New Mexico Historical Review* 65, no. 2 (April 1990): 251–266.

Matsumoto, Valerie. "Japanese American Women During World War II." In *Unequal Sisters: A Multicultural Reader in U.S. Women's History,* 2nd ed., edited by Vicki Ruiz and Ellen Du Bois, pp. 436-449. New York and London: Routledge, 1994.

Meyer, Leisa D. "Creating G.I. Jane: The Regulation of Sexuality and Sexual Behavior in the Women's Army Corps during World War II." *Feminist Studies* 18, no. 3 (1992): 581–601.

Moore, Brenda L. *Serving Our Country: Japanese American Women in the Military During World War II.* New Brunswick, NJ: Rutgers University Press, 2003.

Moore, Shirley Ann Wilson. "'Not in Somebody's Kitchen': African American Women Workers in Richmond, California, and the Impact of World War II." In *Writing the Range: Race, Class, and Culture in the Women's West,* edited by Elizabeth Jameson and Susan Armitage, pp. 517–532. Norman: University of Oklahoma Press, 1997.

Noble, Antonette Chambers. "Utah's Rosies: Women in the Utah War Industries during World War II." *Utah Historical Quarterly* 59, no. 2 (March 1991): 123–145.

Smith, Susan L. "Women Health Workers and the Color Line in the Japanese American 'Relocation Centers' of World War II." *Bulletin of the History of Medicine* 73, no. 4 (1999): 585–601.

Spickard, Paul R. "Work and Hope: African American Women in Southern California During World War II." *Journal of the West* 32, no. 3 (July 1993): 70–79.

Stewart, Jennifer Nichol. "Wacky Times: An Analysis of the WAC in World War II and Its Effects on Women." *International Social Science Review* 75, nos. 1–2 (2000): pp. 26–37.

Taylor, Quintard, and Shirley Ann Wilson Moore, eds. *African American Women Confront the West, 1600–2000.* Norman: University of Oklahoma Press, 2003.

Wei, William. "Sex, Race, and the Fate of Three Nisei Sisters." *Colorado Heritage* (Autumn 2007): 2–17.

Yesil, Bilge. "'Who Said This is a Man's War?' Propaganda, Advertising Discourse and the Representation of War Worker Women During the Second World War." *Media History* 10, no. 2 (2004): 103–117.

Zhao, Xiaojian. "Chinese American Defense Workers in World War II." *California History* 75, no. 2 (Summer 1996): 138–153.

Conclusion

After World War II, nothing would ever be the same again for women in the West. For years historians focused on the facts that employers laid off tens of thousands of women when the war ended and that racial-ethnic minority women lost their jobs at a much higher rate than white women, and concluded that the gains women made during the war did not last. But women's participation in the paid work force rebounded rapidly by the late 1950s, as more women entered the paid workforce than had worked during the war. By 1950 half of the black working women who had found skilled industrial, white collar, or professional positions during the war had regained those positions. Some even moved back into those jobs much more quickly than white women did. Tina Hill remembered, "When North American [Aviation] called me back, was I a happy soul!" She quit her garment factory job immediately and worked for the company for the next forty years.

More importantly, no one could take away the memories and the pride western women had earned during the war. Women knew they played critical roles in helping to win the war. Employers, unions, the federal government, and much of the American public might have reverted quickly to saying women could not do certain jobs, but women knew better. Postwar social conservatism could not erase Beth Wyrill Jantz's memory that her first paycheck from Boeing was twice as much as she had ever earned before the war. Leona Giddings had worked in the tool crib at Beech Aircraft Company and used some of her wages to help her father buy a gas station. Ruth McLaughlin, an airplane welder, bought a set of false teeth for her mother and a monument for her father's grave. Roseva Lawrence, the first female x-ray technician at Beech, bought her parents a new set of living room furniture. Katherine Abraham used her savings to help buy a restaurant that she and her husband managed together. In all of these cases, the women knew that their higher wartime incomes gave them greater influence in their families' financial decisions and gave them the ability to help their families directly.

The women recalled many other positive aspects of their war work in addition to the bigger paychecks. Marceline Hendrixson appreciated that war work put her in contact with a broader range of women than had been possible before. For her it made a big difference, because she learned to interact with other people and accept their differences. Ruth McLaughlin suggested that because of the war experience, women of her generation had much fuller lives than their children did. Helen Volmer believed that she and other women had broken some of the barriers that restricted the types of jobs that employers considered women capable of performing. Ramona Snyder thought that after the war it was perhaps more acceptable for women to work with tools. Vera Sims believed that women's war experiences altered both male and female perceptions about the jobs women could do if given a chance. And after dealing with inadequate housing, food rationing, and raising her son alone while her husband was away in the military, Mary Jane Babcock of San Diego said "it made me almost cocky about being able to tackle most everything that comes along. I'd much rather be that way than to be fearful."

During the war, many nurses in the Army Nurse Corps (ANC) had taken on more responsibilities than they had during their civilian nursing careers. Phyllis Johnson of Nebraska found it hard to settle back into peacetime nursing for that reason, as well as because the civilian hospital's priorities were so different: "You didn't do the important things first." Bernice DeLong did not like having to treat some patients with special care because they were important people and not because they were critically ill. She said it "infuriated" her because "boys gave up their lives to let us be equal." In spite of the difficult conditions and the awful things that many had witnessed, the western nurses were proud of their contributions and believed that their wartime service had made them better people. One said she had learned that "there was nothing you couldn't handle." Jeannette Davis said, "the fact that this little farm gal was able to be there and do something was important."

That newfound confidence would shape the postwar West dramatically. Not only did women re-enter the paid work force in large numbers and shape the new western suburbs, but many of them also got involved in the civil rights movements of the 1950s and 1960s. For example, the National Association for the Advancement of Colored People (NAACP) of Richmond, California, found a lot of its new members and held a lot of meetings in the clubs that black women had opened during the war. Women were in the forefront of the organization, and the Richmond branch became the fastest-growing and most active one in the nation. As Margaret Starks said, African American women got involved in the postwar struggles because they "weren't going into some white woman's kitchen and make five dollars a week again. They said they did that back home in the South and they weren't going to do that out here."

The overlapping themes of agency and opportunities, continuity and change, and choices and constraints can be seen in the lives of women in the West in the decades after the war, too. The changes included the dramatic growth in the population of the West, the ongoing shift from rural to urban and suburban living, and entirely new economic opportunities. These changes were not felt equally across the West, however: most occurred on the west coast or in Texas. The old overland trails took on a new life in the twentieth century. In the thirty years after World War II more than thirty million Americans moved west of the Mississippi, the single biggest internal migration in the country's history. Even the population of western states like the Dakotas, Nebraska, and Montana dropped as their residents headed to the coast. By the mid-1960s, California was the most populous state in the nation, and Texas moved up to second spot in the 1990s. The West's cities continued to grow, and cities like Los Angeles, Houston, and San Diego were soon in the top ten. By the end of the twentieth century, nine out of every ten western women lived in cities.

Not all of them lived in specifically urban areas, however, because another significant postwar change in women's lives was the dramatic growth of the suburbs, low-density residential communities in between the high-density cities and sparsely populated rural areas. Suburbs developed first in the West because only western cities had huge empty areas around them into which they could spread. Homes in the suburbs were marketed to nuclear families on the assumption that women were full-time mothers and homemakers, with no need for convenient access to any services except a nearby school. Most suburbs were also segregated at first, with strict rules barring African Americans, Jews, and other minority groups from buying homes there.

The continuities and constraints in the postwar era are thus equally clear. Even in the face of great changes, women retained primary responsibility for childcare and housework, were not generally treated as equal, independent workers and citizens, and race and ethnicity continued to limit or afford opportunities. The continuing limits on women's lives are particularly evident in the wide range of political movements that western women participated in during the latter half of the twentieth century. African Americans organized the most successful civil rights campaign of the century, while Native Americans, Hispanics, and lesbians fought their own separate battles for rights and recognition. Western women often played key leadership roles in these movements. African American Barbara Jordan became the first black Texas state senator in 1966 and was elected to Congress in 1972. Hispanic activist Dolores Huerta helped

César Chávez organize the United Farm Workers in California in the 1960s to improve the working conditions of Mexican American agricultural workers. As the century progressed, women in the West continued to demand more choices and changes and accepted fewer constraints and continuities. Women's roles, experiences, and contributions remain at the heart of the history of the U.S. West.

In this way, the lives of women in the U.S. West are much like the lives of women elsewhere in the country and around the world. The historians who have studied other times and places rarely placed women at the center of their narratives either, but those who did have often uncovered the same themes running through the incredible diversity of women's experiences and contributions that this book has emphasized: agency and opportunities, choices and constraints, and continuity and change. It's no coincidence that the field of women's history has developed in recent decades alongside women's demands for equal rights in all aspects of their lives. When women are left out of the history books, it seems obvious to leave them out of the world of electoral politics and big business, too. But when we begin to see a balanced and more complete picture of the past, we can start to ask what else might look different with women at the center.

When we put women at the center of the history of the U.S. West, a different history emerges than the one which tells the more familiar male-centered story of explorers, warfare, and railroads. This history is both significantly harsher and somehow also more optimistic. For example, narratives about "the frontier" start to look a lot less heroic when one realizes the extent to which the westward expansion of the United States relied on raping Native American women. However, the West was also a place where women felt entitled to and sometimes had more opportunities, more chances, more choices, and they seized or created such opportunities whenever they could. Western women were explorers and adventurers, workers and environmentalists, and miners and ranchers, and they came from many different racial, ethnic, and religious backgrounds. Native American women supplied much of their communities' food, as well as having important social, political, economic, and spiritual roles. Native women played crucial roles in the development of the fur trade and helped their cultures persist despite the onslaught of disease, warfare, and policies intended to eradicate their ways of life. Women of all racial groups were vital intermediaries as different races and cultures began to encounter each other across the West. White and black women followed the overland trails westward, sometimes with their families and sometimes on their own, all of them seeking a better life. Women's work was economically important whether they took supporting roles or worked their own mining claims or farmland. Women flocked to western cities in greater numbers than men because of the wider range of economic, personal, and political opportunities available to them. When the Great Depression hit, women of all racial groups did whatever was necessary to keep their families together and fed, and when World War II started those women also did whatever they could for the war.

With women at the center, we can see that the history of the West was vibrant and complex and that race and class and religion intersected continuously with gender to shape what happened. Women made their choices and they took their chances, and the history of the West would have been very different if they hadn't.

Index

["

Choices and Chances: A History of Women in the U.S. West
Development editor: Andrew J. Davidson
Copy editor: Catherine Cocks
Production editor: Linda Gaio
Proofreader: Claudia Siler
Typesetter: Bruce Leckie
Cartographer: Jason Casanova
Printer: McNaughton & Gunn

The Buffalo Bill Historical Center, Cody, Wyoming

The vast American West—its unmatched beauty and broad horizons—was home to diverse wildlife populations, Native American peoples, and eventually an equally diverse group of explorers, pioneers, and settlers. The wildlife and human cultures, sometimes in harmony, sometimes in conflict, made an indelible mark upon the West and its history.

Much of that western spirit is embodied in a man, William Frederick Cody, a unique American who defined America's West for the world. Known as Buffalo Bill, Cody brought his version of the American West to international audiences through his renowned Wild West show. The story Cody told was rooted in a region—wild, beautiful, and vast—that reinforced the myth of rugged individualism and the reality of community.

By the time Cody died in 1917, the West in which he lived was vanishing—and needed to be remembered. At his passing the Buffalo Bill Memorial Association was chartered. A nonprofit educational organization, the Buffalo Bill Historical Center is dedicated to exploring, preserving, and promoting the American West—its people, its wildlife, its landscapes—which Cody first introduced to the world stage more than a century ago.

Much has happened since Cody left the stage, and the passage of time has broadened our perspective. The story of the West grows increasingly robust and complex. As the writer Wallace Stegner put it, the story of the West is the story of America, "only more so."

By illuminating the highly diverse natural and cultural faces of the American West, the Buffalo Bill Historical Center brings new knowledge to bear on this distinctive region.

www.bbhc.org